TORT LAW AND SOCIAL MORALITY

This book develops a theory of tort law that integrates deontic and consequential approaches by applying justificational analysis to identify the factors, circumstances, and values that shape tort law. Drawing on Kantian and Rawlsian philosophy, and on the insights of game theorist Ken Binmore, this book refocuses tort law on a single theory of responsibility that explains and justifies the broad range of tort doctrine and concepts. Under this theory, tort law asks people to appropriately incorporate the well-being of others into the decisions they make, explains when that duty applies, and explains the scope and limits of that duty. The theory also incorporates a theory of the evolutionary development of social values that people use, and ought to use, in meeting that duty and explains how decision making from behind the veil of ignorance allows us to evaluate the *is* in light of the *ought*.

Professor Peter M. Gerhart is a graduate of Northwestern University and Columbia University Law School. He practiced law with Weil, Gotshal, and Manges before entering teaching in 1975. Before serving as Dean of the Case Western Reserve School of Law from 1986 to 1996, he was an expert in antitrust law, publishing widely in the area and serving as consultant to both the ABA Commission on the Future of Antitrust Law and the Carter Commission for the Review of Antitrust Laws and Procedures. Since 1996 he has specialized in international economic law, tort law, and legal theory.

Tort Law and Social Morality

PETER M. GERHART

School of Law, Case Western Reserve University

CAMBRIDGE
UNIVERSITY PRESS

CAMBRIDGE UNIVERSITY PRESS
Cambridge, New York, Melbourne, Madrid, Cape Town, Singapore,
São Paulo, Delhi, Dubai, Tokyo

Cambridge University Press
32 Avenue of the Americas, New York, NY 10013-2473, USA

www.cambridge.org
Information on this title: www.cambridge.org/9780521768962

First published 2010

QM LIBRARY
(MILE END)

Printed in the United States of America

A catalog record for this publication is available from the British Library.

Library of Congress Cataloging in Publication data
Gerhart, Peter M.
    Tort law and social morality / Peter M. Gerhart.
        p.   cm.
    Includes bibliographical references and index.
    ISBN 978-0-521-76896-2 (hardback)
    1. Torts – Social aspects – United States.   I. Title.
    KF1250.G47   2010
    346.03–dc22   2010005462

ISBN 978-0-521-76896-2 Hardback

Brief Contents

Contents

PART IV   SUMMARY AND IMPLICATIONS

Preface

This book owes its origin to my dissatisfaction with the current state of tort doctrine and theory. When I began teaching tort law more than a decade ago, it became clear that the schisms in tort theory and the verbal patches holding tort doctrine together signaled the need for a deeper understanding of the normative theory that justifies tort law. Among the animating conundrums I faced were the deep, antagonistic, and seemingly unbridgeable divide between corrective justice and economic theory, the multiple goals that tort law is said to serve, and the inadequate justifications given for (among other things) duty and no-duty rules, proximate cause, and the injection of strict liability into the otherwise dominant negligence regime. Clearly, I thought, there must be a better way to understand tort law.

My search for a new way of looking at tort law led me to believe that the underlying problem was a failure of justification – that is, a failure to understand the reasons why tort law finds one person responsible for the well-being of others, and the limits of that responsibility. As I explored the justification for various decisions, I saw that too often our understanding of why the courts decide one way rather than another was not supported by sound analysis of the factors that would lead to a just outcome. The decisions were supported instead by bland appeal to generalized ideas that did not reveal the normative basis for the decision. My search for a better way of understanding tort law also convinced me that the positive and normative core of tort law emanates from tort law's foundational concept: the requirement that one person take into account the well-being of others when deciding how to behave (an expression of the requirements of the reasonable person). As I explored the concept of other-regarding behavior in various contexts, I began to see it as the thread that runs through tort law and brings it unity and coherence. I saw that it allows us to justify a range of tort doctrines that would otherwise be disparate and disconnected. This book presents the current state of my analysis.

This book, however, seeks not only a better positive and normative understanding of tort law; it also seeks a better methodological approach. I seek a
methodology that is justificational, integrative, and coherent, as is explained
immediately below, and those methodological goals become a theme that ties
the various chapters of the book together.

THE JUSTIFICATIONAL PROJECT

My primary aim is to provide an account of tort law that is analytically justificational. As I hope this book illustrates, this term has a particular, and specialized, meaning that distinguishes it from existing theoretical approaches.
I seek to present an account of tort law that identifies the circumstances, factors, and values that justify the imposition of liability in tort and an analytical
framework that links those circumstances, factors, and values with a normative theory that makes it legitimate for the state, acting through courts, to
compel one person to repair the harm another has incurred. A justification is a
well-specified statement of the attributes of a dispute that compelled the court
to decide the case the way it did. A justification cannot be complete unless it
is founded on, and reveals, a normative vision of the law's values and explains
the attributes of a dispute that are relevant to implementing those values in the
context of the dispute, given the institutional character of the law.

All theory is justificational in a broad sense if it seeks to bring deeper understanding to a welter of disparate outcomes. The justificational theory I present
is, I hope, distinctive in its specificity and coherence, bridging the gap between
a normative theory of responsibility and its application in a way that links normative theory to determinate analysis. Theory can be conceptually coherent
in its generality but not determinate in its application, or it can be specific in
its application but untethered from an overarching theory of responsibility or
from the values that animate the theory. I hope to combine the two in this
book. My focus is on *how* we think about tort cases – a methodology of specific
assessment – rather than on *what* we think about them. This is an important
distinction, for it distinguishes between saying that tort law embodies a theory
of corrective justice or wealth maximization (i.e., *what* we think about tort
cases) and saying: "Here is the sense in which we can understand the corrective justice or wealth maximization notions embodied in tort law."

Because of its focus on specificity and coherence, this book bears a special
relationship to the existing theory, building on much of what exists, but ampli-
fying it in ways I believe to be important to fulfill theory's promise. First, the
book is a reaction to, and an antidote for, what many regard as the considerable indeterminacy and overconceptualization of much existing theory. As

I illustrate throughout the book, tort theory is seriously underspecified because it fails to reflect and incorporate the circumstances, factors, and values that are necessary to apply the theory to particular instances of injury. My aim is to get underneath tort law's doctrine, principles, and central concepts to establish a framework that explains why and how they are applied to determine whether one person is responsible for the harm that befalls another. Thus, I seek to get a richer understanding of the meaning of the concepts of ordinary care, duty, proximate cause, and strict liability in order to give a fuller account of the factors, circumstances, and values that impel a court or jury toward one outcome over another. My project therefore seeks to develop a theory of tort law that overcomes what I view to be the major flaws in much existing theory: excessive generality and lack of specificity, the associated problems of lack of analytical rigor, and theory that is outcome-driven.

Let me elaborate.

Corrective Justice Theories

Theories of tort law tend to be conceptual in one of two ways, corresponding to the two main bodies of tort theory. Corrective justice theories are conceptual in that their concern is the form and function and interrelationships between tort concepts. This focus on form, function, and interrelationships allows theorists to understand tort law holistically, but not in a way that points to the specific circumstances, factors, or values that are relevant to deciding cases and evaluating in a particularized way whether the case was correctly decided. The indeterminacy of corrective justice is well known[1] and even acknowledged[2] (and sometimes celebrated[3]) by its practitioners. Corrective justice simply leaves too many questions open to do the kind of work that provides a satisfying and full understanding of tort law.[4]

My concern with the excessive indeterminacy of corrective justice must be understood through appreciative inquiry. My indictment is too generalized itself; some theory that can be grouped under the corrective justice rubric

---

[1] Jody S. Kraus, *Transparency and Determinacy in Common Law Adjudication: A Philosophical Defense of Explanatory Law and Economic Analysis*, 93 VA. L. REV. 287 (2007).

[2] Ernest Weinrib, *The Disintegration of Duty* in Stuart Madden (ed.), EXPLORING TORT LAW, Cambridge University Press (2005).

[3] Jules L. Coleman, THE PRACTICE OF PRINCIPLE, Oxford University Press (2001). Among the justificational agnostics is Benjamin J. Zipursky, *Rawls in Tort Theory: Themes and Counter-Themes*, 27 FORDHAM L. REV. 1923, 1939 (eschewing the priority of justification in the analysis of law).

[4] I will not support this claim specifically here, for each chapter of the applications section of the book reviews the literature and the kind of justificational problems that arise.

is highly specified (even if unconvincing).[5] My project is not to dethrone or criticize corrective justice; it is to supplement it and build on it. The theory developed here is neither a brief for the supremacy of law and economics nor a claim that corrective justice theory is wrong. My claim is narrow: corrective justice theory can be made more meaningful by understanding it in the context of justificational analysis linking the relevant concepts to their applications.

In particular, much of this book follows the conceptual road carefully crafted by Arthur Ripstein, providing justificational analysis to implement his underappreciated conceptual analysis.[6] Like him, I view tort law to be working out "fair terms of interaction" and "social cooperation"[7] under terms of equality in a way that accounts for each person's interest in both liberty and security. Like him, I view the objective of analysis not as an inquiry into how much of one person's liberty must be sacrificed for another person's security – as if those two values could be balanced across persons – but rather as working out an accommodation between liberty and security that is acceptable to all people, as both injurer and victim, when their larger interests as part of the social collective are separated from their immediate interests in either freedom or security. And I follow Ripstein's lead in identifying the relevant foreseeability inquiry as neither an epistemic nor an ideal requirement, but instead as an integral part of what a reasonable person would understand. Above all, I take a theme developed by Ripstein – the notion that "[t]he point of the reasonable person standard is to specify the respects in which people can be required to take account of the interests of others"[8] – and raise it to be the central organizing feature of tort theory.

But I do two things with Ripstein's account of tort law that correspond to the two goals of my project. First, I make Ripstein determinate in a way that he does not, showing how we analyze the requirements of "fair terms of social interaction" and tying that analysis back into an overarching normative theory that explains the content of the concepts of equality and fairness that drive

[5]   I am thinking of the work of Gregory Keating, who has developed a highly specific and grounded rights-based theory for distributing the burdens and benefits of activity between persons and requiring an actor to repair the damage so distributed. Gregory C. Keating, *Reasonableness and Rationality in Negligence Theory*, 48 STAN L. REV. 311 (1989) and Gregory C. Keating, *Rawlsian Fairness and Regime Choice in the Law of Accidents*, 72 FORDHAM L. REV. 1857 (2004).

[6]   Arthur Ripstein, EQUALITY, RESPONSIBILITY, AND THE LAW, Cambridge University Press (1999).

[7]   *Id.* at 7. Ripstein traces this view to T.M. Scanlon, *Contractualism and Utilitarianism* in Amartya Sen and Bernard Williams (eds), UTILITARIANISM AND BEYOND, Cambridge University Press (1982).

[8]   Ripstein, EQUALITY, RESPONSIBILITY AND THE LAW, at 8.

the application of the theory. Second, I follow that normative and analytical theory of fairness and equality to its logical application as part of a coherent theory of responsibility that emanates through tort law.

My claim that corrective justice theory is not fully justified will be resisted by those who misunderstand what counts as a justification in the theory I develop. For my purposes, justificational analysis cannot rely on a description, a definition, or an unspecified concept (like fairness or duty) without trying to articulate, with as much analytical power as can be mustered, the meaning of the concept and how it is applied. The central normative concept of corrective justice is a "wrong," which involves the obligation to do something in a certain way and a breach of that obligation. Without providing a theory of "wrong" and "obligation" that gives those concepts analytical content – one that allows them to be applied by identifying the circumstances, factors, and values that justify the law in saying the defendant has committed a "wrong" or violated an "obligation" – the theory remains, in my terms, nonjustified. Under this reading, current accounts of corrective justice remain incomplete. Understanding the concepts of "wrong" and "duty" in their function and form – the goal of prominent collective justice theorists[9] – does not provide an understanding of their meaning or content.

Under the justificational analysis I champion, we understand concepts such as "wrong" and "duty" not as self-defining ideas with self-referential applicability. Rather, we understand them as placeholders for analysis that gives them content and makes them determinate. Too often, theorists write about concepts like duty as if they were inputs into deciding cases. We should not confuse inputs and outputs. What is important in understanding the law is the input – the considerations that an analyst takes into account and the way the analyst takes them into account. A concept like duty is an output not an input; it is the result of analysis, not an input into the analysis. Duty has no defined meaning that allows us to use it as an input into analysis; its role is to express a conclusion that flows from the appropriate analysis. The concept of duty is the concept that we are working to define as we analyze a case. Of course, we ask, for example, whether a store owner had a duty to the customer. But we do not ask this question as if the concept of duty would yield a determinate and justified answer. Instead, we are asking the following kind of question: Given the circumstances as we understand them and the way that we understand how the store owner ought to think about the well-being of her customers in light of those circumstances, how do we understand the obligation of the store

---

[9] John C.P. Goldberg & Benjamin C. Zipursky, *The Restatement (Third) and the Place of Duty in Negligence Law*, 54 VAND. L. REV. 657 (2001).

owner to take on more burdens for her customers? Duty is a summary of the
results of our analysis, not an input into the analysis. It is the concept that we
are trying to elucidate in the context of analyzing the case, and points to the
analysis we ought to use, but its content comes from the analysis not from the
concept.

Law and Economic Theories

Law and economic theories are conceptual in a different way. They are built
around a central concept – that tort law seeks to maximize individual benefit
under some measurable notion of benefit. These theories appear to be determinate (which is what makes law and economics so attractive). Because this is
a functional conception, its theorists present an understanding of tort law that
appears to be analytically justificational – that is, they present a well-specified
set of results that follow directly from the assumptions behind a proposed
model. Both the model and the conclusions flowing from the application of
the model are justified in the analysis. The conceptual lacunae of economic
theory is not in its analytical apparatus, but in the assumptions it makes in
order to undertake the analysis. Economics is specified without being justificational because it contains no normative basis for justifying the assumptions
on which the relevant analysis is based.[10]

We can take it to be self-evident that it makes sense to spend $500 to avoid
a loss of $501, that it makes no sense to spend $501 to avoid a loss of $500, and
that in those terms minimizing losses (or maximizing wealth) makes good
sense for all individuals. But we have an incomplete theory of tort law until
we have a normative theory for thinking about how we figure out the value of
the relative investments and returns. Where do the figures of $500 and $501
come from? The determination of those values is not self-identified from the
fact that we would want to maximize wealth or minimize losses; no economic
theory is complete until the methodology of the valuation is specified.

One can, of course, "do" welfare economics without specifying the origin of
the values that one assumes in the maximization process (just as one can "do"
corrective justice at a conceptual level). The ability of economists to strip out
the value formation part of the analysis has been an important development
in our understanding of tort law (and law in general) because it lays bare the
underlying structure of the analysis that sets up the maximization problem to

---

[10] Arthur Leff, *Economic Analysis of Law: Some Realism About Nominalism*, 60 VA. L. REV. 451
      (1974). For a more recent statement of the need to integrate normative values into economic
      analysis, see Joseph William Singer, *Normative Methods for Lawyers*, 56 U.C.L.A. L. REV.
      899, 915 (2009).

be solved. The formal modeling of the maximization process has revealed the many insights that are not easily seen without it – including the relationship between injurer care and victim care, the difference between due care and activity-level decisions, and the nature and role of externalities. Ultimately, however, welfare economics depends on some specification of the values that determine which trade-offs between various human capacities are important to society. That can be done only by specifying what makes a decision moral and how we identify decisions that we think were made with the appropriate deference to the well-being of others. Once we have a basis for specifying the necessary social values, we can solve the maximization problem that characterizes the law and economics approach, but without it we have only a guess as to the appropriate normative response of the law.

More generally, the statement that the goal of law is efficiency can be made determinate only by specifying the values that are to be taken into account in the allocation process. Slavery is efficient if society devalues the worth of Africans; by devaluing their worth, we are saying that the loss of freedom is not important in the allocation process, so its loss produces benefits without waste. On the other hand, if society values the worth and freedom of each individual, slavery is inefficient. The relevant normative analysis is in the valuation. In the context of tort law, we need to know which costs and benefits are relevant to determining the efficient result and how society understands those values. When a driver with epilepsy has a seizure and crashes into a bicycle shop, we can say we want an efficient resolution of the conflicting claims, but we cannot resolve the conflict without specifying how we understand the trade-off between the freedom of an epileptic to drive and the personal safety of those in the store. After we have made that specification, we can call the result efficient, but specifying the goal of efficiency or wealth maximization does not help us make the valuation.

Economic theory shares with corrective justice a common characteristic of nonjustificational theory: reliance on words whose meaning is not known or specified. We can all agree that tort law functions to internalize externalities, but that concept just begs the issue of how we recognize and define externalities. At one level, the externalities perspective is simply a statement of the problem that society faces. People engage in activities that impose costs on others. Society needs a mechanism for determining which of those costs ought to be internalized into which activity. Although we can conceptualize this as the need to balance external costs and benefits, for justificational analysis we cannot escape the obligation to identify which costs ought to be internalized to which activity and why. Not all externalities are internalized. If they were, the costs we impose on others would come close to deterring us from acting at all. Whether to call a cost or benefit an externality (and therefore whether to internalize it) is itself a social choice that depends on which activities we value and why we value them. Some external costs of activities we internalize; some we do not. The choice depends on how we think we should allocate the costs and benefits from various activities and on the incentive effects of different allocation schemes.

We can therefore agree with welfare economists that legal outcomes should be chosen solely on the basis of their effects on the well-being of individuals in society. That is not a controversial statement. What is controversial, and is not sufficiently addressed in the economic literature, is the basis on which one values the effects that the decision of one person has on the well-being of others in society, given the inability to simultaneously achieve desirable effects for both parties. The theory presented here provides a basis on which we judge an actor's decisions, but that basis is not determined by the actor or even by the comparative general well-being of injurer and victim; it is determined by the community of individuals. Society creates a social index of the ranking of projects and preferences of different people that allows tort law to determine whether the projects of the victim or the projects of the injurer should be burdened. The values that determine which projects and preferences must be burdened are not derived from outside the social system; value creation is what the social system does. The social system, through the decisions of many individuals, determines, for example, whether a person should be required to drive more slowly so that others face less risk. It determines the means that are acceptable for separating two dogs and those methods that impose too much risk on society. It determines these factors based on the experience of people in everyday life and in how that experience shapes the values that determine how reasonable people behave. It gives economic theory the values needed to make the theory normatively determinate.

THE INTEGRATION PROJECT

Because both dominant theories of tort law are underspecified (although in different ways), it could be that these theories are less at odds than is conventionally thought. Could it be that the differences in the theories reflect the different levels of generality that each has chosen and that once we add specificity to them, we will see the theories converge? A second aim of this project is to explore the possibility that corrective justice and law and economics can be integrated into a single theory that harnesses the power of each while paying attention to the lacunae that keep them from being fully specified theories.

My approach is to recognize what the theories have in common, to understand the additional elements that must be added to each theory, and then to fill those lacunae in the hopes that what is added to each also integrates one theory into the other. This is not the first attempt to reconcile and integrate the two dominant theories of tort law, but none has achieved satisfactory traction with proponents of the opposite camp.[11]

From the time of Holmes (at least), tort law has been understood to "require a policy decision on how to mediate an actor's interest in liberty with the conflicting security interests of others."[12] All tort theory embraces this image. For economists, the liberty interest (the freedom to engage in valuable activity) is represented as the burden of precautions necessary to reduce risk and prevent harm, while the prevention of harm has been represented by the expected harm of not taking precautions. This is summarized in the Hand formula: that a reasonable person will take precautions – that is, curtail one's freedom to engage in valuable activity – whenever the actor's loss of liberty is less than the expected harm that would otherwise occur (or, more familiarly, when the burden of precautions is less than the expected harm to the victim). A similar image animates corrective justice theory, either explicitly or implicitly (although not in the form of the Hand formula).

From that common starting point, we can specify the considerations that are relevant to addressing the mediation between the two interests, essentially building our understanding of tort theory from the bottom up, specifying what society is trying to achieve, the causal mechanism society has chosen to achieve its goals, and the kinds of considerations that are relevant in implementing the causal mechanism. When we do, we find an integrated theory that is consistent with, and makes determinable, both corrective justice and law and economics.

THE COHERENCE PROJECT

This book also seeks to rethink how we understand and express tort doctrine. We should not be satisfied with our present understanding because too much turns on distinctions and devices that, on examination, seem artificial. As I make clear in this book, the lines between various doctrines are porous and malleable. We understand tort liability to be built around the fault concept, but we simultaneously believe that there are "pockets" of strict liability in the

---

[11] Louis Kaplow & Steven Shavell, FAIRNESS VERSUS WELFARE, Harvard University Press (2002).
[12] Mark A. Geistfeld, ESSENTIALS OF TORT LAW 13, Wolters Kluwer (2008).

tort landscape. This bifurcated system is coherent and sustainable only if we have a sound way of determining when the "pockets" of strict liability ought to be invoked as "exceptions" to the general "default" rule of the negligence regime. But do we? Similarly, we understand an actor's general duty to be reasonable and the simultaneous existence of "no-duty" rules. Without a coherent theory of duty that encompasses both the duty and non-duty rules – for they must surely act as a coherent whole – our understanding is unstable and incomplete. And the doctrine of proximate cause – the doctrine that relieves admittedly negligent actors from responsibility – begs an understanding of proximate cause that grows out of the fault concept rather than cutting holes through it.

Many will find the story I tell to be disorienting, for each of the fault lines I have identified is addressed by well-known devices. The theory of abnormally dangerous activities, for example, is thought to distinguish strict liability from negligence liability. The distinction between nonfeasance and misfeasance is thought to justify the duty and no-duty rules. And the scope of the risk concept is thought to justify proximate cause. As I hope to show in subsequent chapters, such justifications are unsatisfactory because they rely on distinctions that do not work. The fault concept that I portray is able to do away with what I consider to be artificial distinctions and to present a single (albeit unconventional) theory of fault that makes tort doctrine coherent.

My dissatisfaction with the current justifications for bringing order to the various tort doctrines reflects my conjecture that too often theorists have been outcome-oriented – assuming the answer they were trying to justify. Theorists believe that tort law embodies a concept of strict liability, so they develop a theory to justify a negligence regime with pockets of strict liability. Theorists think of no-duty rules as "policy-based" limitations on a general obligation to be reasonable and then construct a theory to explain the exceptions. Theorists think of proximate cause as a way of relieving an actor who has acted unreasonably from liability, so we understand proximate cause as an exception to duty or breach. I hope to do away with theory that is designed to reach preconceived outcomes. The purpose of justificational analysis is not to justify law as we think it to be, but to reason from a normative theory of responsibility to understand what the law *ought* to be and therefore *must* be.

A COMMENT ABOUT OUR CONCEPTION OF LAW

The kind of justificational theory I present reflects, and is derived from, a different concept of law and legal theory than the standard jurisprudential approach. The dominant conceptions of law – law as command, law as principle, and law as function – assume that the law has content that is separate from, and imposed on, the subjects that the law is affecting – that is, on the parties to the suit and the social relationships that will be governed by the outcome of the case. Under this view, the task of legal analysis is to find the right "fit" between a concept of law and the particular dispute or social problem the law addresses. These conceptions assume, for example, that law starts with a set of rights and obligations, or with a set of goals, or with a set of principles from which rights and duties can be derived. Under these views, the law operates by discovering or addressing rationally – that is, by legal reasoning – how the law is expressed in commands or principles or functions and then applies that conception to resolve particular disputes. These are top-down approaches, moving from a concept of law to the facts of a case. They define the law separately from the law's understanding of how people interact; they address the problems that people bring to the law by imposing law or a conception of justice on the problems. These approaches assume that the words and concepts of the law – words like *fair* or *efficient* – have meaning that can be determined and applied independently of how people interact in the nonlaw world.

This work challenges that view by suggesting that we understand the central concepts of the law to be a reflection of how communities construct and understand, and ought to construct and understand, the concepts of the law – concepts such as justice, obligation, fairness, efficiency, and responsibility. If we conceive law to be derived from the social arrangements that allow society to flourish, then we need to understand the concept of law as a method of analysis. We start with the way that humans interact (with each other and with nature) and perceive the law to be a way of examining human interactions to see which are best (as measured by some standard of what is best). If our sense of justice is socially derived rather than imposed from the outside by law – if our sense of right is created by, and facilitates human interaction – then we need a concept of law that is premised on, rather than separate from, an account of social interaction. That is what I present here – a theory that derives law from an appreciation of the kind of social arrangements that are normatively compelling and socially productive and that, for that reason, guide lawmakers in determining whether and how to intervene in human affairs through private law.

Conventional jurisprudential understandings of law search for a concept of law that asserts the primacy of law; this formalist approach has been a natural part of the evolution of thought designed to legitimize the use of power by the state. However, the formalist approach has largely been a dead end, for it is not fundamentally a normative enterprise. It is either descriptive ("the law is what the institutions of the law say it is") or it is disconnected from well-specified and empirically grounded normative theories (resulting in, "I know justice when I see it"). Legal realists came along to challenge the primacy of law but were not able to replace the formalist concept with a normative theory. Then legal functionalists (such as law and economics scholars) began constructing the normative basis for understanding and evaluating law, but only within a narrow behavioral and philosophical model. The approach developed here is the natural next step in this evolution, for it allows us to form a concept of law that is normatively and analytically sound. When we turn our concept of law upside down and make the law the handmaiden of social morality, we have a concept of law that is normative, responsive to human behavior, and socially relevant.

The starting point for this conception of law is not the law at all. Tort cases present social problems: a claim by one person that a relationship with another in the community should be repaired with the award of damages, a claim by a victim that another failed to regard the victim with sufficient solemnity. The analysis of the claim depends on situating and evaluating the social problem that gave rise to the claim – the conflicting claims to resources, space, capacity, or autonomy. The social problem, not the legal problem, is the starting point for analysis; the law simply describes the way the social problem is resolved. The law and its output are determined by the analysis of the social problem, but the input into the analysis is independent of the label attached to the output and is therefore independent of law as commands, principles, or functions.

This conception of law – one that would embed the law in an evaluation of the requirements of social morality – moves law from outside the social system to inside the social system. Law may be independent, but its independence comes not because it sits outside the social system but because the social system demands an independent method to evaluate social relationships and to select those that seem to embody traits that are good for the community. Under this conception, the law is the analysis and is not separate from the analysis. Law is the analysis that appropriately determines what circumstances, factors, and values influence the shape of the law and whether the law, thus shaped, is moral. To understand the normative content of law, and its institutional force, we need to understand the justification for the law – that is, we need to understand what it is that gives law its hold over human behavior and its claim to be called just or appropriate. The theory presented here supports a radical reconceptualization of law so that we see it as a method of analyzing human interactions and choosing an array of rights and obligations that enhance social interaction. Under this reconceptualization, law should not be understood by its output – its commands, principles, or functional doctrine – but by its input: the modes of thought and empirical understanding that allow lawmakers to make decisions that they believe will improve what I call social cohesion.

What gives law its force as an engine of social cohesion is not *that* it commands but the reasons that it commands. The law's force comes from its appeal to a sense of justice that people find to be worthy of following and therefore use to guide their behavior. The force of the law, and therefore its content, is not in the command but in how we think about the justification for the command – the congruence between the sense of justice that is embodied in the command and the sense of justice that people use to decide whether and how to follow the command. The law is continually renegotiated in light of technological, demographic, social, and behavioral forces until the justifications for the commands of the law are congruent with the requirements of social cohesion. The way we think about the normative requirements of social cohesion provides both the reasons for calling the law just and the reasons for obeying the law.

To implement a concept of law as the analysis of social morality, we need to develop analytical theories that specify the determinants of social cohesion and the meaning of the concepts (like efficiency and fairness) that we use to determine the social arrangements that are best for social cohesion. When we do, we have a kind of theory, an analytical theory, that is distinct from traditional legal theories. Then, we have an output and can describe the behavior as wrong in the sense that we have defined it under the analysis we have undertaken, and we can articulate a theory of responsibility under the relevant analysis. We can conclude, in other words, that it is wrong to speed under the circumstance with which the defendant was charged and that the defendant violated a duty to the plaintiff by acting unreasonably in this or that way. We should not, however, confuse inputs and outputs. What is important in understanding the law is the input – the considerations that an analyst takes into account and the way the analyst takes them into account – not the command that results from the analysis.

Although an analytical theory of the kind I proffer reflects a radical reconception of the concept of law, the theory does not seek to overthrow conceptual or functional theories; the theory is purposefully integrative. The theory seeks to approach conceptual and functional theories from a different direction, moving from the social problems that the law addresses to an understanding of how the law identifies its concepts and functions to take account of the appropriate resolution of social problems. The theory here thus stands in relation to conceptual or functional theories not by denying them on their own terms but by embracing them as reflections of the way social problems ought to be addressed. The analytical theory fills out conceptual and functional theories from the bottom by assessing how human interaction can be improved, but it does not seek to replace conceptual and functional theories.

Analytical theories are not conceptual in the traditional sense because they do not seek to identify *ab initio* the abstract concepts or principles that courts rely on to decide cases, as if the concepts or principles could be known separately from their derivation or application. It seeks rather to identify the empirical propositions – propositions about how people interact with one another and with the physical world – that, because of their appeal to people's well-specified sense of justice, have moral force in resolving a dispute and that justify a court in deciding one way rather than another. Accordingly, an analytical theory is unlike that constructed by philosophers; it is not a theory about the central legal characteristics of tort law or the core legal concepts that courts espouse. It does not seek, as philosophers do, to examine the practices that the participants in the legal system understand to be the central characteristics, ideas, and beliefs that give the system underlying coherence.

Nonetheless, an analytical theory of the kind I posit bears an important relationship to philosophical conceptual analysis, as I hope this work makes clear. The analytical theory I present is, I believe, both consistent with, and linked theoretically with, conceptual analysis. It does not defile conceptual analysis to say that once we understand how the law approaches the kind of social problems that give rise to tort cases, we can understand that the concepts of the law are shorthand ways of expressing the values that exist in a healthy society for addressing social problems. The analytical theory therefore helps us understand the content of legal concepts, giving law determinacy and transparency.

Analytical theories are also not functional in the usual sense because they do not assume that the law serves a particular function or external goal (like efficiency or deterrence) that exists outside the law. True, the analytical theory presented here assumes that the law functions to advance social cohesion, but social cohesion is not thought to be defined outside of social interaction that makes the community better off. Social cohesion is the goal of the law because it is the legitimate goal of people interacting in a community, and it takes its content from the appropriate way of thinking about human behavior in an interdependent world. Social cohesion is an analytical goal, and analytical theories do not assume that the law is designed for any purpose other than to undertake the analysis of the law provided by the theory. Under this view, the analysis is the function to which the law is aimed, just as the concept of law is law's analysis. Rather than the function controlling the analysis, the analysis controls the function. In the terms used here, analysis shows us that the function of tort law is to encourage people to take into account the well-being of others in a socially appropriate way when making decisions. Confirming appropriate other-regarding behavior becomes the function of the law because that is the function of the analysis. Although this concept of law would seem to deny that economic theory can be known by any particular function, the theory does not deny the value of economic analysis; it seeks simply to deny that economic theory is functional in a teleological sense.

In summary, the conception of law underlying this book sees law as an institutional basis for addressing problems of social interaction by drawing on an appreciation of the values people normally use in social interaction, addressed in light of a theory of social morality.

Acknowledgments

A book with a gestation period as long as this one owes many debts. For more than a decade the students in my section of torts, the Advocates, have encouraged this work, putting up with my attempt to make obsolete their commercial outlines and canned briefs, and struggling to sharpen and then apply the theories as they developed. Had they not bought into the theories as they unfolded, the task would have been harder; had they not asked probing questions, the theories would be less precise. Several Advocates who served as my research assistant over these years are worthy of special mention: E. Bart Kalnay, Gus Makris, Bill Manske, Namrata Mohanty, Andrew Thompson, Justin Thompson, Ku Yoo, and Ryan DeYoung. Paul Knupp provided insight and research while a law student at Notre Dame Law School and sustained helpful ideas after he graduated. Special thanks to Lisa Board-McShepard who has worked and reworked the manuscript so magnificently.

My colleague, Ronald Coffey, schooled me in the methodology of justificational analysis and continually pushed me to be more precise and more, well, justificational. He stands as the model of intellectual thought. Together with my accomplished colleague Juliet Kostritsky, we have shared many stimulating discussions and debates over the years about the nature and content of legal analysis; many of the ideas stimulated by that collaboration have found their way into this book (although professors Coffey and Kostritsky should not be charged with my derelictions from their thought). Professor Wendy Wagner encouraged me at every step and kept me on track when I was about to wander. Our series of e-mail exchanges after she moved to the University of Texas provided the seeds for much that germinated here. My colleague Max Mehlman read several papers that found their way into this book and was always encouraging.

I was also lucky enough to have Jules Coleman sponsor a workshop at Yale Law School at which some of the top torts scholars commented on an earlier draft of the book. In addition to Jules, there were Mark Geistfeld, Scott Hershovitz, Catherine Sharkey, Wendy Wagner, and Ben Zipursky. They may not be persuaded by the product, but they were tremendously helpful in sharpening my ideas and challenging me to better connect them to existing tort theory.

My family has been supportive throughout this process. Much of this book was written in Little Italy, whose spirit continues to animate my thinking.

OTHER-REGARDING BEHAVIOR

In this part, I set up the framework that supports the theory developed in this book. In Chapter One, I explain that, in order to solve the social coordination problem tort law addresses, society asks each person to think appropriately about the well-being of others when deciding how to behave. This is the basic requirement of the reasonable person, and it asks the analyst to examine not only how people normally behave but also how they would behave if they were thinking appropriately about the well-being of others. I explain that other-regarding behavior is common, and that it allows people to be rational and reasonable at the same time. And I outline my claim that a system that reinforces other-regarding behavior allows society to function efficiently, fairly, and with stability (which achieves the goal of social cohesion).

In Chapter Two, I then illustrate the major attributes of other-regarding behavior by suggesting the broad outlines of other-regarding thought and its relation to the Hand formula. Here I develop the notion that social communities generate values that allow people to make other-regarding choices, and I show the requirements of empathy and reasoning behind a veil of ignorance that allow other-regarding thought to be considered socially moral.

1   Law as a Social Institution

1.1. THE COORDINATION PROBLEM

Tort law provides an institutional mechanism for reconciling conflicting claims of people over things that are important to them: freedom of action, bodily security, property, and emotional well-being. Human interaction entails both conflict and cooperation. As the number of people and interdependencies grow, the potential interference between people grows, and so too does each person's knowledge that his interests and decisions potentially interfere with the well-being of others. Sometimes the issue is apparent conflict; people want to be in the same place at the same time. They want to lay claim to the same resources. In addition, people want to protect their freedom to choose relationships, hoping that others will look for authorization before interfering with their relational freedom. In other instances, human interaction is cooperative. Human interdependence comes from social bonds that are formed to improve individual well-being; individuals rely on those bonds. People form relationships and communities, those relationships and communities entail explicit or implicit commitments among people, and these commitments improve each person's lot by allowing each person to rely on the commitments of others. At times, those commitments lead to conflicts over the terms of commitment.

Such conflicting claims between people are often irreconcilable in the sense that to honor the claim of one person would disable society from fully honoring the claim of another person. Because society must reject or modify one of the claims to honor the other, tort law is coordinating between the conflicting claims of people in a community of people. By resolving conflicting claims when several actors' activities are otherwise irreconcilable, tort law endorses and establishes patterns of behavior and attitude that determine how people in a community cooperate. The crucial issue that tort theory faces is how we understand and evaluate the nature of the conflicting claims and the sense of justice that underlies various ways of adjusting the burdens and benefits of citizenship in an interacting community.

Consider one of the most difficult trade-offs that tort law makes – the trade-off between the freedom of movement of one person and the physical security of another. In *Hammontree v. Jenner*,[1] a person with epilepsy was under a doctor's care but had a license that allowed him to drive if he followed his prescribed treatment. He crashed through the window of the plaintiff's bicycle shop, testifying later that he had blacked out. The owner of the bicycle shop sued and the court applied the negligence standard, refusing to hold, as the plaintiff requested, that the defendant should be responsible under strict liability for the harms caused by his condition because the risks of a seizure from epilepsy could not be eliminated with medical treatment.[2] Because the jury found insufficient proof of negligence, the defendant won. This case presents the kind of social coordination problem that tort law must address. How do we conceive of the rights and responsibilities of the two parties, given their activities, when their activities clash? We have to burden either the victim or the injurer with the obligation to absorb or insure against a loss – that is, society must put burdens on either the driver with epilepsy or on the owner of the bicycle shop to insure against the injury or absorb the loss. What mode of thought do we use to determine, in Ripstein's phrase, "the fair terms of interaction" between these two parties, and what is the relationship, if any, between that conception of fairness and the larger interests of society?

Given the nature of the social coordination problem with which tort law deals, it makes sense to understand tort law in terms of the dynamics of human interaction. In this book, I develop a theory of one person's responsibility for the well-being of others with respect to the risks the others face and explain the theory's implications for tort law's doctrine, social function, theory, and analysis. Tort law determines when one person is responsible for the well-being of another if injurer and victim have not bargained directly over their mutual well-being.[3] A court that orders the defendant to repair the plaintiff's

---

[1]　20 Cal. App. 3d 528 (Cal. Ct. App. 1971).

[2]　Plaintiff's lawyer cleverly argued that if an auto manufacturer is "strictly liable" for defective products, then a driver should be "strictly liable" for his defective condition. The court found "some logic" in this syllogism, *id* at 531, but declined to apply it because it would upset the negligence regime that applies to automobile driving.

[3]　The notion that tort law determines when one person is responsible for the well-being of others runs throughout the tort literature. In addition to the prominence given to this notion by Arthur Ripstein in EQUALITY, RESPONSIBILITY, AND THE LAW, see e.g., Ariel Porat, *The Many Faces of Negligence*, 4 THEORETICAL INQUIRIES L. 105 (2003) (showing that this conception is inherent in the Hand formula); Ernst Weinrib, THE IDEA OF PRIVATE LAW 3–21

damage has made a judgment that the defendant is responsible for the well-being of the plaintiff; the compensation represents the value of the plaintiff's well-being that the defendant is asked to assume. When a court finds the defendant not liable to the plaintiff, the court has made a judgment that the defendant is not responsible for the well-being of the plaintiff, either because the defendant bears no relevant relationship to the plaintiff's well-being or because the defendant has fulfilled her responsibility for the plaintiff's well-being.

Because findings of liability and no liability are both judgments about the defendant's responsibility for the plaintiff's well-being, tort cases call for an inquiry into whether the defendant has been sufficiently other-regarding. A judgment of liability is a determination that the defendant has been insufficiently other-regarding (which requires the defendant to correct the failure to be other-regarding), while a judgment of no liability is a determination that the defendant has thought appropriately about the plaintiff's well-being. In this way, tort law exists to define the extent to which an actor is expected to incorporate the well-being of others into the actor's choice set; it determines when and how an actor must consider the well-being of others when deciding how to act. This assessment rests on a theory of responsibility, and that theory embodies a theory of nonresponsibility – a theory of when one person is not responsible for the harm that befalls another because that person has, when making decisions, adequately considered the well-being of another. A single theory determines when an actor is responsible for the harms that befall another and the limits of that responsibility. It is a theory of other-regarding behavior.

I present the theory of other-regarding behavior as the single guiding star of tort law – a unifying theory that treats tort law as founded on a coherent and consistent conception of an actor's responsibility for harms that befall another. In this book, I show its significant doctrinal, functional, theoretical, and analytical implications.

The context for this theory, of course, is personal well-being. Life is dangerous and uncertain, nasty and brutish. People face risks – of nature, of our

---

(1995); Stephen R. Perry, *The Moral Foundations of Tort Law*, 77 Iowa L. Rev. 449 (1992), and Benjamin J. Zipursky, *Slight of Hand*, 48 Wm. & Mary L. Rev. 1999, 2036 (2007). Lord Acton, writing in *Donoghue v. Stevenson* [1932] AC 562 (HL), captured the thought this way: "You must take reasonable care to avoid acts or omissions that you can reasonably foresee are likely to injure your neighbor. Who, then, in law is my neighbor? The answer seems to be persons who are so closely and directly affected by my act that I ought to have them in contemplation as being so affected when I am directing my mind to the acts or omissions which are called into question." However the other-regarding notion has not yet been made the center of a well-specified theory of responsibility in tort law.

own making, and of others' making. We are subject to luck, good and bad. We sometimes embrace luck and sometimes flee from it; sometimes it catches up with us. We impose risks on others for our own gain, and we face risks imposed by others for their gain. We can buy our way out of some dangers if we have the resources and knowledge, and we can sell our chance at security if we do not. Our well-being is only partially in our control. As already mentioned, we seek refuge from life's vagaries in community and we depend on community to shield and soften life's challenges. We construct community by banding together to address life's uncertainties and we count on others to help us. We join and we commit; we learn and we protect. We act as if we were interconnected with others and we count on others. We hope that others will look out for our well-being, just as we look out for the well-being of others. Those on whom we can count become our community.

Human beings therefore interact in a world driven by expectations about how one person will look out for the well-being of others.[4] Often these expectations are embodied in a relatively explicit contract that spells out each person's responsibility for the well-being of another. At other times, the expectations are formed without direct bargaining; expectations about how one person will take responsibility for the well-being of another are implicit in being a member of a community, drawn from the practices of the community. The theory of responsibility advanced here concerns the latter type of expectation – those subject to an implicit social contract formed in a social community that determines when one person will think about his own well-being in light of the well-being of others. The theory recognizes, as do many theories of torts,[5] that communities develop norms and expectations of other-regarding behavior that form the basis on which the law develops a theory of responsibility. Those expectations allow the community to flourish because they provide the best way by which each person in a community can explore his or her capacity for a meaningful life in light of shared expectations about the responsibilities that each will assume for the well-being of others. Together, these social expectations of appropriate other-regarding behavior provide the glue that holds society together and that allows individuals to flourish in a community of individuals with minimal conflicts – what I call social cohesion.

---

4   In Garrett Hardin's felicitous phrase, "human beings are the environment for other human beings." Garrett Hardin, FILTERS AGAINST FOLLY 12, Penguin Books (1985). Robinson Caruso is a central figure in jurisprudence precisely because he did not need a morality of social responsibility until he was forced to confront the existence, and therefore the well-being, of other people.

5   Marshall S. Shapo, TORT LAW AND CULTURE, Carolina Academic Press (2003).

1.2. OTHER-REGARDING BEHAVIOR AS A COORDINATION DEVICE

The mechanism society uses to coordinate interpersonal relations is what I call other-regarding behavior. The theory of other-regarding behavior posits that society has as its coordinating device to address interaction between people the requirement that each party's interests be other-regarding – to evaluate his or her own behaviors in light of the interests of others and to make decisions that appropriately integrate those interests as a part of the actor's self-interest. Under this view, the responsibility of each person is to be other-regarding in a particular way; the law functions to determine what other-regarding decisions are appropriate and to impose the obligation to compensate another on a party that has failed to fulfill her responsibility to be other-regarding. Because the obligation to be other-regarding in an appropriate way is a constant and universal social obligation – the heart of the social contract – the law needs only to evaluate human behavior to see if it reflects appropriate other-regarding decisions and declare when the social obligation has not been met. And because the obligation to be other-regarding is socially constructed to reduce conflicts and maximize coordination, it results in obligations that advance the health of the community with minimum judicial intervention.

Each person freely chooses the goals he or she wants to achieve and the means used to achieve them. Naturally, an actor's choices reflect that person's projects and preferences – that is, the goals the actor has and the means the actor chooses to reach those goals.[6] But equally naturally, an actor's projects and preferences can conflict with or burden the projects and preferences of others. That is the coordination problem that gives rise to the need for tort law – the conflicting and irreconcilable projects and preferences of people in a community that represent conflicting claims on each other. As we have seen, a person with epilepsy wants the freedom to drive, and the owner of a bicycle shop wants bodily security; given the defendant's epilepsy, both cannot be accommodated.

The competing projects and preferences mean that an actor exists both as an individual decision-making unit and as part of a community of individuals

---

[6] The term "projects and preferences" is intended to convey the notion that people have objectives – projects – and that they adopt attitudes and means for achieving those objectives – preferences. Going to the beach is a project; trying to get there as quickly as possible expresses a preference. A project denotes an activity an actor undertakes; a preference denotes how the actor undertakes the activity. These are not the only ways that the terms can be understood. A person naturally has a preference for her projects, and a preference like taking risks might in fact be a project. But "projects and preferences" simply acknowledges that people have objectives and ways of reaching them.

who are decision-making units, and an actor must make choices that meet the actor's personal projects and preferences in the context of a community of projects and preferences. In such a community, it is a mistake to think that rational interest means narrow self-interest or that a rational person will think only about his own projects and preferences. In fact, rational decisions often account for the well-being of others because people regularly make decisions that incorporate a range of other-regarding sentiments. Any debate about whether self-interest is good or bad is quite irrelevant to the theory presented here, for the relevant distinction is not between decisions that are self-interested and those that are altruistic. The relevant analytical distinction is within the category of self-interested decisions. It is between decisions that fail to take into account the well-being of others – ones that are therefore rightly understood to be narrowly self-interested – and decisions that incorporate the well-being of others into the decision-maker's own well-being – and are therefore self-interested but other-regarding. The latter category arises whenever an actor makes the well-being of others a part of the actor's decisions; by accounting for the well-being of others as part of an actor's decision, the actor makes a decision that is both rational and reasonable.[7]

[7] The distinction between the rational and the reasonable is important to both deontic and consequentialist scholars. Deontic scholars emphasize the distinction in order to marginalize the brand of law and economics that makes revealed preferences a means of valuing relational choices. Gregory C. Keating, *Reasonableness and Rationality in Negligence Theory*, 48 STAN. L. REV. 311 (1996). Consequentialist scholars, on the other hand, emphasize the dichotomy because they cannot imagine that people would not choose means and ends that they find to be pleasing, and because it gives them a single model of personal behavior. I, by contrast, desiring to integrate across deontic and consequential theories, employ the notion of other-regarding behavior to remove the dichotomy, arguing that it is rational to be reasonable.

At first glance, this appears to be contrary to John Rawls's famous distinction between the rational and the reasonable, but I think that the context in which Rawls was writing shows that his distinction does not apply in tort law. For Rawls, "rational is ... a distinct idea from the reasonable," one based on the following: "what rational agents lack is the particular form of moral sensibility that underlies their desire to engage in fair cooperation as such, and to do so on terms that others as equals might reasonably be expected to endorse." John Rawls, POLITICAL LIBERALISM 50–51, Columbia University Press (1993). His distinction reflects his desire to make sure that "there is no thought of deriving one from the other; in particular, there is no thought of deriving the reasonable from the rational," and he defines "the reasonable agents as having no ends of their own they wanted to advance by fair cooperation" (*Id* at 52). If this were taken to describe the relationship between the rational and the reasonable when working out the fair terms of cooperation in private law, it would be inconsistent with my position. My claim is that the reasonable can be derived from the rational because individuals who would be moral can subject their own ends to the requirements of socially fair cooperation, making the desire for fair cooperation an end in itself for individuals.

But I think that Rawls ought to be understood to be writing in the context of distributive, not corrective justice, and therefore not to be contrary to my proposal. Rawls's concern was to develop the basic structure for thinking about how society distributes rights and basic

Sometimes our self-interested decisions are purely selfish in the sense that we ignore the impact of the decisions on others, taking into account our personal projects and preferences only. This is generally thought to be true, for example, if we choose a flavor of ice cream. We do not commonly think that our choice has meaningful implications for the well-being of others and we therefore take into account our own well-being only. But our self-interested decisions can easily become other-regarding. For example, if an actor is ordering ice cream to share with a loved one who is allergic to certain flavors, the actor is likely to incorporate that information in the actor's decision, forgoing an otherwise preferred flavor to pick one that promotes the well-being of the loved one while sacrificing some of the actor's well-being. The actor is acting in a rational, self-interested way, but his self-interest is now influenced by his regard for the well-being of another. In that context, giving up some narrow self-interest is the reasonable way for a rational actor to make decisions.

It is through self-interested but other-regarding behavior that the community is built. Other-regarding behavior is instinctual and reflexive; it is second nature to people because it is what allows them to have meaningful relationships and to coordinate activity in a community. We know from common experience that we take into account the welfare of those we care about, whether in interpersonal affairs, in transactions, or in a broader social context. We also know that sometimes we take care not to impose costs on others unnecessarily, which is also a form of other-regarding behavior. For example, within many communities people generally stand to one side on an escalator, exerting energy to allow those who want to walk ahead to do so. This is not selfless or altruistic behavior. It is self-interested behavior in which

goods within a community. In that context, we can endorse his statement that we are asking individuals to put aside the ends they want to achieve as individuals when deciding on the basic distribution of rights and primary goods, and we do not expect them to develop a moral sensibility to engage in fair terms of distributive cooperation from the fact that they are rational. If we allowed the reasonable to be derived from the rational in distributive settings, we would violate the notion that people have to put aside their ends when making distributive decisions. That Rawls was writing in the distributive context is confirmed when Rawls goes on to say that "a further basic difference between the reasonable and the rational is that the reasonable is public in a way that rational is not (*Id* at 53, footnote omitted).

Corrective justice is different because it involves interpersonal relationships in which the fair terms of cooperation do not require that one person put aside his ends and in which an individual can, I claim, develop a moral sensitivity. It therefore does no harm to integrate the reasonable and the rational by deriving the reasonable from the rational.

The concept presented here – that with other-regarding behavior, it is rational for people to be reasonable – is also consistent with W.M. Sibley's classic account of the difference between the rational and the reasonable. See W.M. Sibley, *The Rational Versus the Reasonable*, 62 THE PHILOSOPHICAL REVIEW 554 (1953). His rational person would consider not only her own ends but also the ends "of others affected by [her] actions." *Id* at 555.

one determines one's self-interest by taking into account the effect of one's behavior on others. When we walk down the sidewalk, we generally take pains to avoid obstructing another's way, both to protect our own well-being and to make their way easier. Our own sense of well-being often depends on feeling that we have acted in a way toward others that we find to be virtuous or worthy or for which we receive implicit social benefits.[8]

Other-regarding behavior therefore becomes the glue that holds communities together; it is the essence of community. And other-regarding behavior does not necessarily require an external monitor to force the behavior. It only requires each member of the community to make decisions giving appropriate weight for the well-being of those who might be affected by the decision, relying on others to reciprocate and on reputational sanctions to enforce the reciprocity.

Appropriate other-regarding behavior is the central characteristic of the reasonable person, for reasonable decision making means giving appropriate regard to the well-being of others when making decisions. When one examines human behavior under this notion, the question is not whether a person is self-interested or altruistic. If an actor defines her interest to be totally other-regarding, she may well give all her time and money to the needy, and therefore appear to be altruistic; but her altruism is also self-interested in the sense that she has decided that her interest is defined by the well-being of others. Self-interest is constructed from a mix of selfish and other-regarding motivations. The relevant issue is to determine what forms of other-regarding thought influence a person's decisions and are made a part of a person's self-interest. The relevant prescriptive issue is what forms of other-regarding

---

[8]   The causal source of the impulse to be other-regarding is intricate but not crucial to the theory developed here. People become other-regarding out of personal need for relationship or community, for survival, as a kind of exchange, from social pressure or reward, or out of an inner compunction that comes from spiritual teaching or belief. The causal mechanism that induces people to engage in coordinating behavior is subject to a lively theoretical debate. Among the theories that explain why people engage in cooperative behavior are those of altruism, inequality aversion, reciprocity and conditional cooperation, identity, and institutions. See, e.g., Stephan Meier, chapter two in Bruno S. Frey and Alois Stutzer, ECONOMICS AND PSYCHOLOGY, A PROMISING NEW CROSS-DISCIPLINARY FIELD, MIT Press (2007).

We need to understand the variety of causal elements behind other-regarding behavior if we want to understand how communities build social capital and how it is torn down, and causal mechanisms are crucial to a general theory of social cohesion. For the theory developed here, however, what is most central is how courts recognize and reinforce other-regarding behavior that allows people to freely pursue their projects and preferences in a community of people with projects and preferences, and how courts participate in a social dialogue that strengthens and reinforces other-regarding behavior. The causal question is always in the background, but we will try to understand tort law without an elaborate inquiry into what makes people other-regarding.

behavior a person *should* follow in a particular context in order to make a socially appropriate decision. Tort law defines behavior as reasonable when it is appropriately other-regarding and is unreasonable when it is insufficiently other-regarding.

In summary, the theory propounded here suggests that the core requirement of the reasonable person is to be other-regarding in an appropriate way. The appropriately other-regarding actor takes into account the well-being of those who might be affected by the decisions of the actor and integrates it into the actor's own projects and preferences in order to achieve a fair and equal balance between the projects and preferences of members of an interacting community, one that reflects an appropriate balance between the burdens and benefits of community membership. This characterization of the reasonable person is still rudimentary, for it simply shifts the analytical emphasis from the reasonable person to the appropriately other-regarding person. Yet this shift appears to be salutary, for it is a key way by which we can express the relational duality between injurer and victim as a single event and it explains how a rational actor can rationally be reasonable. The rest of the book develops a theory of social morality that provides a moral foundation for other-regarding behavior and an analytical framework to distinguish appropriate from inappropriate ways of taking into account the well-being of others. Before doing so, however, it is helpful to highlight a crucial characteristic of other-regarding behavior – the relationship between an actor's conduct and the decisions the actor makes to determine her conduct.

1.3. OTHER-REGARDING BEHAVIOR AND PERSONAL DECISION MAKING

Tort law examines how people behave and insists, in a negligence regime, that the behavior be reasonable. Yet when we ask whether an actor has taken due care, we are really asking *not* what the actor did but whether an actor who was appropriately other-regarding would have behaved the way the actor did. We are comparing the actor's behavior in its context with the behavior that an appropriately other-regarding actor would have undertaken, and we are calling the behavior unreasonable to the extent that the actual behavior diverges from the ideal. In order to determine the behavior an appropriately other-regarding actor would have undertaken, we must examine the way an other-regarding actor would have made decisions in that context and the conduct that would result from those decisions. In this way, underlying the question of reasonableness is a question of what kind of decision-making process a reasonable person would use to decide what to do.

Such decision-making centrism is essential to the methodology adopted in this book. Underlying the question of reasonableness is the question of how a reasonable person would decide what to do. The theory is a behavioral theory, but it focuses on the kind of decision making that a person would undertake in order to be engaged in appropriately other-regarding behavior. The decision-making process used by an ideal, reasonable actor is often the relevant unit of analysis in tort law: It looks to determine the way a reasonable person would process information about the world to be appropriately other-regarding.

This is not a new insight; many theorists implicitly refer to decisions rather than conduct in their analysis. I highlight it because of its normative and analytical appeal. As later chapters reveal, it is the foundation of the normative theory by which we understand social and interpersonal morality. Moreover, as we see in the application chapters, focusing on the way an actor makes decisions helps us address the incoherence of tort doctrine. It explains, for example, why an actor who behaves unreasonably is not responsible for the actor's harm (under proximate cause), why an actor who behaves reasonably is nevertheless sometimes responsible for the harm he causes (the *Vincent* doctrine), and the origin and limitation of the no-duty rules. By considering how a reasonable person makes decisions that take into account the well-being of others, we can understand how a collection of appropriately made decisions by people in a community could help the community reduce conflicts and maximize the freedom of members of the community to invest in their projects and preferences.

1.4. OTHER-REGARDING BEHAVIOR AND SOCIAL COHESION

But tort law is about more than just identifying and enforcing appropriate other-regarding behavior. When it is successful, tort law works in tandem with social practice to shape and enforce shared values and understandings. Under the view presented here, tort law reflects an evolving definition of the morality of interpersonal or social responsibility – the challenge of finding a morally sound way of ordering the various wants and desires of people in a community in a way that minimizes interferences between them, maximizes the possibility that individuals will achieve their projects and preferences, and provides a sense of shared destiny that binds the community together.

As Arthur Ripstein emphasizes, tort law provides the basis for determining the fair terms of interaction and cooperation between free and equal people. It is both aspirational and grounded in human behavior, expressing what people ought to do as a reflection of an ideal extracted from what people normally do. The concept of law reflected in this work therefore sees law as a socially developed reflection of the values that are important to, and developed by, a community of people – values that are important, instrumentally (because they lead to good consequences) and morally (because they align with speci-fied conceptions of the right way to think about human interaction). The book adopts a social evolutionary concept of law of the kind recognized by social scientists. It relates law to morals that are understood in the following terms:

> Human life is – and has to be – a moral life precisely because it is a social life, and in the case of human species, cooperation and other necessities of social life are not taken care of automatically by instincts as with social animals. In commonsense terms, morals are socially agreed upon values relating to conduct. To this degree morals – and all group values – are the products of social interaction as embodied in culture.[9]

Ken Binmore, in his magisterial synthesis of social, biological, and moral principles important to understanding human cooperation put much the same thought in the following terms:

> The moral rules that really govern our behavior consist of a mixture of instincts, customs, and conventions that are simultaneously more mundane and more complex than traditional scholarship is willing to credit. They are shaped largely by evolutionary forces – social as well as biological. If one wishes to study such rules, it doesn't help to ask how they advance the Good or preserve the Right. One must ask instead how they evolved and why they survive. That is to say, we need to treat morality as a science.[10]

These views of social morality do not deny that deontic thought plays an important role in "socially agreed upon values relating to conduct" or the "evolutionary forces" of social behavior. Rather, as I argue in this book, the coordinating device that society has chosen is to follow a process of interper-sonal accommodation that is fully consistent with, and implements, Kantian obligations.

Virtually all tort theorists understand that the challenge of tort law is to find a methodology for assigning rights and obligations to individuals that maxi-mizes the possibility for productive interaction and minimizes social conflict. Because the obligation to be other-regarding is socially constructed to reduce conflicts and maximize coordination, it results in obligations that give coher-ence to being a member of the community and a warrant for the community to correct the behaviors that increase conflicts and reduce coordination. What

---

[9] Clyde Kluckhorn, *Systems of Value-Orientation*, in Talcott Parsons & Edward A. Shils, (eds) TOWARD A GENERAL THEORY OF ACTION 388, Harper Torchbook (2001)

[10] Ken Binmore, NATURAL JUSTICE 1, Oxford University Press (2005).

the law is looking to advance is a kind of social cohesion in interpersonal affairs, where members of the community take on rights and obligations so that the community might flourish.[11] Social cohesion in interpersonal affairs does not connote the suppression of dissent or the absence of conflict. It expresses instead the orderly resolution of conflicts over time, by both socially and legally corrective means, in a way that promotes the acceptability of the resolution by relying on basic indicia of efficiency and fairness and the adjustment of the burdens and benefits of membership in a community in response to changing social perceptions and circumstances.

I posit social cohesion as a worthy goal for the law because in a liberal democracy it implies that the collective is able to thrive by allowing individuals to thrive, and it responds to individual capacity and choice.[12] When understood as a concept that is neither predefined nor self-defining, the concept of social cohesion in interpersonal affairs allows the implicit social contract to be continually reevaluated and renegotiated in response to technological and demographic changes, and in light of evolving perceptions of principles that enhance the community by appealing to values that *ought* to influence people's choices. The goal of social cohesion therefore allows the law to be flexible and adaptable in response to changing patterns of behavior and thought, in an evolutionary way. It also supports our positive, normative, and analytical understanding of the law. It is explanatory in that it helps us determine the origins of social arrangements at any given time and over time; it is normative in that it can explain why the law reaches the outcomes it does and how those outcomes might justly be criticized; and it is analytical in that it points to the factors and modes of thought that form law's central character and content.

Although the content of the concept of social cohesion is not self-defining, the outcomes that will advance social cohesion are capable of being determined through standard methods of philosophy and the behavioral sciences. Philosophical thought provides a defense of values that people ought to use when they make decisions and that must therefore be taken into account when we seek to understand how the social contract is, and should be, negotiated. Under this view, philosophers do not tell the law which behaviors are moral; instead, they speak to the modes of thought that are moral and to how people

---

11   The notion of social cohesion that I develop builds on the individual-focused definition used in sociology (in asking what determines an individual's attitudes and behaviors toward group membership) and the institutionally focused definition used by political scientists. See Noah E. Frudkin, *Social Cohesion*, 30 AM. REV. SOCIOL. 409 (2004) (outlining the various conceptions of social cohesion).

12   Undoubtedly, a complete theory of social cohesion would encompass both distributive and corrective justice. In this book, I take up the role of law in resolving interpersonal conflicts through private law, which implicates only corrective justice.

should understand social morality. The law needs to understand what people find to be moral in their decisions about human interaction because the law must reflect and affect those interactions. Behavioral thought is important because the social contract is negotiated through behavioral interaction between people when they decide which effects of their decisions they will take into account when making decisions in light of the expected decisions of others.

Any theory of social cohesion therefore draws on the work of scholars who are working at the intersection of the behavioral sciences and philosophy. Chief among them is Ken Binmore, whose *Natural Justice* integrates into game theory – the quintessential behavioral model – ideas of Rawls and Harsanyi concerning the way each person's view of how people *ought* to be treated influences how people *are* treated.[13] But this work seeks also to integrate Kant's metaphysics of morals with Kaplow and Shavell's *Welfare versus Fairness*[14] in a way that sees moral fairness and economic welfare to be inseparable concepts.[15]

Here, following Binmore, I sketch the model of social cohesion in interpersonal affairs that is developed in this book, leaving the detailed exploration of the topics to subsequent chapters.

In this model, individuals operate within a system that allows them to choose their projects and define their preferences. Although this attribute follows the Western ideal of individualism, it does not preclude collective identity and social bonding. It assumes, rather, that aspects of identity and collective value will be based on individual choice that can freely be changed. The model then suggests that social cohesion will develop from three concepts:

1. **Efficiency:** The system will try to maximize the ability of each person to achieve his/her own projects and preferences, subject only to the constraint that one person's projects and preferences must sometimes give way to the projects and preferences of others when both cannot be achieved. This is the concept of efficiency: trying to get the most out of what people want to achieve when they operate in a community, and maximizing the capacity of individuals to achieve the projects and preferences in a community of projects

---

[13] Binmore, Natural Justice. Anyone familiar with Ken Binmore's epic work will understand the debt that I owe him, in more ways than I can mention. My thought diverges from him only on our understanding of Kant, whom I interpret to be closer to Binmore than Binmore does.

[14] Louis Kaplow & Steven Shavell, Fairness Versus Welfare, Harvard University Press (2002).

[15] The normative appeal of the theory of social cohesion defended here is laid out in Part II, which consists of Chapters Three, Four, and Five.

and preferences. Efficiency here means "no waste": A system of social cohesion never misses an opportunity to make one person better off if that can be done without making another worse off (Pareto efficiency), and it seeks to ensure that individual projects and preferences are achieved with a minimum of inputs.

2. Fairness: The system will result in rights and obligations that people regard as broadly fair, or fairly arrived at, so that people can pursue their projects and preferences without resentment. This concept provides a neutral principle that assures the community that the distribution of rights and obligations in interpersonal affairs will not be determined by preexisting privilege or social status, but by the equal consideration of the claims of each person. This concept allows humans to devote their energy to achieving their projects and preferences, and serves as a spur to individual initiative and a guarantee against exploitation. Without it, people will invest in wasteful retribution or cease investing in their own projects and preferences.

3. Stability: The system of private rights and responsibilities will be stable, but not frozen, implying that the system will follow procedures to adjust rights and responsibilities that are broadly perceived to be fair, that the system can adjust to changing circumstances without losing efficiency and fairness, and that the system takes into account the long-term interests of the people (given their projects and preferences). In this sense, stability is not the outcome of the system, but is an indication of the procedural fairness from which the system arises and the system's allegiance to values that people are willing to follow.

Finally, the social system must be based on institutions that incorporate the other properties. Viewing social cohesion as the goal of the law allows us to see the law in institutional terms, as part of the socially constructed set of incentives and constraints (some defined by the individual and some defined by the community) that allow human beings to coordinate their projects and preferences in a world of scarce resources by reducing frictions and enhancing shared values.

1.5. SOCIAL COHESION AND OTHER-REGARDING BEHAVIOR

Consider the close relationship between the goal of social cohesion and other-regarding behavior. We can rephrase the central concern of tort law as follows: Tort law asks whether the actor has made a decision that enhances social cohesion by taking into account the well-being of others in a way that fairly accounts for the conflicting claims of others and the fair balance between the rights and obligations of citizens in a community of citizens. Social cohesion is advanced when people make decisions using a certain mental apparatus and with a certain mental disposition. The purpose of tort law is to recognize and encourage decisions that are made in accordance with that apparatus and disposition. We label decisions made in that way as reasonable decisions; as the next chapter explains, we rely on values that society itself uses when determining which decisions are reasonable. Social cohesion results when people make decisions by factoring the well-being of others into how they determine their own well-being in a way that society regards as optimum because it enhances overall efficiency, fairness, and stability. Social cohesion relies on other-regarding behavior and disintegrates in its absence.

Several characteristics of the goal of social cohesion respond to aspects of the current debate in legal theory. Social cohesion is not a goal that exists outside the legal system. It is what the legal system takes into account when it decides cases. As subsequent chapters make clear, the behaviors and attitudes that lead to social cohesion are formed within a community, and they are the raw material to which the law looks to determine the values that society considers to be relevant to the reasonable accommodation of conflicting projects and preferences. Because the law uses social values to evaluate whether an actor is sufficiently other-regarding, the goals of the law and the values of the community are aligned, diverging only when judges think that the community as a whole is not sufficiently other-regarding.

As we will see in Part II, the theory of social cohesion advanced here puts moral decision making at the center of the theory, invoking a theory of moral decision making that draws on the Kantian categorical imperative and Rawls's original position. It is not a theory that emphasizes only "do what is best," but one that also emphasizes "do what is best because it is right." It therefore blends deontic and consequential thought; it is a synthetic goal combining aspects of fairness and efficiency. The precise way in which this is done is elaborated in Part II; for now, it is enough to note that a theory of social cohesion allows us to work toward a theory that integrates the deontic duty to think in the appropriate other-regarding way with an appreciation of which consequences are appropriate to consider.

For that reason, social cohesion effectively merges the goals of deterrence and correction. There is nothing inherently contradictory – indeed there is something reinforcing – about a system that seeks simultaneously to correct and to deter, one just needs to specify what is being corrected and deterred. The concept of correcting an imbalance and the concept of deterring modes of decision making that lead to that imbalance are two sides of the same coin. We hope to deter, but we correct that which we cannot deter in order to ensure that the world is close to the position it would have been in had we deterred. When they are fully specified, the goals of deterrence and correction are correlative. We know what we are trying to deter by recognizing that which we would correct if we do not deter, and we correct to the extent that we would have tried to deter the defendant from failing to account appropriately for the well-being of others. Moreover, we neither deter conduct that we find to be made with appropriate deference to the well-being of others, nor find an imbalance to correct if the other-regarding behavior results in harm.

1.6. AN EXAMPLE

To illustrate how the theory of other-regarding behavior allows us to give analytical content to tort law, let us return to *Hammontree*. The defendant's act-based (due care) decisions were whether to take medication, avoid behaviors that would enhance the risk of seizure, and be aware of the signs indicating that a seizure was possible. Under the negligence rule, a defendant would be responsible for harm caused by failing to reasonably make those decisions because that failure is evidence that the defendant unnecessarily and unjustly preferred his own projects and preferences to those of another. By taking a little effort, the defendant could have completed his own projects and preferences (in particular the desire to drive) without unduly burdening the projects and preferences of the owner of the bicycle shop. In terms of the Hand formula,[16] the cost of due care is less than the expected harm that would have been avoided if the defendant had paid the cost. Failure to take the precautions shows the defendant's inappropriate disregard for the well-being of the victim.

This standard understanding, however, still begs the issue of what basis we have for saying that the defendant's effort was "little" or that the projects and preferences of the victim would have been unduly prejudiced. Before we can say that, we have to have a basis for believing that the burdens are little in comparison to the victim's harm and that the actor should have realized that. If the seizure occurred because the driver failed to take his medicine, it might be fairly easy to say that had the actor been thinking appropriately about the well-being of others, the actor would have taken his medicine. But what results if the actor failed to understand a sign his body gave him that a seizure was likely? And we can see how difficult the assignment of values is if we focus on broader activity-level decisions, such as whether or where to drive.

Once we shift our focus to an actor's decisions and the range of consideration that a rational, but reasonable, actor would incorporate into his decisions, we

---

[16] *United States v. Carroll Towing Co.*, 159 F.2d. 169, 173 (2d. Cir. 1947). The next chapter shows how comparing the burden of precaution with the accident probability and the magnitude of harm if the accident occurs is appropriate other-regarding behavior.

can also better understand the choice between the negligence regime and the strict liability regime. Although making reasonable due care decisions would have reduced the risk of seizure, some residual risk would have remained, and that residual risk would (because of the epilepsy) be greater than the risk of a seizure in the general population. The defendant could control even those residual risks through the choices he made about his driving – the activity-based decisions. He could take public transportation or stay at home, reducing to zero the risk of harm from having a seizure while driving. Or he could have chosen less populated and therefore less risky routes. These are activity-based decisions. A regime of strict liability would base responsibility on causing harm and would therefore make the choice of whether and where to drive the source of responsibility. This is true because under strict liability, the defendant would reduce the risk of having to pay for causing harm by taking the risk of harm into account when deciding whether and where to drive and would ensure against any risk that yielded the defendant more benefits than the expected harm. The strict liability regime would therefore make driving expensive for the defendant with epilepsy (either requiring him to buy insurance or to change his behavior to less-desirable alternatives). The defendant would have to burden his projects and preferences for the sake of the projects and preferences of the owner of the bicycle shop.

Under the theory of other-regarding responsibility, we ask whether the defendant's decision to drive rather than to choose one of his other options was appropriately other-regarding. To assess *that* decision, we must compare the loss to the defendant's projects and preferences from liability for driving with the expected harm to the plaintiff's projects and preferences if the defendant is not required to compensate the victim for accidents from driving. This requires us to compare the defendant's freedom to drive (given the due care he took) against the plaintiff's freedom from bodily injury (which could have been extensive). This is no easy decision, for the conflicting values are incommensurate, but it is a comparison that is inevitable in deciding the plaintiff's claim. In terms of the theory of other-regarding behavior, the question is whether the defendant impermissibly favored his own projects and preferences over those of the plaintiff's when deciding that he would drive rather than avoid driving.

Tort law's general rule, of course, and the one applied in *Hammontree*, chooses the negligence regime, not the strict liability regime. This can be understood to indicate that if the defendant took due care, the defendant did not think inappropriately about the welfare of the plaintiff when deciding whether and when to drive. This outcome indicates that it must have been reasonable for the defendant to decide that his freedom to drive was more socially valuable than the plaintiff's freedom from bodily injury. Proof that the defendant caused the plaintiff's injury is insufficient to show that the defendant impermissibly disregarded the plaintiff's well-being. We can understand this result in two ways. From the defendant's perspective, he did nothing to deserve the epilepsy; it was bad luck and it had already reduced the quality of his life. To subject him to a further disability (the risk of paying damages from driving) because of the existing disability would be a major imposition, not outweighed by the potential harm to the plaintiff. Once he took due care, the accident was caused by bad luck, not by anything within human agency, and there is no reason why the defendant rather than the plaintiff should bear the burden of that bad luck. When forced to choose between his freedom to drive and the plaintiff's safety, it is reasonable for him, in the circumstances of this case, to choose his freedom.

Naturally, plaintiff would see the case differently, for she had done nothing wrong and ended up with a broken arm. But we might ask the plaintiff to consider this question: if the roles were reversed, or if she did not know whether she was the driver with epilepsy or the victim, what rule would she want to govern the situation? What decision would she have made? It is quite likely that behind this veil of ignorance, the plaintiff might well have chosen the negligence rule.[17] If so, then we have a neutral rule – one chosen without regard to the status of either actor – that provides a basis for saying that the defendant's decision to drive did not impermissibly discount the well-being of another. Under this reading, we have a fault-based system to recognize the socially constructed meaning of responsibility for the well-being of others. Every person must be responsible for the well-being of others in the way they would be if they were the other (including the responsibility to reasonably control the risk of seizure) but not for conditions – like epilepsy – over which they have no control.

Notwithstanding this justification of our fault-based system, *Hammontree* is an especially compelling case for the plaintiff, presenting something of a challenge to our fault-based system. The plaintiff contributed nothing to the accident (except to open a bicycle shop on the street where the accident occurred) and the defendant controlled any information that might have shown that he did not take due care, making it hard for the plaintiff to prove, for example, that he had not taken his medicine or had ignored signs that might cause a reasonable person to refrain from driving. Yet the plaintiff's burden of proving fault protects a defendant even when the defendant is lying, giving rise to the

---

[17]   This conclusion is more fully supported in the next chapter. The veil of ignorance is described in detail in Chapter Five.

possibility of false negatives. One reason the legal system tolerates false negatives is that in the absence of sufficient proof that the defendant could have
controlled the epilepsy, the law would risk punishing the honest but unlucky
epileptic, imposing responsibility beyond the defendant's agency. The plaintiff's burden of proof protects the values that the law respects – in this case,
the freedom of the person with epilepsy to drive – from unwarranted judicial
intervention. In addition, however, the negligence rule is flexible enough to
allow the court to lower the burden of proving negligence to test the validity
of the information the defendant gave the court. In *Hammontree*, the judge
allowed the jury to base responsibility on the doctrine of *res ipsa loquitur*. In
this way, if the jury felt that the defendant was lying and could have prevented
the accident with proper precautions, the jury would be entitled to find that
the defendant was negligent.

The conclusion we have reached so far – that under the circumstances
presented in *Hammontree*, the tort system values the freedom of a person with
epilepsy to drive more than the freedom of the victim to avoid injury – reflects
the theory of other-regarding behavior. The conclusion does not project a
rule but a way of thinking about how society expects people to adjust to the
unavoidable conflict in which these two people found themselves. It also projects how society expects people to think about the well-being of others in the
context of those unavoidable conflicts. The resolution is efficient because it
reduces the unavoidable conflict (by requiring the defendant to take reasonable precautions) and reduces the social losses from the trade-off between two
desiderata when both cannot be achieved. The resolution is fair because it
reflects a resolution that we believe would be appealing to both people if their
roles were reversed and because it is attentive to the ability of human agency
to affect the well-being of another. The resolution will be accepted as legitimate because the resolution takes into account, and responds to, the social
and contextual values that influence how society thinks about the defendant's
responsibility to the plaintiff given his disability and options. The resolution
achieves a kind of social contract by asking whether the defendant's decisions
show an adequate regard for the well-being of potential victims of the kind
that the defendant and victim would agree to (as proxies for similarly situated
people) if they did not know whether they were in the position of the injurer
or victim.

This approach allows the outcome of the analysis to change as the circumstances change, allowing the implicit social contract to be continually reimag-
ined or renegotiated. We have been assuming, for example, that the defendant
had a rather low level of risk from epilepsy if he followed the prescribed treatment (in *Hammontree*, the defendant had not had a seizure in 12 years). As

the risk of seizure increases, the relative social importance of the contesting desiderata will shift; at some point the risk of a seizure, even when medically controlled, may be so great that an other-regarding defendant would stop driving. Where the line between the reasonable and the unreasonable is located, we cannot say in advance. But when that line is reached, we can understand it by asking an actor with that kind of epilepsy whether, if the roles were reversed and the actor with epilepsy were the potential victim, the actor would favor an outcome that would rank personal safety higher than the freedom to drive. A reasonable person – one who is thinking about the welfare of those whom he might injure – would incorporate the well-being of potential victims into his own welfare and at some point would decide that the advantages of driving were outweighed by the disadvantages of the potential harm imposed on others.[18]

The analysis is also socially contingent. If we change an implicit background assumption (that the defendant, a California resident, had few alternatives to driving), we can understand that if the actor had good public transportation the outcome might change. An other-regarding person with epilepsy would take public transportation if the burden of doing so was outweighed by the benefit of reducing the risk to others. And if the defendant with epilepsy decided to become a taxi or school bus driver, society might well say that an other-regarding defendant would understand that he should choose another job; alternative employment, although less desirable to the actor with epilepsy, would impose less burden on society than the risk of being on the road more frequently or carrying precious cargo. Under these revised circumstances, the law could well require the defendant to make a different decision.

1.7. CONCLUSION

This chapter has developed the broad outlines of a concept of social cohesion that serves as the goal of tort law (and indeed of private law in general) and as the justification for state intervention into the lives of private citizens. Although the requirements of social cohesion have not been fully specified, the theory responds to the two ideas already introduced in this book: that (1)

---

[18] Notice that we need not resort to the doctrine of strict liability to reach this conclusion – we need not determine that some persons with epilepsy are abnormally dangerous and others are not. We simply ask whether the decision to engage in the activity – the activity of driving – was unreasonable in the circumstances because it failed to give adequate attention to the social ranking of the freedom to drive and the freedom from risk of injury. It is the analytics of reasonableness, not the analytics of strict liability, that determines whether and where the defendant should have driven that day.

tort law ought to focus on whether an actor's decision (rather than simply the actor's conduct) is reasonable and (2) that decisions are reasonable when they are made with an appropriate socially cohesive regard for the well-being of others. This can be understood in terms of traditional tort doctrine to encompass duty and reasonableness. Duty is the obligation to think of the well-being of others when making certain decisions.[19] Reasonableness is the obligation to reason appropriately about the well-being of others when one is under a duty to do so, which requires the actor to incorporate appropriately another's well-being in the actor's projects and preferences.

Central to this approach is the notion that communities themselves, by the way that people continually interact and coordinate their projects and preferences, generate and reflect the values that a reasonable actor must take into account when determining how to be other-regarding. In healthy communities, people continually adjust their decision making to take into account the well-being of others and adjust their conduct accordingly. We can see this if we look in detail at how reasonable people make decisions and if we develop a theory of decision making that reflects how healthy communities develop patterns of behavior and attitude toward others that enhance both efficiency and fairness. This will address the problems of value-formation that tort theory has thus far been unable to address: The first is to determine where the actor gets the values that allow the actor to compare the social value of different options the actor faces, and the second is to determine the relative ranking of those options in light of the projects and preferences of potential victims. I develop this aspect of the theory of other-regarding behavior by discussing, in the next chapter, the requirements of the reasonable person.

---

[19] Although this is not a free-wheeling duty to take care of others, it is a duty that an actor has whenever the actor is attached to the risk that another faces in a relevant way. I defer to Chapter Six the discussion of which decisions require an actor to take into account the well-being of others and which decisions the actor is permitted to make without taking into account the well-being of others.

2   Social Cohesion and Social Values

The Reasonable Person

Open-ended, undefined, and context-contingent, the reasonable person standard is both the central pillar on which tort law is built and a source of mystery
about the content and function of tort law. The standard definitions are circular, not a source of analytical or justificational understanding.[1] And the attempt
to give the reasonable person concept an analytical and justificational core by
invoking the relative costs and benefits of various courses of action – the Hand
formula – has fueled the divide between consequential and deontic theories.

But the mystery and division are unwarranted if we understand the reasonable person in light of the theory of other-regarding behavior. In this chapter,
I give the reasonable person concept analytical and justificational content
by advancing my claim that the reasonable person is one who appropriately
accounts for the well-being of others in a way that promotes social cohesion.
Central to this account is a portrayal of the source of the values that reasonable people use in order to be appropriately other-regarding. An actor's responsibility is to adopt a method of making decisions that allows the actor to give
appropriate weight to the projects and preferences of others – to internalize, in
an appropriate way, the social value of the projects and preferences of others
into the decisions the actor makes.

2.1. THE CURRENT UNDERSTANDING

This conception of the reasonable person builds on our current understanding of the analytical and functional content of tort law.[2] Like existing accounts

---

[1]   In common formulations, unreasonableness is doing something that a reasonable person
      would not do or failing to do something that a reasonable person would do. Alternatively, a
      reasonable person is one who takes "due care" or "ordinary care." Dan B. Dobbs, THE LAW
      OF TORTS 277 West (2000). Both are descriptions with little analytical content.
[2]   The typology in this paragraph draws heavily from Ben C. Zipursky, *Sleight of Hand*, 48 WM.
      & MARY L. REV. 1999 (2007).

of the reasonable person, the account here acknowledges the importance of social norms and conventions, but it goes beyond existing accounts by showing why and how the values underlying those norms and conventions are important and why courts feel free to substitute their judgment for social conventions. Like virtue accounts of the reasonable person – those that view reasonableness to be a personal virtue that can be nourished – it looks at the actor's attitude as the significant focus of analysis, viewing the ability to adopt an other-regarding attitude as a virtue of the same order as the virtue of being self-regarding. Like many existing accounts, the account here understands tort law to be a form of social contract, but it specifies the terms of the contract and how courts identify them. This conception begins where most accounts of the reasonable person begin, by understanding the reasonable person in terms of the need to reconcile the conflicting interests of the actor and the victim (which have been given various names, including rights, liberty and integrity, freedoms, social value or, as I have put it, well-being).

However, existing accounts of the reasonable person are incomplete and underspecified because they do not make clear how we understand the values that a reasonable actor takes into account when reconciling conflicting claims – that is, the basis on which a reasonable person determines how much weight to give the well-being of those who might be affected by the actor's decisions.

Rather than focusing on questions of value formation, scholarly appraisal of the reasonable person standard has been diverted to a sort of winner-take-all debate about the role of the Hand formula, a debate made current by the inclusion of cost–benefit analysis in the *Restatement Third* description of the reasonable person.[3] The debate is multifaceted and complex, depending, as it does, on what version of the Hand formula the author seeks to attack or defend and on the meaning the author gives to various concepts that haunt the debate, such as the impartiality and the equality principles. My approach is to elide the details of that debate, preferring to offer my own version of the reasonable person under the Hand formula that builds on much of the debate but casts it in a new light.

The central question governing the Hand formula, and our assessment of its application, is the thought process the reasonable person is expected to use when making decisions and choosing among options. I adopt the Hand formula as an organizing device for the simple reason that it expresses the basic requirement of other-regarding behavior and the trade-off that the reasonable actor must make between his liberty and the security of the victim. But

---

[3]   Richard W. Wright, *Justice and Reasonable Care in Negligence Law*, 47 Am. J. 143 (2002).

I do not choose among the theories of evaluation that have been advanced to implement the Hand formula, nor do I suppose that there is one method of economic valuation.[4]

Rather than wade into the cross-currents that constitute the debate about the Hand formula, I instead develop a theory of value that allows that trade-off to be understood in terms of a theory of interpersonal morality that both reflects and guides human behavior. Given the baggage that the Hand formula now carries and the existing battle lines, I risk being misunderstood. But one who reads this chapter with an open mind and without prior conceptions about what the Hand formula means may find that my rendition of the Hand formula avoids the divisiveness that otherwise haunts the literature, and that, in fact, it extracts the best features from the current debate. In other words, I present a rendition of the reasonable person that is consistent with Richard W. Wright's conclusion that corrective justice (which he calls interactive justice) "requires that others who interact with you in ways that may affect your person or property do so in a way that is consistent with your equal right to negative freedom, and vice versa."[5] I also expect my rendition to be consistent with Kaplow and Shavell's notion that the only criterion for judging a legal intervention is to determine whether it advances human welfare. Just as social cohesion embodies concepts of both fairness and efficiency, I expect to present a version of the Hand formula that is both deontic and economic.

Because the Hand formula has been the domain of economists, and because my version incorporates the concept of corrective justice into the application of the Hand formula, it may be helpful to comment briefly on the relationship between the theory developed here and the theories of deontological scholars that have tried to explain the reasonable person in relatively determinate terms.

Ronald Dworkin's approach is to consent to the basic trade-off between the well-being of two people that is implied in the Hand formula, and even to use the willingness to pay criterion as a basis for valuing the trade-off, creating a market-simulating approach.[6] However, he subjects the trade-off to severe

4   Stephen G. Gilles has identified five valuation methods: the willingness to pay approach, the utilitarian approach, the social contract approach, the egalitarian approach, and the virtue-based approach. Stephen G. Gilles, *On Determining Negligence: Hand Formula Balancing, The Reasonable Person Standard, and the Jury*, 54 VAND. L. REV. 813, 819–21 (2001). The notion that a reasonable person would weigh the costs and benefits of various ways of acting has been around a long time. Judge Posner seized on it, to be sure, to advance a particular economic vision of the Hand formula, but his goal was as much to make our understanding of the reasonable person determinate as it was to advance a particularized and narrow agenda.

5   Wright, *Justice and Reasonable Care in Negligence Law*, at 166.

6   Ronald Dworkin, LAW'S EMPIRE 295–309, Harvard University Press (1986).

constraints by imagining that the injurer and victim have equal resources, such that their willingness to pay is not affected by their ability to pay or other circumstances that ought not affect the distribution of burdens and benefits in a community. This puts a distributional constraint on a utilitarian exchange in a way that, along with other important qualifications, is thought to result in a just allocation of rights and responsibilities. The basic intuition is that if people start from a position of equality, then willingness to pay reflects how important the resource is to them; it reflects the choices that people feel are important to them given the other things they would like to accomplish in their life (subject to our ability to agree on the relevant conditions of equality).[7] Comparing these values then allows us to determine the priority of one person's freedom versus another person's security. It has never been clear whether Dworkin adopted this suggestion simply to illustrate how one might take a utilitarian, market-simulating approach and move it closer to a distributionally fair approach, or whether he indeed thinks that it is the best approach for the trade-off that must be made. But it overcomes many of the objections to a utilitarian approach by overcoming the distributional drawbacks of utilitarianism.

The Dworkinian solution is important in at least one respect. Dworkin uses a hypothetical device (what people would pay for freedom or security if everyone had equal resources) to determine which person's claim should have priority. Indeed, it is difficult to see how to ascertain of relative values without relying on a hypothetical device, and my approach joins Dworkin in that respect. In the end, however, the theory presented here rejects the Dworkinian approach because he assumes that the interpersonal comparison of value is based on the (distributionally neutral) evaluation made by the injurer and victim. This seems to me to be too individualistic and possibly idiosyncratic to reflect a social valuation. Even if the injurer and victim were idealized to average reasonable people, this approach makes it look as if individual values, and not social values, matter. The hypothetical device I employ allows individual value systems to be important in giving content to the system of evaluation, but allows a social ranking of claims that is more representative of trade-offs that are likely to support the goal of social cohesion.

---

7   One of the important qualifications, of course, is the one that Amartya Sen raises. Amartya Sen, DEVELOPMENT AS FREEDOM 54–6, Anchor Books (2000). If one person has a disability – say the risk of epileptic seizures – and the other does not, are we to judge their equality by ignoring the disability or by adjusting for it even before we ask about the willingness to pay for a resource. That is, to what extent is the equal capacity to achieve one's goals the measure of equality that we impose before we ask about willingness to pay for a particular resource?

The other relevant account of the reasonable person by one firmly in the deontological camp is the "civil competency" notion developed by Ben Zipursky.[8] Although he does not purport to provide a detailed account, his theory, like that here, emphasizes that society socializes its members to have certain attributes, including the attribute of carefulness. He portrays this not as just a skill or performance level, but as "the very activity of taking others' well-being seriously in conducting oneself."[9] And he illustrates that other-regarding behavior with the example of a camper who would not leave rotting meat at the campground when she left, lest it attract animals who would make camping risky for others. His explanation foreshadows the one I provide: "Part of being reasonably prudent, under such circumstances, is being able to think through an appropriate way to behave that does not unduly imperil others," which involves not only skill, intelligence, and reasonable foresight but also "being other-regarding to a certain extent."[10]

Building on that idea, the theory of other-regarding behavior developed here specifies the basis on which the actor's and the victim's conflicting claims to well-being are reconciled, the source of the values that are used to make that reconciliation, and the relationship between those values, social norms, and social cohesion, on the one hand, and, on the other hand, the behavior requirements of one who would appropriately integrate the well-being of others with the actor's own well-being. This gives us a more precise and integrated way of thinking about the attributes of the reasonable person and how those attributes can be evaluated, communicated, and debated. It therefore specifies the analytical content of the reasonable person in a way that allows us to give tort law determinacy within a normative framework for ascertaining fair terms of interaction.

I first show, in Section 2.2, that the Hand formula embodies the theory of other-regarding behavior and argue that it can therefore serve as the central organizing model for justificational analysis of the reasonable person. But the Hand formula provides an incomplete understanding of the requirements of the reasonable person because it does not itself specify the values that a reasonable person will take into account when determining how to account for the well-being of others. I therefore go on, in Section 2.3, to show how people in a community act and interact on the basis of values that are important to them and how those values provide the raw material from which a reasonable person is expected to take into account the well-being of another. This allows

---

[8] Zipursky, *Sleight of Hand* at 2034–41.
[9] *Id.* at 2035.
[10] *Id.* at 2036.

me to show, in Section 2.4, how the values that underlie norms influence the decision making of the reasonable person, and also to introduce the device of the veil of ignorance to describe how conflicting values are reconciled. The remainder of the chapter addresses several objections that have been raised to the use of the Hand formula as the central justificational model of the reasonable person. In Section 2.5, I address the claim that so-called compliance errors cannot be explained by the Hand formula. I use this discussion to demonstrate how the reasonable person standard, even within the context of the Hand formula, responds to evidentiary reality by creating presumptions of unreasonableness and how it responds to the need for legal determinativeness by inducing people to develop relatively straightforward rules of behavior. In Section 2.6, I address the claim that the Hand formula cannot explain the heightened standard of care that tort law sometimes imposes.

2.2. THE HAND FORMULA AS OTHER-REGARDING BEHAVIOR

The theory of other-regarding behavior suggests that the Hand formula is both under- and overappreciated; it is more insightful than corrective justice theorists admit but less formulaic and deterministic than law and economic theory suggests. The approach here unpacks the Hand formula to show that it advances our understanding of other-regarding behavior, grounding our interpretation in a description of how people coordinate their activities in order to advance social cohesion. In this version of the Hand formula, the reasonable person is one who incorporates the well-being of another into the person's decisions in the way that is socially appropriate, taking into account the central attributes of other-regarding behavior and the requirements of social morality.

Literally, the Hand formula suggests that an actor is unreasonable if the actor could have invested in precautions that are less costly than the expected harm that would occur without the precautions. To be reasonable, an actor must make the reasonable investment in precautions, requiring the actor to accept burdens or sacrifices to his own projects and preferences. Failure to make the investments gives those injured by the actor a claim against the resources of the actor to repair the damage. This requires the actor to incorporate the well-being of others into how the actor thinks about his own projects and preferences – to be other-regarding. Or, to put the matter another way, under the Hand formula a potential victim has a claim on the resources of an actor when the actor's resources that are required to prevent harm have less social value than the social value of the potential victim's resources that would be lost if the actor does not use his resources to protect the potential victim.[11]

When we unbundle the Hand formula, we see that it expresses two fundamental judgments about relationships between persons in a community. The first is that an actor has an obligation to take into account the well-being of potential victims when making certain kinds of decisions. The second judgment is that an actor ought to integrate another's well-being into decisions about his own projects and preferences in a certain way. Specifically, the actor must invest in the well-being of a potential victim – that is, burden his own projects and preferences to recognize the projects and preferences of the other – up to the point where an additional burden on his projects and preferences would be assigned a higher social value than the well-being of the other that it preserved (the expected harm to the projects and preferences of the other). However, an actor need not burden his own projects and preferences with sacrifices that would not have a commensurate beneficial impact on the social value of the well-being of another, for to do that would diminish the social value of the actor's projects and preferences without any offsetting increase in social value. The Hand formula, thus interpreted, calls for a comparative evaluation of the projects and preferences of different people in order to maximize the extent to which each of the projects and preferences can be achieved, as measured against the values that people ought to use if they want to advance social morality.

Understood in this way, the Hand formula embodies the theory of other-regarding behavior. It focuses on an actor's decisions and asks the actor, when making decisions about his projects and preferences, to take into account the projects and preferences of others in a way that enhances social cohesion. The actor is required to give up assessments that seek to disproportionately advance his own projects and preferences from a social perspective. The reasonable person integrates the well-being of others into his own well-being, reflecting

---

[11]   That the Hand formula is a form of cost–benefit analysis is not surprising. Cost–benefit analysis is unavoidable because people who decide how to behave inevitably consider the relative merits of alternatives and choose the one that seems to be best. The specter of cost–benefit analysis should not deter us from determining how reasonable people ought to value the relevant costs and benefits, which is the significant question. If I am deciding how fast to drive and I take into account only my own projects and preferences – that is, how quickly I want to get to my destination and what I am willing to risk to get there – my cost–benefit analysis is of a particular (selfish) type, and I have not taken into account the external costs of my choices. On the other hand, if I take into account the possibility that my behavior will adversely affect others, and internalize the external costs, it is of a different type. Either way, it is cost–benefit analysis. The issue is not whether cost–benefit analysis is required or used, but the nature and value content of the cost–benefit analysis that decision makers use.

a broader vision of how individuals in a community coordinate their various projects and preferences when those projects and preferences potentially
conflict.

We thus understand the Hand formula as a device that people use to coordinate their behavior. In particular, well-functioning communities rely on
each person to make decisions that take into account the well-being of others
in addition to the person's own well-being so that each decision maximizes
the potential for successful coordination and minimizes interference between
the projects and preferences of different people. The Hand formula is a summary view of what makes one person's decision making appropriate in light
of the projects and preferences of other people. It works as a coordinating
device when it is reciprocally used under the circumstances – that is, when
both an actor and other people incorporate the well-being of others into their
own well-being using similar social values. When all actors make decisions in
accordance with the same version of the Hand formula, the actors collectively
minimize interference between their projects and preferences and allow the
projects and preferences of people to flourish to the maximum extent possible.
The law recognizes and reinforces the standards of cooperation that communities use and improves the standards when an improvement would advance
social cohesion.

This conception can be understood in both economic and corrective justice
terms. From an economic perspective, the other-regarding person is one who
internalizes externalities; one person's claim on social resources must take into
account another person's claim on the same resources (i.e., the social opportunity cost of any claim). From a corrective justice perspective, the right of the
actor to act is conditioned on considering the interests of potential victims and
ensuring that the well-being of the injurer and the victim are appropriately balanced in the decision. If the appropriate balance is not achieved, the actor is
disrupting social cohesion and the state is justified in correcting the wrong.

In the way I have interpreted it, the claim that the Hand formula embodies the obligation to take into account the well-being of others when making
decisions should be uncontroversial. It is, however, an incomplete account of
the justificational content of the reasonable person. First, the Hand formula
does not provide a means of understanding when a person must be other-
regarding. It provides a framework for thinking about how an actor must act
when the actor has the duty to take the well-being of others into account, but
no framework for understanding when an actor has that duty. That aspect of
the reasonable person is taken up in Chapter Six. More to the point of this
chapter, the Hand formula does not tell an analyst how a reasonable person
ought to think about the values that will allow her to determine the nature

of the integration of the conflicting interests of actor and victim. We need to understand how the reasonable person views the projects and preferences of others and how the reasonable person understands the sacrifices she must make to protect another's well-being. In terms of economic analysis, we need to define the basis on which externalities will be defined and internalized. In terms of corrective justice, we need to determine what balance of interests between injurer and victim must be preserved. Or, more concretely, we need to know whether a driver with epilepsy who can reasonably control the risk of a seizure should be responsible for the harm he causes if he has an unexpected seizure while driving home from work. Does the freedom of the driver have to give way to the security of those he puts at risk? As another example, one suggested by Gregory Keating, Don is driving to the beach, is late, and has to decide how fast to drive. How do we understand the requirements of the reasonable person in that context?[12]

2.3. THE CREATION OF SOCIAL VALUES AND OTHER-REGARDING BEHAVIOR

In the account of the Hand formula that I advance, the reasonable actor uses appropriate values to integrate another person's projects and preferences into the actor's. We therefore need an account of how a reasonable person identifies the relevant values, both as they affect a person's behavior and as they affect the comparison of the projects and preferences of different people.

In this section, I develop a theory of value formation, both for individuals and for society. I do that by turning the usual presentation upside down. It is well known that tort law responds to norms and customs that govern people's behavior. When the norms are reasonable, they are the ones a reasonable person is expected to follow. When they are unreasonable, they are behaviors that the law is trying to change. But too often these norms are thought of as independent rules of behavior, as if they formed magically and inexplicably from human interaction. And too often, the norms are thought of as establishing behavioral values by looking at what the norms induce people to do. If there is a norm that those standing on the escalator will move to the left, the value expressed by the norm is thought of as a form of behavior. This view deemphasizes the values that go into creating and supporting the norms and emphasizes, instead, the resulting behavior. I want to reverse the emphasis. To understand norms and their use in the analysis of the reasonable person, the

---

[12] Gregory Keating, *Reasonableness and Rationality in Negligence Theory*, 48 STAN. L. REV. 311, 324–5 (1996).

approach here is to focus not on the norms themselves but on the values that underlie the norms and what those values tell us about the requirements of the other-regarding person.

In this formulation, values are inputs used in making decisions. Values identify the factors that are (or should be) given weight in making a decisions and they determine how those factors are (or should be) balanced against each other. Reasonable people use appropriate values when they make decisions – that is, they give appropriate weight to the various considerations that have to do with their own well-being and with the well-being of others. This usage of the term *value* can be distinguished from the sense of value as an output – that is, the notion of what people like to achieve. If we say that society values social cohesion, we are using the term "value" as an output, as something that people want to bring about. If we say that a person values leisure, we are using the term *value* to signify a goal or desideratum. So too, if we say that a person values the freedom to drive fast. The distinction between values as an input and values as an output is significant. A person who values leisure (an output) may nonetheless decide to work because the factors (values as inputs) the person uses when making decisions show that work is better for some reason for that person. A person who chooses not to work (value as an output) may choose that because of one of several inputs (time to think, laziness, or various preoccupations).

This emphasis on values as inputs rather than as outputs is important because it is the best way by which we understand the decision-making process that a reasonable person would use to be appropriately other-regarding. It is therefore our basis for evaluating the norm to see if it is one that a reasonable person would follow. When people stand to the side on the escalator, what is important is not their behavior *qua* behavior, but their recognition of the social value of standing aside so that others may move more quickly.

Social values – the weight to be given various projects and preferences when they clash – reflect the decisions people make in the infinite variety of circumstances they face. People act on the basis of things they value. They decide, for example, whether to drive, walk or take public transportation, how often to drive, how fast to drive, whether to drop an unneeded wrapper on the ground, and whether to pick up a wrapper left by someone else. These decisions reveal the kinds of factors that people take into account when they decide between alternatives. Individually, these decisions are context- and person-specific, reflecting the myriad of circumstance that make up human decision making. Each such decision represents value judgments an actor makes in a particular context – a personal statement about what factors are important to the person making the decision at that time and place and under those circumstances. These decisions are influenced by habit, convenience, emotion, reputational returns, self-interest, and how the decision maker thinks of the interests of others. Often, the decisions are conditioned by how people think they should act – those internal compulsions that constrain and guide people's choices. Often, the value judgments are influenced by how the decision maker thinks others make similar decisions; in the face of uncertainty, people gain a measure of confidence when they do as others do.

Individual decisions become aggregated and interlinked. One person's way of living influences another's; through their behavior, individuals communicate with each other about the beliefs and values that seem to be satisfying to them and about those they find to be unsatisfying. Some behaviors are nonconformist; of those, some are mimicked until they become part of mainstream norms, while others wither away. Despite the heterogeneity of beliefs and values that guide behavior, certain beliefs and values find a critical mass among people, a center of gravity that expresses a kind of community or social value. These social values reflect an unstable but self-reinforcing consensus, a set of heuristics that most people follow most of the time and that express – and influence – the beliefs and values individuals hold. These social values help people form belief systems about the questions they face: What is the value of driving rather than taking public transportation, how should people think about the frequency with which they use their car, what value do people normally assign to getting to their destination quickly, and how important are clean sidewalks?

The values that individuals reflect in their behavior often coalesce into norms – that is, into constraints on behavior that become reinforced by practice and that guide and constrain individual behavior. Imperceptibly, people are conditioned to behave in ways that reflect the social values created by the collective, and the values reflected in certain behaviors in turn are taken up by others when they make decisions. The cycle of reflecting and creating social values continues as people interact in light of norms and putative changes in norms. Although norms sometimes influence how people behave when their behavior has no effect on others, most often norms help coordinate the activities of members of the community. Coordinating norms reflect a set of values that people use when one person's projects and preferences conflict with the projects and preferences of others; the norms of behavior help to coordinate the various projects and preferences. A norm may suggest that people stand to the side on an escalator to allow walkers to pass them. That norm coordinates activity between those who would walk up the escalator and those who would not, allowing the conflicting projects and preferences to be coordinated. Similarly, people entering a building routinely stop to let others go through the door first. Drivers signal to each other when the right of way is not clear.

These and countless other forms of coordinating norms are norms of other-regarding behavior. The behavior occurs because the social norms suggest that one person should take into account the well-being of others when making decisions. Such other-regarding behavior is the social glue that holds communities together and that allows the projects and preferences of many people to be coordinated with a minimum of interference and a maximum of individual well-being. The norms express a set of values about the burdens that actors should make part of their own projects in order to improve the well-being of others in the community, given the projects and preferences of others. Under these norms, one actor incorporates the well-being of another into the factors the actor takes into account when making decisions. The norms therefore reflect the social cohesion of other-regarding behavior.

In this way, norms and behaviors that coordinate the various projects and preferences of people in society reflect values that allow a person who wants to contribute to social cohesion to understand when he or she should assume burdens in order to spare other people from having their own projects and preferences burdened.[13] They therefore help us define whose behavior seems to be ignoring the importance of social cohesion. Coordinating norms are highly reciprocal. Norms define the circumstances under which one person can expect to receive benefits from others who take on burdens to advance social cohesion. People assume burdens as part of their decisions and advance the well-being of others because they can expect others to bear burdens to advance *their* well-being. Reciprocal burden-sharing advances social cohesion.

Socially developed norms are, of course, unstable, because the projects and preferences of various individuals are unstable. But the norms move toward equilibrium – a situation in which decisions made by individuals reflect the projects and preferences of other individuals in a way that is broadly acceptable to all – the condition of social cohesion. Interaction of people in the community continues to refine beliefs and values until conflicts are

---

[13] The formal study of norm formation and evaluation resides in game theory – the study of how actors arrive at coordinated behavior given the costs and benefits of the behavior of one actor in light of the potential behavior of other actors. Game theory – like tort law – involves a potential conflict between the projects and preferences of different actors that can be ameliorated with successful coordination – coordination that requires each actor's decisions to be other-regarding by taking into account the well-being of the other actors, given various possible behaviors by each actor. When the decisions are sufficiently and reciprocally other-regarding, coordination is enhanced and the actors flourish. When the decisions are insufficiently other-regarding and/or nonreciprocally other-regarding, the well-being of the actors is diminished. On game theory, *see generally*, Douglas G. Baird, GAME THEORY AND THE LAW, Harvard University Press (1998). and, Cristina Biccheiri, THE GRAMMAR OF SOCIETY: THE NATURE AND DYNAMICS OF SOCIAL NORMS, Cambridge University Press (2006).

minimized, people are able to pursue their own projects and preferences with relative freedom, and the burdens and benefits of being part of a community are perceived to be equally shared. These equilibrium norms, because they are perceived to be both efficient and fair, are accepted as legitimate and constitute the implicit social contract. They are supported as long as no other norm could advance the interests of the collective as a whole by being more efficient and fair.

Because coordination norms are socially created, we can understand the law as an institutional means of recognizing and influencing coordinating norms in order to promote social cohesion. Tort law is, as we have said, a claim by one person that her projects and preferences should have been given greater attention by another. We can therefore see why tort law revolves around a standard rather than around rules.[14] The reasonable person standard is open-ended, undefined, and context-contingent precisely because tort law does not deal with behavior in the abstract.[15] Tort law deals with behavior as it relates to an actor's attention to social values that require the actor to consider the well-being of others. Driving fast is not a concept that is especially relevant to tort law; driving fast becomes unreasonable only when it is done under circumstances that show an inappropriate regard for the well-being of others. The focus is not on how fast the driver goes when measured against some external standard of appropriate speed. The question is what we can infer (from the defendant's speed and other circumstances) about the defendant's attitude toward the well-being of those who might be injured. We can tell from the circumstances whether a reasonable person, taking into account his or her own projects and preferences, would think about the circumstances that might affect the well-being of others in a different way and implement those thoughts with different decisions. These circumstances are so variegated and contextual that our quest is not for rules of behavior but for a way of thinking about and describing the requirements of the reasonable person that allows us to evaluate behavior by understanding the values the defendant is required to take into account when making decisions.

---

[14] Even the "rule" of strict liability functions as a standard. The rule of strict liability often allows exceptions for acts of God or the victim's own negligence. More important, a court can invoke the rule of strict liability only by determining whether an activity is "abnormally dangerous" or meets some other basis for applying the rule. Because the basis for applying the rule is not self-defining, a court must use a standard – for example, the standard of "abnormally dangerous" – in order to invoke the rule, making the rule function as a standard.

[15] As Justice Cardozo said, citing Pollack, there is no negligence in the air. *Palsgraf v. Long Island Ry. Co.*, 162 N.E. 99, 100 (N.Y. 1928).

2.4. APPLYING THE HAND FORMULA

Despite the inherently contextual nature of the reasonable person inquiry, the standard need not be indeterminate. As we see in this section, the theory of other-regarding behavior provides determinacy by specifying the contours of the inquiry into the values an actor would adopt if the actor were to be other-regarding in an appropriate way. This includes the kinds of empathy that one person is expected to have for the projects and preferences of others and the kind of interpersonal comparisons between various projects that the person is expected to use. In this way, the theory of other-regarding behavior, while reflecting the moral responsibility of one person to others in the community, allows us to make the reasonable person standard more determinate, avoiding the kind of vague and circular definitions that now dominate tort law.

We can use our two paradigm cases to illustrate the other-regarding, and therefore reasonable, person, building the appropriate analytical model from its simplest form. Don, who is driving to the beach to meet friends, is in a hurry; perhaps he overslept or wants to get the best spot on the beach. If no other drivers are on the road (and Don can do no damage to others by going off the road), Don is free to think only of his own well-being when deciding how fast to drive. He will weigh the risks of driving fast against the benefits of achieving his project of getting to the beach in a hurry. Speed limits and state criminal enforcement aside, Don has the right to pick his projects and preferences in his self-interest, without interference from any other person.[16]

Once other drivers are on the road, however, Don's decision about how fast to drive affects others. If he is reasonable, Don will consider the well-being of others when deciding how fast to drive; he will integrate into his projects and preferences (the reason he wants to drive fast and his taste for risk) the projects

---

[16] The framework developed in the text allows us to be more precise about how we understand rights and obligations. When we say that Don has a right to select his projects and preferences (and to behave in accordance with them) we mean that society has no legitimate basis for questioning those projects and preferences in the abstract (which is why Ronald Dworkin calls them "abstract rights"). Whether they are good for Don or wisely chosen, and whether they are rational in some sense, is not open to question in the abstract. We call them rights because we respect Don's ability to make the decisions, even if they are not decisions that others would make and even if they are not ones that we think are good for Don. This right to choose projects and preferences is an important one, for although the right must sometimes be made subservient to the projects and preferences of others, it is not questionable on its own. This meaning of right confirms Don's human autonomy and capacity. The approach suggested here is thus "rights based" in the sense that it reflects and, in fact, endorses the world as Don sees it. Moreover, to say that sometimes Don's right must be subservient to the rights of others is not to denigrate Don's right in its own terms. It is only to say that in order to coordinate the way Don exercises his rights with the rights of others, communities must make choices between conflicting abstract rights. That is what tort law does.

and preferences of those who may be on the road for a different purpose or with different reactions to risk. To be reasonable, Don must follow socially developed and morally mediated values (or the norms reflecting those values) that govern human interaction in that situation. The norms and values that Don evidently adopted, based on his behavior, can be compared with the norms and values that Don would adopt if his behavior were to be reasonable, based on social values that correspond to those necessary to build social cohesion. Don will not be able to argue that he should be able to go 90 miles an hour because of his interest in getting to the beach early or his taste for risk. Social values show that society values the physical and emotional integrity of other drivers more highly than it does the marginal increases in Don's early arrival or thrill of driving fast.

But how are we to understand the values that a reasonable person should use to determine whether his projects and preferences must give way to the projects and preferences of another? The theory of other-regarding behavior allows us to go beyond current understanding and specify the source of those values, and how we can recognize and assess them.

To evaluate whether a defendant's behavior was appropriately other-regarding, we must ask whether the defendant's behavior, in the context in which it occurred, is sufficiently empathetic to the projects and preferences of others, and whether the behavior gives appropriate weight to conflicting projects and preferences when the actor determines whether to take on burdens or to allow the burdens to fall on others. The weight that is appropriate is determined by the requirements of coordinated behavior in a crowded world; the actor's comparison between her projects and preferences and those of others must be sufficiently neutral and universal to result in a ranking of conflicting projects and preferences that achieve social acceptability.

This requires the actor to appreciate the world as others experience it and to evaluate the interpersonal claims of injurer and victim from a neutral position (i.e., without regard to the actor's circumstances that are extraneous to the appropriate balance between injurer and victim). The first requirement is empathy; the second is a neutral and universal evaluation of the social ranking of various projects and preferences, which is achieved by undertaking an evaluation of disparate projects and preferences from behind Rawls's veil of ignorance.[17] These are intertwined requirements. Empathy is required because a reasonable actor who makes decisions behind the veil of ignorance must understand the range of personal characteristics that differ from hers. The reasonable actor must understand that other people are risk averse (even

---

[17]   This is discussed in greater detail in Chapter Five.

if the actor is not), that some have preexisting heart conditions (even if the actor does not), and that some people have less information than she. Then the reasonable person must consider what course of action she would choose if she understood the trade-off between the projects and preferences of injurer and victim but did not know which characteristics she had and whether she was injurer or victim.

Consider first the quality of empathy: Don must be able to appreciate and respect the projects and preferences of others through the value system that others are likely to employ, not through the value system he uses. He must be able to stand in the shoes of others and try to appreciate the world as those people understand it. Tort law revolves around a modified golden rule: Do unto others as you would have them do unto you if you had their projects and preferences. This requires Don to be respectful of the fact that others will see the world differently than he does, with different goals and objectives and drawing on different value systems to make decisions. He must recognize the general range of hopes and fears that influence people's view of the world, and take those into account when making decisions.

More specifically, with respect to driving to the beach, Don must be able to understand and appreciate from common human experience that others may not be as comfortable with risk as he is, or may give less importance to getting to their destination quickly (perhaps they were in a previous accident or have a heart condition that might be aggravated in an accident). Others could have time on their hands and might enjoy a leisurely drive, or they could be pursing less time-sensitive projects. Don must anticipate those kinds of evaluations and must not impose his own valuations on others. Empathy is integral to the application of the Hand formula, for when determining the expected harm from his decision, Don must include the harm as others would experience it. If Don were to assess the well-being of others through his own set of values, Don would underappreciate their right to reflect their value systems, reducing the chance that the various projects and preferences of those he encounters could be coordinated. Coordination requires that each actor accurately understands the situation of other persons as the other persons are likely to perceive it and the range of values that they are likely to adopt to guide their lives. Without that, one person will make decisions that impose a loss on the well-being of others as the other defines it, and the social cohesion that is meant to flow from coordinated behavior would be decreased.

The methodology of empathy – the socially appropriate way of thinking about the world as others are likely to comprehend it – is itself socially constructed; social interaction teaches people how to stand in the shoes of others and how to understand values that others use when making their own decisions. When tort law distinguishes the benign, attention-getting tap on the shoulder from offensive groping, tort law is reflecting the kind of empathetic appreciation that one person must give another. In the same way, a reasonable actor is expected to know, as a member of the community, the range of attitudes of others toward the world and their place in it. Just as it is straightforward for an actor to understand (or learn from experience) that others like to walk up the escalator (even though the actor likes to stand and ride), the range of human experience encompasses an appreciation of how others behave and therefore an ability to appreciate the world as others see it.

The empathy required of the reasonable person is a central concern of tort law; sometimes empathy alone tells us what is reasonable in the circumstances. For example, the agency relationship between landlord and tenant gives a landlord the duty to look out for the well-being of her tenants, requiring the landlord to be other-regarding even when he or she has not created the risk the tenant faces.[18] The scope of this obligation to be other-regarding is governed by the empathy required of a landlord – that is, the ability of the landlord to think about the world as a tenant would. When, for example, the landlord knows that it would be hard for the tenant to discover that the shower glass is not shatterproof (because the tenant cannot tell by observing it), the landlord is responsible to tell the tenant that the glass is not what it appears to be.[19] The landlord must see the world from the standpoint of the tenant and must understand that information about the shower glass is important to the tenant. The empathy required of the landlord – recognizing that information important to the tenant would be hard for the tenant to acquire – establishes the scope of the landlord's duty to warn the tenant and overcomes the landlord's self-interest in not being asked to replace the glass.[20]

Consider also the thin-skull rule: A driver who negligently causes an accident with a person who has a preexisting condition is responsible to the victim for the harms that result from the preexisting condition, although the driver did not cause the preexisting condition. This, too, reflects the empathy required in tort law – the ability to understand the world as others experience

---

[18] I elaborate on this statement in Section 6.4.

[19] *Trimarco v. Klein*, 436 N.E.2d 502 (N.Y. Ct. App. 1982). When the glass was initially installed, shatterproof glass was not a practical option, so the landlord was not negligent in creating the risky situation. Nonetheless, because of the asymmetry of knowledge about the existence of a hazard and how it might be addressed, the landlord had an obligation to warn the tenant once the technological option of shatterproof glass became available.

[20] In *Trimarco*, evidence showed a custom by landlords to replace nonshatterproof glass at the request of the tenant. The landlord's duty to inform tenants of the condition of the glass was not a part of custom, but the jury imposed the duty to allow the tenant to exercise the right that custom gave the tenant.

it. A driver is expected to know that some percentage of people drive with preexisting conditions that might enhance injuries in an accident, cause an unexpected heart attack, or trigger latent schizophrenia, for example. A driver is also expected to know that social mobility is highly valued by society, so that driving with preexisting conditions is socially acceptable; under ordinary circumstances it is not unreasonable for the victim to do so. Drivers are therefore expected to consider that matter when they decide how to drive carefully, reducing the risk of an accident to reflect the need to protect the well-being of drivers with preexisting conditions. Because the obligation to be reasonable includes the obligation to be empathetic to those with the preexisting condition, it is hardly surprising that a person who negligently causes harm from a preexisting condition is responsible for that harm.

But empathetic reaction simply places an actor in the position of comparing burdens on his projects and preferences with burdens on the projects and preferences of others in a way that respects the others' projects and preferences. The actor must also employ a methodology that allows the actor to rank the projects and preferences of others against his own, determining, in terms of the Hand formula, the relative social value of burdening his projects and preferences against the expected social harm to the projects and preferences of others if he does not. This is the heart of most tort cases. In Don's case, society must have a methodology for determining whether Don's desire to get to the beach soon is more important than the desire of other drivers to get to the beach safely. Or, as in the case of the driver with epilepsy, society must determine the relative values that help us decide whether a victim's right to be free from absorbing an injury is more socially important than the freedom of a person with epilepsy to drive reasonably. With rankings, people can change their behavior to take into account social expectations about the degree of deference to be given to the projects and preferences of others. Without rankings, the accommodation of conflicting projects and preferences would be based on who could get away with what, with each person valuing his projects and preferences in ways that reflect not social coordination but personal gain and power.

The ranking of the relative burden on various projects and preferences is often thought of as a form of interpersonal comparison of welfare or utility, but that does not quite capture the kind of comparison that tort law expects the reasonable, other-regarding person to make. The law does not expect a reasonable actor to compare her lost utils from having to take precautions with the utils the victim would thereby gain. As is well known, the law cannot reliably calculate utils; the actor and victim determine their utils on different, incomparable scales. Moreover, converting utils to comparable preferences by asking what each person is willing to pay would result in a comparison that was unduly influenced by the preexisting distribution of wealth. But these are not the main reasons why the law does not use an interpersonal comparison of welfare or utility.

Instead of making an interpersonal comparison, the actor is making the others' well-being a part of the actor's well-being, putting them on a common scale derived from requirements for cooperation that are essential to social cohesion and deciding what is best for the actor's well-being in light of the social advantages of incorporating the well-being of others.[21] When an actor stands to one side on an escalator to allow others to pass, the actor is not simply comparing the cost of moving to one side against the benefit to the person who wants to walk up the escalator, for that would justify the actor in accentuating the burden of moving to one side. Instead, the actor is determining that as a member of society the actor is incorporating the other person's projects and preferences into his own, using a valuation method that takes into account the importance of such cooperative behavior to the enterprise of building a community. We can think of the value as a kind of a reciprocal venture in which one person finds it in his interest to burden his projects and preferences because he knows that in other situations he will be benefitted when someone else does the same for him.

In other words, in any comparison of well-being, a reasonable actor ranks the burdens on the various projects and preferences of different people in a way that allows the projects and preferences to proceed with minimum interference, using an implicit social index of relative values that reflects neutral valuation criteria and a weight that reinforces social cohesion. The reasonable actor thinks about the neutral criteria that society uses to identify and rank the various projects and preferences, and he uses those criteria to rank the

---

[21] This conception collapses the two forms of other-regarding thought that enable interpersonal comparisons in the Harsanyi–Binmore approach to interpersonal comparisons. Ken Binmore, NATURAL JUSTICE, 113–6, Oxford University Press (2005). They distinguish between sympathetic preferences (where an actor changes her preferences because she takes on the preferences of another, as occurs when people fall in love) and empathetic preferences (where people keep their individual preferences but coordinate their behavior with others in light of the others' preferences). The distinction between sympathetic preferences and empathetic preferences is important if we need to distinguish between how an actor would feel and what an actor would do. But in tort law the issue is whether the actor made a decision with sufficient deference to the well-being of others, so the law expects the actor to change her behavior on the basis of sympathy with another's situation. When we ask one person to live by a rule that she would be happy to live with were she the victim not the injurer, we are asking her to incorporate the other's well-being into how she defines her own well-being. I adopt the term *empathy* to describe the nature of the comparison because it avoids the connotation of sorrowfulness that the word *sympathy* might convey.

burdens on his own projects and preferences against the burdens on the projects and preferences of others. A person who moves to the side on an escalator accepts the social valuation that the small inconvenience of moving over is worth it to avoid the inconvenience to those whose way would otherwise be blocked, given the contribution that this other-regarding behavior makes to shared benefits and burdens in a community.

Social cohesion demands that the social ranking of burdens on competing projects and preferences be stable and acceptable. Social rankings meet these criteria when they reflect a degree of detachment that filters out the situation of particular individuals, either as to their position in society or as to their idiosyncratic projects and preferences, and ranks projects and preferences in a way that advances social cohesion. We can understand this as a valuation that would be chosen by most people if they adopted an empathetic attitude toward various projects and preferences but did not know whether they would be in the position of the victim or the injurer – that is, the valuations that people in a community would make if they were behind Rawls's veil of ignorance. The social ranking of projects and preferences becomes enduring only if it reflects values that individuals would choose if they did not know the particulars of their circumstances and how the rankings would affect them because of those circumstances. Only the social rankings that have that kind of neutrality are likely to be accepted as fair in a way that will promote their use. Only those social rankings are likely to enhance the stability of social cooperation.

Consider again the driver who has epilepsy and therefore has a slightly higher risk of seizure than most drivers. He decides to take the risk and drive, and he has a seizure and hits the victim. Let's call the driver Jenner and the victim Maxine. Should Jenner's decision be a source of responsibility to Maxine; should it be called unreasonable? To make a reasonable decision about whether to drive, that actor must determine whether his freedom to drive without insurance against non-negligent harm is worth more than the possible harm from driving and having a non-negligent seizure. What is the reasonable way for Jenner to think about his well-being in light of Maxine's well-being?

To understand the social value of the trade-off, Jenner must consider what rule would be chosen if both injurer and victim were behind a veil of ignorance. Naturally, once there is an accident, Maxine will feel aggrieved by the injury and will desire compensation; she will, in fact, assume that justice demands compensation. We might, however, put Maxine behind the veil of ignorance and ask her what maxim should be chosen to determine the outcome if she understood Jenner's predicament but did not know whether she was the injurer or the victim. She is likely to pick a rule that ranks a driver's freedom to drive without insurance against non-negligent liability as more important than the freedom of the victim to be free from risk. She would know that if liability were imposed on the decision to drive, the epileptic driver would be under a disability that other drivers are not under (having to buy insurance for non-negligent accidents). She is likely to rank the general freedom of the driver with epilepsy above the projects and preferences of the victim. First, she is a driver and knows the importance that the community places on the freedom to drive. Second, she would understand that nonliability in that situation would also privilege others who had a risk of seizure from whatever source – a preexisting heart condition or old age. Third, she would understand that nonliability might also privilege her if she had a sudden seizure from whatever source. Fourth, she would know that the social harm of a rule putting special disabilities on those subject to a seizure is broad and certain, whereas the harm to potential victims who must bear the risk is likely to be particular and uncertain. Finally, she would know that the driver with epilepsy has an incentive (self-protection) to avoid driving if the risk of seizure were perceptible (and would therefore know that the epileptic driver is likely to avoid driving unless he also accepts the risk of seizure).[22]

For all these reasons, it is reasonable to conjecture that behind the veil of ignorance most people would choose to be the victim without compensation rather than the injurer with epilepsy who has to pay compensation. Once we filter out the knowledge of which person is the injurer and which is the victim, we can reason our way to a neutral rule that seems to present an acceptable balance between the projects and preferences of people in a crowded world – one that privileges the freedom to drive under those circumstances over the freedom to be free from injury in those circumstances. This veil of ignorance is the device that helps us establish the social ranking of various projects and preferences in a way that is likely to lead to social cohesion. As long as Jenner is not otherwise unreasonable, his decision to drive with a slightly higher risk of seizure than is normal is not unreasonable and not the source of responsibility to others for the decision. Jenner is making a decision that comports with social cohesion because society recognizes the importance of the freedom to drive. When Jenner decided to drive he did not think inappropriately

---

[22] Behind the veil of ignorance Maxine is evaluating two states of the world without knowing whether she is Maxine or Jenner: Maxine's good state (Jenner's bad state) and Maxine's bad state (Jenner's good state). For the reasons mentioned in the text, we have some confidence that the disadvantages of Maxine's bad state were she Maxine are smaller than the disadvantages of Maxine's good state were she Jenner. We therefore have confidence that we can place Jenner's freedom above Maxine's freedom on a socially derived scale of values.

about the well-being of others simply because he had a higher than normal risk of a seizure while driving.

Of course, Jenner did not go through the thought process just described when making his decision. But this thought process reflects the instinctual and reflexive way in which people think about their decisions when they are coordinating their activities with others. Without a thought process like this, communities would crumble as people advance their own projects and preferences without regard for the projects and preferences of others. This induces communities to continue to adjust to the various projects and preferences that people present and to do it in a way that leads to stable and predictable relationships, even between strangers. Tort law adopts the best of that process by endorsing those forms of other-regarding behavior that seem to reflect the moral ranking of projects and preferences from behind a veil of ignorance and reforms those that do not by requiring them to meet the standards that would be chosen from behind the veil.

The neutral valuation criteria for social rankings are socially derived in the same way that individual values develop from social interaction, but those that survive have the quality of neutrality that makes them socially acceptable and therefore enduring. People develop methods of comparison between various projects and preferences that others choose by deciding how to act in light of the projects and preferences of others. When a person is required to confront the projects and preferences of another, the person is forced to make social comparisons. A person who is thinking of a relationship with another, whether social or commercial, is continually ranking her own projects and preferences against the projects and preferences of another. The person decides on the scope of a relationship with another by deciding how many burdens on their projects and preferences they are willing to give up to adjust to the projects and preferences of another. They pick the projects and preferences of another that they find to be relatively appealing (compared to their own projects and preferences) and reject those they find to be less appealing. Even in nonrelational settings, people constantly develop methods of interpersonal ranking. A person who decides whether to stand by to let others get off the elevator first is making a social comparison. Social comparisons are at work whenever a person changes her behavior because she prefers the behavior of someone else.

Not only do individuals continually make social comparisons, but people also exchange views about their interpersonal comparisons through conversations and behavior. People, say, for example, "Look at how that maniac is driving. He is either on the way to the hospital or has a death wish." That is a form of expressive social comparison – that those speeding under the circumstances either have a very good reason to do so or are acting illegitimately. People also exchange views about interpersonal comparisons by their imitative behavior. When a large number of people behave in a certain way in a given circumstance, others are likely to find that behavior to be comparatively preferable. Over and over, people show by their behavior the ways in which they rank various projects and preferences that confront them and that therefore require social comparisons.

Not all rankings of projects and preferences are going to lead to social cohesion. But over time, the rankings that are perceived to be widely beneficial (efficient) and neutral (fair) are likely to emerge as rankings that allow people to coordinate their activities by considering those rankings in their decisions. These rankings will tell people, for example, at what speed a preference for driving fast is less important than a preference for road safety and when it is permissible to impose a risk on others to accomplish a certain project. From the individual rankings that seem to promote social cohesion, a methodology of social comparisons emerges, a kind of social aggregation of the various behavioral and verbal interchanges about interpersonal comparison that seems to promote social cohesion. As this social ranking of projects and preferences emerges, it tends to be self-reinforcing if it yields wide benefits and responds to a neutral distribution of burdens and benefits. A deviation from the behavior that conforms to the rankings called for by those comparisons is subject to social sanction. These social sanctions help to reinforce the community's view of the appropriate comparisons; if the comparisons move the community toward a more comfortable and accommodating place, they are more widely adopted and reinforced. Because the ranking of projects and preferences is a social, not an individual ranking, no actor can make a special claim for her particular desire to drive fast or for the high valuation she places on driving fast. Society can easily distinguish between the desire to drive fast and the desire to drive fast to get someone to the hospital.

A social ranking of projects and preferences promotes social cohesion when it leads to decisions that are efficient and fair. When people make decisions in accordance with the ranking that leads to social cohesion, they are acting reasonably. And because rankings are fair when they have the neutrality called for by the thought process behind the veil of ignorance, a court can easily determine whether the ranking of projects and preferences the defendant used in a particular setting is one that will lead to social cohesion. A court can easily police the border between what *is* and what *ought* to be by asking whether what *is* could be improved if the decisions reflected a social ranking determined behind the veil of ignorance.

2.5. THE HAND FORMULA AND COMPLIANCE ERRORS

A persistent problem of tort theory is how to understand compliance errors – those errors that occur when a person is trying as hard as he or she can to comply with the reasonable person standard but, through mistake or inadvertence, falls short of the standard. As Mark Grady develops the concept, reasonable actors adopt performance standards to deal with risky situations they face.[23] Surgeons determine that they will leave no sponge in a patient. An apartment owner determines how often to inspect an external fire escape to make sure that it can still be used safely. A driver determines to check the mirror's blind spot before changing lanes when traffic is in the area. In order to meet such performance standards, reasonable actors must also adopt a precaution plan to help meet their standard. A surgeon will establish checks and double checks to count the sponges as they are inserted in, and removed from, the patient. An apartment owner will set up a tickler system to ensure that periodic inspections are done and will be attentive to signs that more frequent inspections are necessary. A driver will develop habits of checking the blind spot in the mirror and will understand patterns that tell her when the habit of checking the blind spot can safely be omitted. The reasonable person is therefore determining a standard to follow and a precautionary plan to meet that standard.

Yet despite their best efforts, people sometimes fail to comply with the standard they have adopted (either because their precautionary plan is inadequate or because they make a mistake), and sometimes the failure to comply with the standard causes harm. Courts generally find such compliance errors to be the source of legal liability. This raises three types of questions: The first is why the inability to comply with a standard is a source of responsibility if it reflects merely a momentary or one-time lapse? Why should a doctor who is both generally vigilant and pursuing a good precaution plan be subject to liability on the one occasion when a sponge is inadvertently left in a patient? This is the justificational question. The second question is what relationship these examples have to the Hand formula. The Hand formula is clearly helpful in analyzing a precaution plan, for that is an overall plan that directly aims at balancing the cost of greater effort and the harm prevented by that effort. But what is the relationship between the Hand formula and the problem of compliance error – that is, the problem that people make mistakes in compliance efforts even if they try as hard as is humanly possible to avoid mistakes? The third issue is whether liability for compliance errors ought to be thought

---

[23] Mark F. Grady, *The Negligence Dualism* 13–6 (UCLA School of Law, Law & Economics Research Paper Series, Paper No. 09–02, 2009), available at http://ssrn.com/abstract=1337275.

of as an example of strict liability or whether the law simply deals with compliance errors by creating presumptions of unreasonableness that can be rebutted under certain circumstances. Situating these compliance errors on the continuum between negligence and strict liability is important to our conception of the unity and coherence of tort doctrine.

Before addressing these questions, it is relevant to recognize that an actor's inability to comply with the applicable standard is a more pervasive problem than was just described. Professor Grady mentions the well-known problem of the actor who does not have the mental capacity to meet the reasonable person standard, illustrated by the *Menlove*[24] case. Although such a person is incapable of complying with the applicable standard, if the person acts unreasonably, the person is nonetheless responsible for the harm she causes, just as is one who makes a compliance error. The range of relevant questions is identical: the justificational question of why a person who does the best he can should be responsible for another's harms, the question of whether the Hand formula helps in analyzing this case (because the actor is unable to do the Hand formula calculus properly), and the issue of whether we should call this strict liability (because the mental attitude of the actor was not blameworthy, we might call this liability without fault).

Moreover, the same problem arises in product liability law. The problem of manufacturing defects is essentially a compliance problem. Despite their best efforts, manufacturers cannot always reasonably ensure that their products perform as intended. As a result, products sometimes malfunction. An example might be the bottle of soda that explodes because of excessive carbonation, despite the best efforts of the manufacturer to prevent this. To prove that the product was defective in this respect, the plaintiff only needs to show that the product deviated from its intended design and caused harm, a form of proof that does not depend on whether the seller exercised reasonable care. Again, we can ask what the justification for this treatment is, how this is related to the Hand formula, and whether this is an example of strict liability?

This issue of manufacturing defects is enlightening because it illustrates the unrecognized commonality between compliance errors in the service sector and compliance errors in the product sector. The examples used in the "compliance error" literature are drawn from the service sector, whereas in the product sector the similar phenomenon is referred to as a "manufacturing defect." We will have occasion to consider the implications of this unrecognized commonality later in Section 10.7.

---

[24] *Vaughn v. Menlove*, 132 Eng. Rep. 490 (1837).

The most comprehensive exploration of the compliance error problem is by Mark Grady, although we will consider the related concept of inadvertent error propounded by Ben Zipursky when we discuss the role of the Hand formula. We can readily agree with Professor Grady that it is difficult to determine whether the failure to comply with the relevant standard was reasonable. Examining compliance costs is difficult because we cannot easily know, within the range of acceptable evidentiary costs, whether the failure to comply is systematic (and therefore unreasonable in the sense of a failure to regularly comply with the rules) or whether it is simply a one-time error (i.e., a reasonable failure to comply because it is a mistake or inadvertent error that could not have been prevented with more effort). We can also admit that compliance errors are impossible to avoid, no matter how hard a person strives to do so. Everyone makes mistakes from time to time, no matter how hard they try to avoid them. But I part with Professor Grady when he says that reasonable persons "routinely commit compliance errors."[25] The problem with this statement is that in litigation we are not asking whether the defendant was a reasonable person; we are asking whether a reasonable person would have committed this compliance error in this situation. Tort law does not judge the person but judges the conduct or decision making behind the conduct. And I depart from Professor Grady again when he says that the "reasonableness of the error will not be a legal defense."[26] What he means is that it is not a defense to point out that the defendant is normally careful and that this was a "mere" mistake. As we shall see shortly, even under Professor Grady's scheme of strict liability for compliance errors, the jury is allowed to excuse the conduct, which means the jury is allowed to find the conduct to be reasonable under the circumstances.

The conundrum is to explain why a person who did the best she could, and exhausted all reasonable means of avoiding the mistake, should be held to have committed a tort when something goes wrong. Why should a person who has taken reasonable pains to avoid a mistake be held accountable for a "mere" mistake? Acknowledging the narrow point that one who commits a compliance error is not allowed to show that she is normally careful or that she tried as hard as she could to avoid the compliance error, what is the justification for imposing liability when the conduct is not morally blameworthy in the moral sense of doing less well than one could?

We can begin our justificational analysis of this problem by recognizing that most people would assume without much thought that a surgeon who leaves a sponge in a patient was at fault for having done something that he

---

[25] *Id.*
[26] See Chapter Ten.

or she ought not to have done, unless extraordinary circumstance explained how it happened. We can assume that most people would understand that an apartment owner who omitted a planned inspection required of a reasonable person was also at fault for failing to do something that she had an obligation to do (again unless the apartment owner had some overriding reason for omitting the inspection). And most people would say that if a driver fails to look beyond the blind spot while changing lanes, he has omitted something that he ought to have done, assuming that there was no overriding reason for the omission.

Our task then is to explain the common intuition that compliance errors of this type are normally a wrong that needs to be corrected.

The response I give turns, as does Professor Grady's, on an evidentiary, not a substantive, understanding of compliance errors. Analytically, an error that looks like a compliance error could happen in one of three ways: if the surgeon failed to adopt reasonable procedures that would avoid the mistake, if there were an "inadvertent" error or reasonable mistake, or if the surgeon was distracted by something that would excuse the mistake. The first error is one that is observable and assessable. The actor can be asked to testify as to the precaution plan, and its reasonableness can be evaluated under the usual application of the Hand formula. The third reason for the supposed compliance error is situational and uniquely in the knowledge of the defendant. It would apply only to unexpected and unusual circumstances that justified the compliance error by showing that the lack of attention served some greater purpose. An example might be a bomb scare in a hospital that justified the compliance error by justifying the surgeon's deviation from the precaution plan because the risk of harm from the omission was necessary to avoid some higher cost.

The second error – the compliance error – is the difficult one to evaluate. The challenge is to develop a methodology for distinguishing between reasonable and unreasonable compliance errors. It is difficult to establish an evidentiary basis for determining whether one has invested reasonably in the iterative process of complying with the reasonable standard. The precaution plan is a general description of the steps an actor expects to take to avoid compliance errors. It is a description of reasonable effort and what that means in a particular context. It is difficult to compile an evidentiary basis for determining whether the required effort was, in fact, made in the instance where the harm occurred. Take an instance in which a doctor leaves a sponge in the patient. Whether this is a reasonable deviation from the precautionary plan (one that cannot be avoided even with reasonable care) will depend on the particularized circumstances that justify the deviation. Perhaps the doctor was in a hurry to get to a dinner party and was therefore unreasonably hasty. Perhaps she was overtired and perhaps she should have known that the fatigue might affect her ability to comply with the plan (which might have then called for her, in order to be reasonable, to have modified the plan to have someone else execute it). Factors such as these affect whether the compliance error was a reasonable mistake or an unreasonable one. But how will the plaintiff prove this?

Generally, the relevant evidence is in the hands of the defendant, who alone knows whether the required reasonable effort was in fact made. It is often effectively unverifiable in its particularity and personal nature. Moreover, evidence that the defendant is generally careful and generally avoids this kind of mistake is not relevant to the question of whether the defendant acted reasonably on the occasion the mistake occurred. The reason for the compliance error is effectively unknowable and unprovable to the plaintiff because of the difficulty of distinguishing an inexcusable deviation from the precautionary plan and an excusable one. Yes, mistakes happen and, yes, they may not be blameworthy. But compliance errors also occur because the actor may deviate unacceptably from the compliance plan. Distinguishing these two situations is nearly impossible and putting the burden of distinguishing the two relevant causes of compliance errors on the plaintiff would result in false negatives – cases where the defendant was unreasonable in compliance, but the plaintiff cannot prove it.

Because of evidentiary problems, the problem of false negative will be great if the law puts the burden of distinguishing an unreasonable from a reasonable compliance error on the plaintiff. Some cases of unreasonable compliance error will go undetected. Moreover, we expect an other-regarding actor to be very careful to avoid compliance errors; we want surgeons, apartment owners, and drivers to invest heavily to avoid them. The fact that a compliance error occurred may itself be strong evidence that the compliance error was unreasonable.

Under these circumstances, the law creates a rebuttable presumption that a compliance error is unreasonable. The fact that a mistake happened is consistent with unreasonable compliance and will be strong evidence of unreasonable compliance if mistakes of this type do not ordinarily occur in the absence of an unreasonable compliance error. This is not a substantive or normative statement about one person's responsibility for another; it is an evidentiary statement. In other words, the compliance error problem is one of burden shifting, the device usually associated with the doctrine of *res ipsa loquitur.* When the mistake does not ordinarily occur in the absence of negligence, proof that the mistake occurred is strong evidence that it occurred unreasonably; it is sufficiently strong to shift the burden of proof to the defendant to prove otherwise. That explains the common intuition that leaving a sponge in a body after an operation is enough to shift the burden of proof to the defendant to explain how it happened in a way that is consistent with appropriately considering the well-being of the plaintiff. In the classic case, *Byrne v. Boadle*,[27] a barrel of flour came out of a warehouse window and struck the plaintiff. This was a compliance error, for certainly the defendant had a plan for making sure that this did not happen. We do not know whether the plan was inadequately drafted or inadequately executed, but the fact that the mistake happened shifted the burden of proof to the defendant to prove that the mistake happened despite the defendant's investment in reasonable care. We exclude evidence that the defendant is generally careful (as not relevant to the issue of what happened on that occasion) and ask the defendant to prove that reasonable efforts could not have avoided the compliance error.

Here we draw another distinction: the distinction between a defendant claiming that he took all due precautions on that occasion and the defendant's proof that something extraordinary occurred that explains why the compliance error was not unreasonable. In general, we can understand that the law excludes the defendant's proof that he acted reasonably because such testimony is effectively unchallengeable by means of ordinary proof. What is the plaintiff to say when the defendant testifies that she worked very hard to avoid the error but it occurred anyway, or that it was a "mere" mistake? How is the plaintiff to rebut this testimony? On the other hand, the defendant's claim that something extraordinary justified the mistake must rely on proof that is external to the situation and therefore capable of being rebutted. The owner of the flour warehouse may seek to demonstrate that an unanticipated earthquake jarred the barrel of flour loose. The doctor may try to prove that a bomb scare made the benefits of rushing to finish the surgery outweigh the risk of error. These are events that can be (and normally are) subjected to evidentiary evaluation and justificational assessment. The law deals with compliance errors by discounting claims that they were mere mistakes (because the claims are nonfalsifiable) and shifting the burden to the defendant to show the mistakes to result from a more socially important goal that can be verified. This system may err on the side of false positives, but its justification is to avoid false negatives where the evidence of what happened is in the hands of the defendant.[28]

---

[27] *Byrne v. Boadle*, 159 Eng. Rep. 299 (Ct. of Exchequer 1863).
[28] This characterization of the implementation of the reasonable person standard shows the flexibility and reach of the negligence concept, and its ability to adapt the requirements of proof to get access to the information that the system needs to reduce administrative costs

This justificational analysis then helps us explain the relationship between the problem of compliance errors, the Hand formula, and strict liability.

Because justificational analysis has shown that the compliance error problem is really an evidentiary problem, we can understand it to be an application of the Hand formula rather than a refutation of the relevance of the Hand formula. The Hand formula requires an actor to invest reasonably in precaution plans and to comply reasonably with those plans. But because it is so difficult to assess individual compliance errors, the law sometimes presumes that a compliance error was unreasonable and requires the defendant to demonstrate why the compliance error was not unreasonable. This is an application of the Hand formula rather than a different analytical methodology.

Moreover, even the definition of a compliance error requires the application of the Hand formula. Because a compliance error is so closely related to precaution errors (being a failure to execute the precaution plan), we cannot evaluate compliance errors without also evaluating the reasonableness of the precaution plan. Consider, in this connection, the claim that harm that seems to have been caused inadvertently must not be subject to the Hand formula, a claim akin to the claim that we need a different way to think about harms that appear to result without a decisional basis. Professor Zipurksy offers the case of *Waiter v. Patron*, where a "waiter is in a restaurant and accidentally spills hot soup on Patron, burning him and ruining his suit."[29] This seems not to involve the kind of decision that allows the actor to compare the costs and benefits of various courses of conduct and therefore seems not to be a case where the Hand formula has traction.

But the requirement to be appropriately other-regarding is not a requirement to be deliberate and does not depend on any particular type of decision for its application. It requires reference only to the kind of other-regarding behavior people normally assume in that situation when they are thinking of how they would like to be treated. The central issue in *Waiter v. Patron* – why the waiter spilled the soup and whether the waiter could have avoided the spill – invite inquiry into whether the waiter could have thought differently about the well-being of the patron by thinking differently about the costs and benefits of various forms of behavior. Consider the evidence the parties will offer. The waiter will suggest that he was distracted or that some event beyond his control contributed to the accident (i.e., that the waiter could not have taken precautions against this event). The waiter will testify that he had plenty

and to avoid its own errors. This reduces the need to use the doctrine of strict liability to serve the same function, a point elaborated in Chapter Eight.

[29] Zipursky, *Sleight of Hand* at 2017.

of sleep, had not been drinking, and was concentrating on his work (i.e., that he took all relevant precautions). By contrast, the patron will suggest that the waiter carried the soup in a way that invited the accident (i.e., that the waiter did not take cost-justified precautions). Or, relying on the notion that proof of the accident is proof of negligence, the plaintiff will try to convince the jury that accidents of this type do not normally happen unless the waiter fails to do what waiters reasonably do. All such offers of proof are implementations of the kinds of considerations an other-regarding person must take into account and all relate to the intersection between general precautionary plans and the particular instance in which a compliance error occurred. To forestall the relevant analysis by calling these inadvertent errors is to deny that we have a way of thinking about these matters systematically. Once we undertake the analysis of inadvertence, we are squarely in the cost-benefit analysis that the Hand formula asks the analyst to undertake (subject to evidentiary considerations designed to decrease inaccuracy errors).

Finally, it is not clear to me why we would want to call this form of responsibility "strict liability," or why some torts scholars are interested in doing so. True, making compliance errors a basis for finding liability allows a jury to impose liability merely because a mistake occurred, but the negligence concept has always encompassed that possibility through *res ipsa loquitur*. It is certainly a high standard of responsibility, but that is only because the danger of making compliance errors is great and the cost of avoiding them is low. Moreover, it seems strange to use the term strict liability when the defendant is allowed to show that the compliance error resulted from extraordinary circumstances that make the error a reasonable one in the circumstances.

But the fundamental damage from trying to fit compliance errors into the "strict liability" box is justificational. I see at least two problems. First, as is well known, it confuses the concept of responsibility in tort law with the concept of blameworthiness, ignoring the distinction between conduct that justifies the state in forcing an actor to repair another's harm and conduct that we might find to be objectionable as a human failing. The argument that the negligence regime harbors a kind of strict liability by making an actor responsible for acts that are not blameworthy is circular, reasoning as follow: Negligence is a fault-based system; someone who cannot meet the standard of care of the reasonable person is not faulty (in the sense of blameworthy), so liability for that person must be no-fault strict liability. But tort law focuses on responsibility not blameworthiness. In tort law, the word *fault* has to be understood in connection with the notion of social interaction. The blameworthiness that is the subject of tort law means "engaging in conduct that a reasonable person would not engage in as part of social interaction."

Tort law is based on the morality of social interaction, not on the morality of human achievement.

In this sense, Holmes was wrong to try to separate the legal from the moral; he could not appreciate the kind of morality that is involved in tort law. It is not morality writ large, but the morality of social interaction. Responsibility in tort law is for conduct that does not reflect the appropriate morality of social interaction; it is in that sense that the word *fault* has moral content.

Finally, calling liability for a compliance error "strict liability" does damage to justificatory analysis by short-circuiting the relevant considerations. Whether a compliance error should be a source of responsibility depends on a host of factors, some of which are capable of proof and some of which are decided on the basis of presumptions. To move from the conclusion that the defendant committed a compliance error to the conclusion that the defendant is strictly liable for that error (unless the defendant can justify it) truncates the analysis that is necessary to determine the nature of the compliance error, to distinguish compliance errors from precaution errors, and to undertake the analysis that would determine whether the compliance error ought to be a source of responsibility. In fact, compliance error issues are given to the jury precisely to evaluate these kinds of questions through the lens of common experience, and juries undoubtedly take into account a host of factors relevant to responsibility in a social setting. It little helps practicing lawyers, and in fact misleads them, to pretend that the analysis is unnecessary because compliance errors result in a form of strict liability.

2.6. VARIOUS LEVELS OF CARE

Another important issue for tort theory is how we understand the various standards of care that tort law applies. How are we to understand, for example, the relationship between the standard of reasonable care and the standard of utmost care, and does the Hand formula help us with that understanding?

It is often thought that the utmost standard of care denotes a kind of super-reasonableness that differentiates it from reasonable care and the calculus of the Hand formula. Yet no one has articulated a meaningful standard of utmost care, except perhaps to say that people should be more than reasonable or really, really vigilant. The analytical content of the standard of utmost care remains a mystery.

The theory presented here suggests that we ought understand "utmost care" not as a different level of other-regarding behavior or as a distinct theory of responsibility. Instead, we ought to understand utmost care as the application of the obligation to appropriately consider the well-being of others, where various required behaviors flow from the contractual relationship between the actor and the victim. And, because the standard of utmost care is a special application of the theory of other-regarding behavior to contractual relationships, once we understand its analytical content, we can safely fold the utmost standard of care into the negligence standard without decreasing the responsibility of actors to be appropriately other-regarding.[30]

Here is the best way to look at the standard of utmost care. Other-regarding behavior is relational, depending on the relationship between the injurer and the victim, so other-regarding behavior depends on each person's position in society. When the injurer and victim are independent actors, their obligation is the general obligation to act reasonably toward each other. But in many instances, the injurer and victim have an interdependent relationship, perhaps the relationship between seller and buyer or charitable organization and client. In such a relationship, one party may depend on the other for protection and the other party may have information advantages that implicate the obligation to investigate, design, or warn in order to make what is supplied safer. These dimensions of reasonable care flow from the relationship between the parties; they reflect the relative distribution of information between the parties and the obligations that one party takes on because of justified reliance by the other party.

We will see the justificational boundaries of these duties in greater depth in our review of product liability law in Chapter Ten, where we will see that the obligations are fully capable of analysis under the reasonable person test (and therefore within the confines of the Hand formula). To require an actor to gather facts or disseminate information or redesign something that might make an activity safer is a normal part of other-regarding behavior because of a seller's obligation to look out for the well-being of its customers. Within this context, we can understand the standard of utmost care as a justificational failure by courts. Because the analysis of tort cases in the 19th century was rudimentary, courts could not impose directly the obligations to investigate, design, and warn; they had no vocabulary to describe the intensity or nature of the obligations that one person had to undertake on behalf of another to be considered reasonable. Instead, they imposed those obligations by imposing the standard of utmost care, which functioned as a proxy to effectively get the supplier to think more closely about those aspects of the actor's activity that were not directly in the supplier's control but might otherwise damage the

---

[30] That is why courts are increasingly folding the standard of utmost care into the standard of reasonable care. *Bethel v. New York City Transit Authority*, 703 N.E.2d 1214 (N.Y. Ct. App. 1998). They realize that analysis under the negligence standard is able to do all the "work" that was formally done by the standard of utmost care.

customer (such as the presence of a low bridge that required stage coach riders to duck). Justificational analysis, however, suggests that we can now abandon the standard of utmost care and do directly what that standard did only indirectly and vaguely. The utmost standard of care can be folded into the standard of reasonable care without any loss of pressure on an actor to investigate, redesign, or warn because we now have an analytical basis for understanding the scope and content of those obligations. Moreover, looking directly at the circumstances, factors, and values that are relevant to determining the scope of those duties makes the justificational analysis far more lucid, tractable, and replicable.[31]

In short, the utmost standard of care reflects the duty to investigate, redesign, and warn when the actor did not create the risk but is aware of the risk and has an obligation to reduce the risk by one of these means. This interpretation is important to our understanding of product liability law, where courts have been imposing the same duties without the rubric of utmost care, effectively imposing the utmost standard under the reasonableness or defect standard. The claim here is that a single standard of care – to think appropriately about the well-being of others – governs tort law, but that the intensity and content of that requirement varies with the circumstances. In this way, the various standards of care that courts have articulated do not replace the Hand formula as the basic organizing framework but are mere implementations of the Hand formula in particular circumstances.

2.7. CONCLUSION

In this chapter I have sketched the basic requirements of the reasonable person, using the Hand formula as the relevant framework for analysis but showing how the law ascertains the values that must be taken into account in applying the Hand formula. I have also met several objections to the relevance of the Hand formula: in particular, claims that compliance errors and the utmost standard of care respond to a different analytical methodology.

My discussion of the values that ought to be used in applying the Hand formula reflects a depiction of individual and social value formation and has

---

[31] The unity this conception gives to tort law avoids the compartmentalization of phenomena that should be integrated. Under the conception here, there is only one standard – the requirement of being appropriately other-regarding – and the application of the standard changes depending on the circumstances in a particular case. The standard is uniform, its application variable. The application of the standard does not depend on the status of the actor; it depends on the aspects of the status of the actor that are relevant to the analysis of the scope of the actor's responsibility. There is no law relating to innkeepers; there is law relating to agents who have information about, and control over, the well-being of their principals.

shown how the reasonable person uses those values to think appropriately about the well-being of others. This not only supports the moral basis for using the Hand formula as an organizing framework, but it also makes the application of the due care standard more determinate and transparent. By invoking Rawls's veil of ignorance as the method by which one can determine the fair distribution of the burdens and benefits among members of society, I have foreshadowed the normative discussion that follows and have demonstrated how the law mediates between the *is* and the *ought*. I now turn to the normative theory – the justification for believing that an appropriately other-regarding person is also socially moral.

PART II

THE NORMATIVE JUSTIFICATION

In this part, I provide a theory of social morality that requires those who would be moral to be other-regarding in the way that I have described, and I justify that theory on the basis of Kantian/Rawlsian ethics. In Chapter Three, I provide an overview of the theory, building on my claim that individual decisions that are other-regarding lead to a social system that is efficient, fair, and socially stable, and I describe the sense in which this theory is both economic and corrective. Chapter Four then explores the foundation of this social morality in Kantian ethics, demonstrating that the categorical imperative not only establishes the deontological duty to be other-regarding but also requires resort to a form of consequentialism to operationalize the notion that people should not use others as means to their own ends. Chapter Five then employs Rawls's device of the veil of ignorance to allow us to analyze which consequences are appropriately considered when an actor is other-regarding.

3 An Integrated Normative Analysis

My aim in this part of the book is to explore the normative basis for requiring an actor to think about the well-being of others in a way that advances social cohesion – that is, to think about others in a way that leads to a balance of rights and obligations that is efficient, fair, and stable. This obligates me both to defend social cohesion (in the way that I have defined it) as an appropriate goal of the law and to defend a theory of morality that allows us to determine when actors have thought appropriately about the well-being of others. Under the theory that I advance, the two tasks are interrelated. Social cohesion serves as an appropriate goal of the law because it rests on a theory of human interaction and value formation that itself responds to those decisions of individuals that can be said to be moral.

3.1. AN OUTLINE OF THE MAIN ARGUMENT

At the level of community, social cohesion requires a mechanism to ensure that the clashing projects and preferences of individuals are adjusted in accordance with values that are endorsed by the community (and that therefore support social cohesion) and have been formed by decisions that might themselves be called moral. As we have seen, the law serves to mediate between conflicting claims to resources in accordance with socially derived and morally mediated values that coordinate and transcend individual projects and preferences. The justification for government intervention is that a breach in the socially derived and morally mediated norms threatens the social fabric and the implicit social contract that binds the community together. The survival of the community requires an independent arbiter of community values and moral decision making that allows the social contract to be renegotiated in light of, without being undercut by, deviant behavior.

A system of moral values in a community responds to the moral claims of each person to the resources of the community, including the resources of other members of the community. Because each person's claims will sometimes conflict with claims of other people, the claims will impair the ability of any person to develop his or her capacity as a human being unless the community develops mechanisms to turn conflicting claims into coordinated human endeavor. A system of coordination can be considered to be moral to the extent that it allows each person to develop his or her individual capacities to the maximum extent possible, given the projects and preferences of other people. That conception of morality is inherent in the conception of human capacity that provides the moral authority for coordinating human endeavor.

As we have seen, the process of value formation in pursuit of social cohesion is an iterative and evolutionary one. As individuals interact, they develop ways of accommodating each other's projects and preferences, taking on burdens so that others need not take on burdens. Those accommodations develop norms that are either stable or not. The stable norms survive. When they are stable, the norms define the social morality – that is, the morality of people's decision making in the face of conflicting projects and preferences and conflicting claims to resources. These norms can themselves be assessed according to standard definitions of morality – the ones explored in this part of the book – and when they are moral, they become the law because they are moral. And because the norms incorporate the ways in which people normally think about what accommodations to give other members of the community, they command a high level of respect and allegiance.

The normative appeal of the concept of social cohesion presented here is that it allows individual human enterprise to flourish in a community that flourishes. Its morality lies in the respect it shows for the claims of individuals and in its ability to reconcile conflicting claims in a way that fosters the decision-making capacity of both individuals *qua* individuals and the community of individuals. Because it sees law as an institutionalized system for enhancing human cooperation by determining when one person can rightfully claim that an actor must incorporate that person's well-being into the actor's projects and preferences, the theory of other-regarding behavior allows the human enterprise to thrive in a community that thrives. At the same time, the theory is relatively determinate.

The theory presented here does not choose between deontic and consequential theories of social behavior.[1] Rather, it integrates deontic and consequential

---

[1] The term *consequential* does double duty. Many people view consequentialism as a philosophy that looks at the impact of a rule or principle on how people act and therefore allows us

concepts into a single theory of how individuals ought to make decisions in a community of individuals if the community is to thrive. The theory relies on the distinction between the duty to think about the well-being of others without regard to the consequences of undertaking that thought (the deontic) and the need for an actor to understand and evaluate consequences in a socially appropriate way when determining how to take into account the well-being of others in particular contexts (the consequential). As I show in the next chapter, the theory is Kantian because it starts with an appreciation of human capacity to reason toward the concept of duty – a capacity that depends neither on the consequences of searching for a suitable principle nor on external sources of authority. At the same time, because it is rooted in a conception of the role of one person in a community of persons, the system is necessarily consequential in the sense that a conception of the rights and obligations of one person in a community cannot be evaluated without taking into account the consequences of that conception for the rights and obligations of other persons in the community. Kantian maxims constrain the range of consequences that matter in determining the content of an actor's duty but cannot rule out the importance of consequences in thinking about duty. And I employ, in Chapter Five, the Rawlsian device of the original position to tell us which consequences matter and why.

In this way, as I develop below, the normative force of the law depends on both the morality of individual decisions and the morality of the aggregate collection of decisions of the people in the community. The morality of individual decisions turns on a Kantian/Rawlsian assessment of the attitude of the decision-making actor toward the well-being of others given the projected consequences of various decisions. The decision must meet the criteria of neutrality and universality to be called moral. The morality of the collective decision turns on solving a maximization problem – the problem of maximizing

to evaluate the rule or principle by examining the consequences of the rule or principle. This is the incentive meaning of consequentialism. We say that one rule is better than another because it gives better incentives (and therefore produces better consequences). I am using the term consequential to denote the kinds of consequences that a reasonable person takes into account and how he or she takes them into account. The view of consequences as incentives understands consequences to be the output of the analysis. I am using the term as the input into the analysis – as the range of factors that are relevant to the decision maker. I believe that input and output are the same. The other-regarding person takes certain consequences into account as inputs because, if the person did not, the consequences would be bad for social cohesion. In other words, before looking at consequences as an output we need to understand how we determine which consequences are desirable and which are not, and we can do that only by identifying the consequences that people should take into account when they make decisions. This is another way of saying that before we try to deter inappropriate decision making we need to know what kinds of decisions we want to deter and why.

the capacity of the individuals in the community to achieve their projects and preferences (given the fact that not all projects and preferences can be accommodated in a world of scarce resources) in a way that reflects individual moral decisions. This maximization problem is not addressed by looking at the weight that individual members of the community give to their projects and preferences; nor does it depend on equating the projects and preferences with the actor's individual well-being, such as happiness or willingness to pay. Rather, the maximization process requires that individual projects and preferences be maximized across the community in accordance with a set of values that reflect the choices made by individual members of the community in similar circumstances and that are themselves measured against the Kantian/ Rawlsian assessment of moral decision making.

3.2. ECONOMICS AND CORRECTIVE JUSTICE

Although my normative argument is built around the interpretation of Kantian/Rawlsian social morality provided in Chapters Four and Five, it may be worth prefacing that discussion with some general thoughts about the relationship between economic and corrective justice. Much of the clash between economic and deontic approaches appears to be based on misunderstandings about the central force of each position. It therefore makes sense to frame the discussion of social morality by considering how we might think about the economic and corrective justice enterprises in a more integrated way. Rather than giving a point-counterpoint assessment of the current debate, I will concentrate on an assessment that shows the complementarity of the two positions, and I will show how that complementarity dispels some of the dichotomies that are thought to separate them: the claim that the economic approach is external to the law (while the corrective justice approach is internal to the law), the claim that the economic approach (but not the corrective justice approach) is aggregative, and the claim that corrective justice (but not the economic approach) is only backward looking.

Because the theory of social cohesion recognizes the importance of maximizing the capacity of humans to achieve their projects and preferences (given the projects and preferences of others), it draws on the efficiency concept. The theory asks how society should organize itself to get the most out of the human capacity to achieve, doing so in a way that minimizes waste and maximizes the sum of individual capacity to achieve. This incorporates the economic notion that any goal (here, the goal of social cohesion) should be achieved with the fewest resources while maximizing the sum of individual contributions to the goal. Because it appropriately balances the burdens and benefits of being a member of the community, reasonable behavior efficiently minimizes the losses to individual projects and preferences when not all projects and preferences can be met simultaneously. This ensures that no project or preference held by an individual is impinged by others unless there is a countervailing, and more socially important, project or preference that could not otherwise be met. Seen in this light, the reasonable person standard establishes a system through which human potential and capacity are maximized (given existing individual capacities).

As the economists say, this is a form of welfare maximization, viewing welfare to be the ability of an individual to fulfill the individual's projects and preferences in nondistributional settings.[2] Efficiency that maximizes human capacity is effective because the social rankings that last over time are those associated with the success of the community (as members of the community have defined their individual success). The surviving values will be the ones that allow the members of the community to achieve their projects and preferences to the maximum extent that is consistent with the projects and preferences of other members of the community. This is a prerequisite for social cohesion because every person must feel that his opportunities to fulfill his capacity are being subjected to obstruction *only* to serve the higher purpose of allowing another to fulfill the other's capacity. As Judge Posner has argued, there is a moral quality to the goal of efficiency simply because it allows people to achieve their objectives with the minimum interference by others. That, of course, is a morality of consequences.[3] It is therefore entirely appropriate that tort law be portrayed as a system that maximizes aggregate welfare by summing up the decisions of individuals that themselves follow an

---

[2] Undoubtedly, the conception of welfare maximization presented here differs from that held by many economists. The conception will seem strange, for example, to any economist who is wedded to a conception of economics as wealth maximization. See, e.g., Charles Fried & David Rosenberg, MAKING TORT LAW, The AEI Press (2003). My approach can nonetheless be understood to be economic for the reasons mentioned in the text. The view presented here must be understood to present an economic understanding of the private law claims of one person to the resources of another and therefore must be distinguished from the Calabresian approach to the general public policy question of addressing the costs of accidents – an approach that is agnostic on the value of a system of private redress for wrongs. Guido Calabresi, THE COSTS OF ACCIDENTS: A LEGAL AND ECONOMIC ANALYSIS, Yale University Press (1970).

[3] Economists frequently pose the efficiency question by asking what decision an actor would make if the actor were both injurer and victim – that is, if the person who decided whether to make the product safer also bore the full consequences of that decision. This question is misleading if the thought experiment does not permit the single person to have a dual set of projects and preferences – one as a potential injurer and another as a potential victim. But as long as the thought exercise is understood to take into account such different perspectives, it is a way of operationalizing Rawls's veil of ignorance, which I draw on in this book.

assessment of the right way to make decisions. Tort law maximizes aggregate welfare in the quite obvious sense that once we determine which projects and preferences must be burdened, so that conflicting projects and preferences need not be, we are minimizing social friction as best as we can, given the values that the community uses, or should use, to resolve conflicting claims to resources. If all decisions that affect the well-being of others were made with the appropriate regard for their well-being, no rearrangement of rights or responsibilities could improve the well-being of any person without reducing the well-being of some other person.

Ultimately, however, welfare economics depends on some specification of the values that determine which trade-offs between various human capacities are important to society. That can only be done by specifying what makes an individual decision moral and how we identify those decisions we think were made with the appropriate deference to the projects and preferences of other people. By ensuring that the social valuations that are used to rank various projects and preferences are neutral and universal, the law ensures that the ranking of projects and preferences and the burdens that must be accepted are distributed in accordance with a standard that is objectively fair. By testing the comparisons of various projects and preferences against decision making behind the veil of ignorance, the ranking of projects and preferences is tested against a modified golden rule that is widely accepted as fair and that commands wide respect.[4]

It is not surprising, then, that efficiency and fairness are both prerequisites to a social system that seeks to be stable and progressive (in the sense of maximizing the ability of each person to achieve her capacity in nondistributional settings). Efficiency is necessary to allow each person to exercise his or her capacity to the fullest extent possible, and therefore for the community to make social progress in light of the projects and preferences of equal and independent people. Fairness is necessary to ensure that the sacrifices that must be made for the sake of another are understood to be responsive to a neutral

---

[4]   It is perhaps worth noting in this context that Coasean bargains – those made when there are no transaction costs – are very much like social bargains made behind the veil of ignorance. This is true because transaction costs generally arise from either too much or too little information about the other party. H.R. Coase, *The Problem of Social Cost*, 3 J. Law & Econ. 1 (1960), William M. Landes & Richard A. Posner, The Economic Structure of Tort Law 5–13, Harvard University Press (1987). For example, transaction costs arise if one transactor has too little information to be able to trust the other transactor, and they arise if some particular about the other transactor casts doubt on that person's trustworthiness. If transactors could treat the other party as if the other party had neutral, other-regarding characteristics, transaction costs would be very much lower. Coasean bargains would then look much as they would if they were behind the veil of ignorance.

standard that determines the burden of being a member of a community. As Ken Binmore reminds us, under the concept of Pareto efficiency, a large number of arrangements of rights and responsibilities are Pareto efficient in the sense that no one person can be made better off without making another person worse off. As a result, the efficiency criterion often does not point to any one unique solution that would govern the interactive cooperation. People who are looking to cooperate therefore choose a solution from among the efficient solutions that is both Pareto efficient and fair – that is, one that has the most appealing distribution of rights and responsibilities because either party would accept the distribution ahead of time if they did not know which share they would get. That distribution corresponds to a notion of fair distribution among equals.

The fair and the efficient must be conjoined because each provides a determinant of rights and responsibilities that the other lacks. The reasonable person standard interpreted through the theory of other-regarding behavior calls for two types of intertwined but quite distinct inquiries. The first inquiry looks at the impact of an actor's various courses of action on the projects and preferences of others. This is a matter of determining the range of trade-offs between an actor's well-being and the well-being of another. The consequences for the potential victim vary depending on the decision made by the actor across a range of behaviors, and the consequences reflect the relative rate at which one kind of decision affects a particular outcome for others. The expected harm from driving 75 rather than 80 miles an hour will be one amount and the expected harm from driving at 85 miles an hour still a different amount. We can consider this to be the technological comparison of an actor's and a victim's well-being that depends on the rate of substitution of one person's well-being for another's. Whenever we compare the projects and preferences of various people, we need to know the rate at which projects and preferences will be traded off, and this is uniquely responsive to the analytical tools of economics, for the heart of economics (and other sciences) is to ask what happens to one variable when another variable changes. The modeling of what happens to demand when the price of ice cream goes up from 8 to 10 cents is the same modeling that helps us determine what outcomes occur when a driver increases speed by 10 miles an hour.

The valuation of that trade-off is a separate matter. Even if the expected harm decreases linearly with the reduction in speed, the social value of reduced harm is likely to be greater at high rates of speed than at low rates of speed. Assume, for example, that a reduction in speed of 5 miles an hour is associated with a reduction in expected harm of X at any speed between 75 and 40 miles an hour (i.e., there is a linear relationship between speed and safety within that range). Although the trade-off is constant, social values may view the increased level of safety differently at different chosen speeds. We might value a reduction in potential harm as more important when the actor is going at a high rate of speed (when the incremental social value of speed is less), but less important if the actor is going at a low rate of speed. This would be true because the loss to the actor of going more slowly will at some point outweigh the benefits to potential victims, reflecting the fact that at that speed the burden to the projects and preferences of the actor of going more slowly would, as valued socially, be greater than the burdens and benefits of the lower speed to the projects and preferences of the potential victims. Were this not true, the appropriate speed of driving would be zero for everyone. The valuation of these trade-offs depends on the social ranking of the trade-offs that is developed behind the veil of ignorance, not on the technical trade-off between the actor's and the injurer's well-being.

Moreover, the social value of the trade-off between speed and harm will, as I have already emphasized, depend on the reasons the injurer is speeding; it will be at one valuation if the injurer is taking a heart attack patient to the hospital and another if the injurer is going to the beach. These kinds of social valuations cannot be made by examining the technological trade-off between the actor's decisions and the victim's harm because the social valuation is not comparing the actor's losses from having to go more slowly against the victim's losses from facing greater risk. What is at stake is the social valuation of those losses, not an individual valuation, and that comes only from the social valuation of the various projects and preferences from behind a veil of ignorance.

These two types of decisions – the technological trade-off between the actor's and the victim's well-being and the social ranking of the various trade-offs – correspond to the consequential and the deontic. The technological trade-offs depend on the consequences of an actor's decisions for the potential victims and the consequences of the potential victim's decisions for the actor. But we cannot choose between two sets of projects and preferences unless we also employ a valuation system that recognizes the social value of the various trade-offs by their relative weight. That is a deontic enterprise because it depends on the interpretation and construction of social values that are not themselves derived from the consequences of the valuation that is ultimately chosen.

In this way, economic and corrective justice theories work together to establish how a reasonable person ought to behave. The account of the Hand formula suggested here is economic in an important and fundamental sense: Its essential feature is the same as the central feature of any economic inquiry because it recognizes the problem of scarcity and searches for a method of

getting the most out of resources and avoiding waste. We can therefore understand the trade-off between the freedom of a driver with epilepsy and the
physical security of a victim shop owner as an essentially economic trade-off.
When we cannot privilege the projects and preferences of both people, we
must choose the rule of legal intervention that seems best aimed at preserving
the ability of each to carry out his or her projects and preferences to the maximum extent possible, according to a ranking index that seems to reduce as
much as possible the burden on resource use. Economic thought allows us to
make the technological comparisons between competing levels of well-being.
Deontic thought cannot do that.

At the same time, economics is not the source of the values that are used to
understand the social value of various trade-offs. Here we must distinguish the
role of economics in specifying values as *outputs* from the problem of values as
inputs. By studying behavior in the face of trade-offs, economics can specify
the output values that people use to make decisions; for example, the valuation people put on an ice cream cone in various price ranges, which allows us
to understand the relative evaluation of ice cream and other consumables for a
particular consumer or class of consumers. Economics can help us model and
analyze the trade-offs that people ordinarily make in noneconomic settings –
specifying, for example, how much approbation we need in order to conform
to social norms. But economics is not the source of the values that people use
to make trade-offs, people are. The behavior that economists study reflects the
beliefs and values that people rely on; those beliefs and values are exhibited in
the choices people make and the behavior they choose, but they are formed
independently of those choices. If we want to understand those valuations
we must not only specify what the revealed preferences are, which is what
economists do, but also draw on a theory of belief formation and choice that
helps us understand why people make a particular decision. Economists can
specify the degree to which people want to buy more of a good at a lower price,
or whether they sometimes buy more of a good when the price goes up. But
economists cannot tell us why this is so without drawing on a theory of valuation that describes the inputs into the trade-off they are measuring.

A theory that conjoins the consequential and the deontic can be understood by wrapping the deontic in the consequential or vice versa. It is a matter
of preference, not substance, which we do. A consequential-first approach posits the need to maximize the welfare (or well-being) of those whose projects
and preferences are affected, and would therefore start with the technological trade-off between conflicting projects and preferences. But because the
method of ranking the projects and preferences relies on the obligation of the
actor to undertake the thought experiment from behind the veil of ignorance,

it cannot escape the deontic constraint. Although, as we have already seen, the economic approach advanced by Kaplow and Shavell is committed to welfare maximization that is unconstrained by any other goal or value, the deontic constraints necessarily must be embedded in the values that are used in comparing the welfare of different individuals. The deontic constraint is necessary to choose between sets of trade-offs in well-being, no one of which has greater moral appeal or legitimacy than another. Although welfare maximization seems to leave no room for deontic thought, deontic constraints are imbedded in the comparisons.

Alternatively, the consequentialist enterprise can be wrapped within the deontic approach. We can posit that people must treat others fairly, and we can understand the standard of fairness to be determined by the modified golden rule: Do unto others as you would have them do unto you if you were in their position. But to apply this standard, we are left with the need to understand the consequences that one person's projects and preferences impose on another person's projects and preferences. Determining how much X one must give up to get Y is a consequential enterprise. We cannot value the trade-off (the deontic enterprise) until we understand what the trade-offs are (the consequential enterprise).

Given this understanding of the deontic and the consequential, the dichotomies that are said to separate the two camps of tort theory largely disappear. Economic analysis is no longer an external view of the law. Although economic methodology and terminology are derived from the study of explicit markets – and therefore appear to be external to the law – economics does not monetize every value or reduce every interaction to a transaction that is fully specified. In particular, economics does not require an assumption that human behavior is necessarily transactional or only narrowly self-interested, and economics recognizes that markets are artificial creations – institutions whose contours and rules are subject to human intervention as the goals, functions, and limitations of markets become better understood. Properly understood, economics is simply the study of the behavior of people when they interact – behavior that is necessarily interdependent – and the study of the institutions that people design to improve coordination between people and groups. Its unit of analysis, in other words, is human decision making when humans interact with other humans, and that necessarily draws economists into the study of how humans set up institutions to help guide human behavior. Economists know that people react to incentives (including the constraints they accept on their own behavior), that incentives can be positive or negative for the community, and that legal institutions are human creations designed to change incentives so that the community can flourish.

Under this view, economics is internal to the law because it involves the same inquiry as law. Economics and law are both behavioral sciences and both require us to understand how humans set up institutional arrangements that guide behavior so that individual decisions are in the collective interest. To be sure, economists cannot succeed in their behavioral mission – or in any attempt to fully support legal analysis – unless economics is merged with other behavioral sciences, all of which seek to understand human behavior and institutions. An economic view of humankind will be incomplete unless it incorporates the sociological, historical, anthropological, political, and psychological view of human behavior and institutions. But because both law and economics are behavioral sciences, it is hard to find a boundary between the internal view of private law and the economic view of behavior. We can simultaneously affirm, as legal philosophers do – that law is a socially constructed and self-reflective social practice – and also appreciate the trade-offs, and therefore the role of economics, in the law.

For corrective justice scholars, the term *efficiency* poses an unnecessary stumbling block. Like law, efficiency too is socially constructed and self-reflective. Corrective justice scholars correctly show that tort law embodies the bilateral structure between right and duty – between the wrong committed by the defendant and the plaintiff's right to compensation – but efficiency, too, is about a bilateral relationship. Efficiency does not have a meaning outside of relationships; it is an inherently relational category and therefore is entirely consistent with the bilateral structure of tort law. In the form of productive efficiency, the relevant relationship is between inputs and outputs, and the value that is being maximized is the sum of outputs over inputs. In terms of allocative efficiency, the relevant relationship is that between those who have various uses for the resources and the resource itself. In a market context, this is exemplified by the relationship between seller and buyer (where the buyer's surplus is being maximized); in a nonmarket setting it is the relationship between various claimants. In terms of transactional efficiency, the relevant relationship is between the two transactors – the parties to an exchange – and the value that is being maximized is the surplus generated by the exchange. In terms of tort law, the relationship is between the injurer and victim, for the efficiency criterion simply asks what outcome will most enhance the ability of injurer and victim to fulfill their projects and preferences with the minimum of interference with the projects and preferences of others.

Nor should we be concerned that the economic approach appears to be aggregative, looking at total social impact rather than looking just at the interests of the injurer and victim. Although corrective justice is focused on the relationship between injurer and victim, corrective justice does not suppose, and could not suppose, that analysis of the dispute is confined to facts relating to that relationship. Often, there is no relationship to examine, except the relationship of injurer and victim, for the parties are complete strangers, bound only by their common membership in a community and by the fact of an accident. The relationship between injurer and victim is important not because of what the injurer and victim perceive about each other as individuals, but because of their symbolic meaning as members of a class of people in similar situations. The relationship between a driver with epilepsy and the victim of the driver's epileptic seizure, for example, is not important as between themselves but because they serve as representatives of two classes of people in the community: people with disabilities and people who might be adversely affected if a driver with epilepsy has a seizure. The justice that we are seeking is not the justice between two individuals *qua* individuals, for very little about the parties as individuals is relevant to our sense of justice. When determining whether a wrong has been committed we do not care about their health, wealth, or personal situation, except insofar as that relates to the kinds of considerations that each of them ought to take into account when making decisions (and even then only as representatives of people with similar characteristics). We care about the individuals as representatives of people similarly situated, and that abstracts from their personal characteristics and prior dealings with each other and focuses on the projects and preferences of people in similar situations.

The focus of corrective justice is therefore naturally aggregative, examining people in the same class and the generality of their experience. To be sure, this is not a broad investigation of social betterment that is independent of the well-being of individuals in the collective, but it cannot escape the generalization that is inherent in treating individuals as representatives of a class of individuals whose well-being is at stake. This corresponds to the economics view, which is not a sweeping assessment of social betterment but is simply an assessment of what must be given up to protect the right of the epileptic to drive and the right of the victim to be free from the risk of physical injury.

Moreover, given the posture of a case, corrective justice cannot help but be both backward and forward looking. It is backward looking because it looks at the characteristics of the plaintiff and defendant and the interests that are at stake to define the general class of people whose interests are affected. It is forward looking because it thinks about the general class represented by the injurer and victim; it determines how in a situation like the one that occurred in the case, a person in the class of the injurer ought to think about the well-being of a person in the class of the victim. The two aspects of the analysis cannot be separated because they are two parts of a single analytical process of specificity and generality. The "backward looking" part identifies the circumstances of the dispute that are relevant when we consider the rights and obligations of the parties: the fact of epilepsy, the decisions of the victim, what the defendant was trying to do when he decided to drive, and so forth. The "forward looking" part of the analysis is not really projecting into the future but is projecting into a general class of people in similar situations to determine how they would want to be treated were they in the shoes of the other person.

3.3. CONCLUSION

In this chapter, we have seen that deontic and consequentialist scholars start in different places but meet in the middle. Deontic scholars start with a conception of duty – one that is independent of the consequences of thinking about duty – but then find a way for a person who would fulfill her duty to take consequences into account while being faithful to the conception of duty. Consequential scholars start with a conception of human welfare and the need to maximize it, but then they need an account of the values that society uses to determine when one person's well-being ought to be sacrificed for another person's well-being, which requires them to specify values that are not themselves supplied by the goal of maximizing welfare. Once we integrate the deontic and the consequential – the views based on moral philosophy and views based on economic philosophy – we have an integrated theory of the moral attributes of social cohesion.

I develop this theory in two steps. Chapter Four describes the system of Kantian ethics that allows us to understand the deontic obligation to think in a certain way when making decisions that might adversely affect others and the general methodology that informs that obligation. Chapter Five then shows how John Rawls elaborated on that moral theory by showing how the deontic requirement of thinking in an appropriate way about the well-being of others could take into account the consequences of one's actions while working within the Kantian methodology.

4   Kantian Duty

The theory of social morality that provides the foundation for social cohesion turns on an interpretation of Kantian metaphysics that bears some elaboration. The Kantian conception of duty is fully congruent with the theory of other-regarding behavior advanced here. For Kant, social morality – that is, the morality of decisions that affect others in the community – involves an assessment of the attitude one person ought to have concerning the well-being of others in order to be moral. Although Kant focused on the deontological content of duty, and was explicit that to be moral the obligation to think in a certain way about one's behavior may not depend on the consequences of undertaking that thought, he did not deny that consequences are relevant to deriving the maxims that should guide behavior. Although Kant spent little time dealing with the application of his moral theory, and left it to others to determine how an actor accounts for consequences when an actor seeks to fulfill his duty to think appropriately about the well-being of others, his deontological concept of duty is fully consistent with the obligations of the other-regarding person.

To complete the system of Kantian ethics described in this chapter, the next chapter draws on Rawls's concept of the veil of ignorance as an analytical device for determining what consequences matter and how they matter to a person who would make moral decisions. The veil of ignorance allows us to: exclude consequences that should be irrelevant as we develop the maxims called for by Kantian duty, identify consequences that can legitimately be considered, and address the question of how consequences matter in interpersonal comparisons. To work out problems of reciprocal conflicts, the reasonable person must establish a calculus of comparison that determines whether the relevant consequences for the actor or the relevant consequences for the victim are more important.

4.1. EXISTING UNDERSTANDING

Kant's philosophy figures prominently as the foundation of corrective justice but is ignored or vilified in economic accounts of tort law. My aim in this chapter is to add specificity to the corrective justice account of Kantian philosophy and to show how this specificity reveals the Kantian foundations of economic theory. Although corrective justice pays homage to Kant, the only extended discussion of his philosophy is by Ernest Weinrib; his interpretation will serve as the jumping off point for the elaboration presented here.[1]

Weinrib's project is to explore, among other things, the "presuppositions about agency and normativeness that underlie the equality of corrective justice."[2] He does this by exploring Kant's "idea of reason that nonetheless has undoubted practical reality; for it can oblige every legislator."[3] Reason is a basis for bringing coherence to the world. Practical reason is reason that can be put into practice – that is, reason that affects behavior. It is reason that is influenced by the will – that is, by purposive action that is able to move toward an end – and because will starts with an end in mind (what I have called the actor's projects), it embodies a kind of purposiveness that reflects the agency of the actor (which Weinrib calls purposiveness that is a causality of concepts).

Purposive action is free when mental representations of a particular end can "be compared with (and revised in favor of) a different mental representation."[4] But to do this, one "must have the capacity to abstract from the immediacy of inclination, to reflect upon the content of the mental representation, and simultaneously to substitute one representation for another."[5] This describes the process of decision making that moves beyond inclination and is able to exercise choices from among a range of alternatives. That means that behavior is self-determining (rather than being determined by inclination or instinct) and that behavior is not determined by the content of the thought but by its "form" – which I take to mean the process by which thought is undertaken

---

[1] Gregory C. Keating correctly relies on Kant to say that the proper resolution of competing claims of freedom of action and security cannot depend "on the bargaining strengths of the affected parties, or on the comparative intensity of their preferences for their own welfare." Gregory C. Keating, *The Idea of Fairness in the Law of Enterprise Liability*, 95 MICH. L. REV. 1266, 1302 (1997). However, other than appealing to general principles of justice, his proposals do not find explicit support in Kantian ethics, and he explicitly rejects the veil of ignorance as a device for determining the requirements of justice. *Id.* at 1301.

[2] Ernest Weinrib, THE IDEA OF PRIVATE LAW 84 (1995).

[3] *Id.* at 87, quoting Immanuel Kant, CRITIQUE OF PURE REASON, A 644/B672 (Norman Kemp Smith, *trans.*, 1929).

[4] *Id.* at 90.

[5] *Id.*

and given content. This distinction between content and form is crucial because it separates what our thought is (its content, as in "I think that doing this is dangerous") from the process of thought (its form, as in "Here is how I need to think about whether doing this is dangerous"). The way we think about our ends – that is, the form of thought – then becomes the focal point of agency and purposiveness and allows Kant to posit a basis on which the form of thought is exercised in its finest form – that is, under the categorical imperative, to "act upon a maxim that can also hold as a universal law." Practical reason (reasoning about how to behave) can therefore exist separately from both the ability to make free choices and the content of those choices. Purposive activity "is the effort to bring *something* into actuality,"[6] but the determining ground of thought is not what the thought says to do, but the way the purposive activity is thought about.

This understanding of purposive agency allows Kant to understand the obligation that forms the normative core of his philosophy, one that is designed to achieve the "organization of humanity ever nearer to its greatest possible perfection."[7] Kant's notion of obligation is inherent in the idea of practical reason because practical reason can make no claim to external forces or standards; it "does not impose any demands on free choice from without."[8] It therefore generates its own obligation by generating all of the reasons for reasoning by reason itself. According to Weinrib, "Normativeness consists in the governance of purposive activity according to a standard arising from the nature of such activity."[9]

Weinrib is careful to provide an interpretation of Kant that downplays any teleological element and construes the normative force of practical reasoning as internal rather than external. Yet even his abstract, conceptual description shows that practical reason has ends that are to be served by practical reason. Weinrib acknowledges that Kant is addressing "the mutual externality of the interacting agents,"[10] that the idea of reason functions to allow people to contract to "give up their inborn external freedom in order immediately to receive it back secure and undiminished as members of a lawful commonwealth,"[11] and that the focus of Kant's legal philosophy is to ensure an action's "consistency with the freedom of all persons."[12] This suggests that even an internal view of practical reason serves an external function of coordinating behavior.

[6] *Id.* at 92.
[7] *Id.* at 93.
[8] *Id.* at 94.
[9] *Id.* at 94.
[10] *Id.* at 84.
[11] *Id.* at 85.
[12] *Id.* at 94.

I start my elaboration of Weinrib's account with just that notion. Contrary to Weinrib's belief, a normative theory can have an external function without necessarily calling on external forces to give it normative validity. We can accept Weinrib's conclusion that the standard governing purposive activity arises from the nature of such activity (rather than from external norms) but still affirm that purposive activity serves an external function. Indeed, we can go further. It is hard to imagine purposive activity that does not have an external function, as I now demonstrate.

4.2. KANTIAN METHODOLOGY OF DECISION MAKING

The central concept of Kantian morality is that human beings can, and should, think about the values that guide their decision making using methodologies that are independent of the goals the person seeks or the means the person uses – that is, without regard to the actor's projects and preferences. This, of course, is the categorical imperative – the obligation to make decisions by reasoning toward a maxim that can be universalized because it is a maxim that is independent of the interests of the person making the decision. In order to be moral, a human being must search for, and make decisions using, a maxim that he or she would have everyone apply in that situation and that the person would apply to him or herself no matter what the circumstances or the consequences of the maxim given the person's individual circumstances.

Importantly, this conception separates the question of how people make decisions from the question of what decisions people make. The focus of the categorical imperative is on how one thinks about the decisional options one has – that is about the methodology of decision making one uses.[13] For decision making to be moral, its methodology must be of a particular type; it must employ a methodology that leads to a maxim that the person would want to make universal. This is quite distinct from an evaluation of the behavior that results from that methodology. In Kant's view, the question of how one behaves cannot be evaluated on moral grounds unless we first address the questions of how one thinks about a maxim that determines how one behaves. Morality is in how human beings reason to a decision rather than in what decision they make or how they behave. To Kant, we can understand morality

---

[13] This is what John Rawls called the categorical imperative procedure. John Rawls, LECTURES ON THE HISTORY OF MORAL PHILOSOPHY, 162–3, Harvard University Press (2000) (Viewing the CI-procedure "as a way of generating the content...of a reasonable doctrine"). The conception presented in the text is not the conventional one. Many people believe the categorical imperative is about behavior rather than about a methodology of thinking about behavior. The conventional view does not do justice to Kant's nuanced thought.

only by thinking about how people think about their decisions and determining whether they have used appropriate decisional methodologies. Kant expressed it this way:

> It [morality] concerns not the matter of the action [not the behavior], or its intended results [the goals of the behavior], but its form and the maxims of which it [the action] is itself a result, and what is essentially good in it consists in the mental disposition, let the consequence be what it may.[14]

For Kant, morality is reflective of the "mental disposition" that a human being brings to decision making and it is the decision-making methodology that must be appraised to determine whether a person is acting in accordance with one's duty. Under this approach, we should not derive our sense of morality from an examination of a person's behavior but from our understanding of the methodology of thought that a person must have used to arrive at the decision that led to the person's behavior.

Kant understood that an actor who is making decisions about a matter that might affect the well-being of others is not only deciding what to do; the actor is also, and prominently, deciding how to decide what to do. The latter decision – the decision of how to decide what to decide – determines how and whether the actor will incorporate the well-being of others into the decision in a way that allows the decision to be understood as derived from a universal maxim. For Kant, this decision (about how to decide) was the source of morality[15] – it is a categorical imperative and a duty that all actors have to all other actors.[16]

Because Kant located morality in how one decides, not in what one decides, it is a mistake to view the categorical imperative as referring to duties about acting this way or that way. Such a view assumes that the "right" or the "law"

---

[14] Immanuel Kant, FUNDAMENTAL PRINCIPLES OF THE METAPHYSICS OF MORALS (1785) (Thomas Abbott trans.) in Allen W. Wood, BASIC WRITINGS OF KANT 174, Modern Library (2001).

[15] Kant was fighting against source of authority that would be external to the human will or human reason. He specifically rejected skyhooks and theology as sources of moral thought. In his view, even moral behavior derived from theology was consequential morality because it was perceived to be the gateway to heaven. *Id.* at 190.

[16] Implicit in Kant's conception of the obligation to think in a certain way about what decision to make is both the obligation to take into account the well-being of others and also the obligation to take into account the well-being of others in a certain way (again, to decide the matter following a maxim that is universal). Kant described only the imperative that the actor uses a methodology that could lead to universality. He left it to others to describe what methodology is moral given the need to use a methodology that would lead to a universal principle, a topic we take up in the next chapter. And Kant spoke only in examples about what decisions a methodology of neutrality would prescribe – that is, what behavior would be moral given the nature of the thought that is required to make it moral.

to which Kant referred is an edict about behavior, as if it were categorically required that one not tell a lie (even if the telling of the lie will save many lives). Instead, the categorical imperative is an imperative to search for and follow a maxim or set of maxims that can be made universal. The categorical imperative is an injunction about how to think about whether to tell a lie and is therefore entirely contextual, not doctrinaire.

Kant's claim that we must separately understand the methodology of thinking about a situation before we can assess the morality of the behavior in that situation has several implications for moral thought and for how we envision the concept of duty. First, it situates corrective justice as a central concept of tort law. For Kant, the concept of duty is not in its content (it does not say that we should act in this way or that way) but in the way a moral actor will think about the content of the actor's obligations to others. That is why corrective justice can be conceptual (and conceptually accurate) without necessarily having any particular content and without undertaking the obligation to articulate the content of the concept in any particular setting. To conceive of a concept such as duty as a complete statement of the conduct that is required by the concept puts too much work on the concept, because the purpose of the concept is to direct the actor to think about the situation in a particular way rather than to act toward the situation in a particular way. Once we understand the concept of duty to demand a certain way of thinking about a situation rather than a way of acting *within* a situation, the concept stands as its own constituent part of the tort morphology.

Kant's detachment of the methodology of thinking about a situation from the behavior in that situation means that even behavior that looks moral may be immoral. Assume that an actor has an opportunity to kill a hated enemy without being detected or punished and decides to flip a coin to decide whether to undertake the killing. The actor has both a methodology of deciding and a behavior determined by that methodology. If the flip of the coin determines that the enemy should be spared, the actor does not kill the enemy. But under the categorical imperative that is an immoral act, even though the enemy was never killed. It is immoral because the decision was made not in accordance with a maxim that could be universalized – that is, not by a methodology that we would regard as legitimate in that context. We would never sanction a killing if the flip of a coin commanded the actor to kill the enemy, so it would be immoral to sanction a decision to spare the enemy that was reached by the same method.[17] We call this decision immoral, even though it resulted in no

---

[17] On the other hand, the methodology of flipping a coin to make a decision would be a legitimate one – that is, one that we would accept as universal (and therefore moral) – if the

harm, because of its arbitrariness and because the only thing that separated behavior that hurt another from the behavior that did not was fate. Using a coin to determine whether someone lives or not is immoral (even if the person lives) because deciding that question in that way is to disregard the value of another's life. The actor himself would not subject his own life to that methodology of decision making, so the actor could not be acting under a maxim that can achieve universal status.

4.3. THE MORALITY OF THINKING ABOUT THE WELL-BEING OF OTHERS

The categorical duty is therefore the following set of obligations: to search for a maxim that will govern one's decision and that can simultaneously serve as a universal maxim, to act in accordance with that maxim, and to do so for the sake of the maxim. This requires a methodology of thinking about the world to develop a universal maxim and a methodology of applying the maxim to the decision the actor is facing. Both methodologies are categorical because neither depends on, or changes depending on, the consequences of the obligation to think using the appropriate methodology. The duty to think in the right way about the world, and then to act in response to the maxim derived from the correct methodology, is immutable, universal, unchanging, and absolute. It is not consequential because the obligation to think in the right way and to act in accordance with that methodology does not depend on the consequences of thinking in some other way. In Kant's terms, the goal of thinking in an appropriate way is an end in itself.

Kant also made it clear why the methodology of thinking about things is the essence of a moral decision. Kant's insistence that to be moral a person must use an appropriate methodology of decision making expresses his concern with the human inclination to rationalize – that is, to provide a justification for action that reflects the actor's projects and preferences. Kant correctly saw that reasoning about morality will always be imperfect if the reasoning is not separated from the object of the reasoning.[18] If the question is, "Is it moral

question were whether all people should drive on the left or the right side of the street (provided that no person had yet invested in driving on either the left or the right side). Because the outcome does not matter (only the uniformity of the conduct), the method of flipping a coin is as good as any methodology for choosing a maxim that would be universal.

[18]   The references within Kant are numerous. For example, when a maxim is conceived as categorical it must, by virtue of being categorical, exclude "from any share in their authority all admixture of any interest as a spring of action." *Id.* at 189. Then, later in that paragraph, he says that "in the case of volition from duty all interest is renounced, which is the specific criterion of categorical as distinguished from hypothetical imperatives."

to lie in this situation?" the reasoning about that issue will be influenced by the individual consequences of the answer for the person doing the analysis. Reasoning can never be pure unless it is separated from its effects on the person doing the reasoning. In other words, when we take action, we can describe it as moral action only if we can take it in accordance with a maxim that has been formed without regard for the consequences on ourselves. Such a methodology of reasoning is moral precisely because we know that the methodology of thinking about the matter excluded from consideration the consequences (for the person doing the reasoning) of invoking one maxim rather than another. The obligation is to reason to a maxim that is neutral in terms of the objectives or status of the person doing the reasoning. When that occurs, we know that the decision could not have been taken because of a contingency or consequence that favored only the decision maker. The decision can be moral only if it can be undertaken in accordance with a maxim that has no contingency because it has no end except to be universal and neutral.

Kant thus understood the concept of duty to exclude acts that are made in one's self-interest. He thought it hard to imagine that an action could be moral unless it resulted from a sense of obligation rather than out of self-interest, ruling out acts of kindness that are done for reputational or reciprocal benefit. If a decision were made out of self-interest, it would be hypothetically, rather than categorically, imperative. Yet Kant understood that it is impossible to distinguish between an act motivated by obligation and one motivated by self-interest. He stated that "it is absolutely impossible to make out by experience with complete certainty a single case in which the maxim of an action, however right in itself, rested simply on moral grounds and on the conception of duty."[19] For Kant, we can never identify a completely selfless act because we can never "infer with certainty that it was not really some secret impulse of self-love" and, if we focus on looking for a selfless act, we will doubt whether pure virtue exists anywhere in the world.[20] He therefore abandoned any quest to differentiate acts that are committed out of duty and acts that are committed out of self-interest. In other words, he abandoned the assessment of conduct and focused instead on duty as an obligation to think in a certain way about what maxim to use when deciding how to act. Although that focus would not use behavior to determine whether the behavior was done out of duty, it would identify behavior that was consistent with behavior undertaken out of the duty to use an appropriate decision-making methodology. The categorical imperative was a way by which Kant

[19] *Id.* at 165.
[20] *Id.*

reconciled the moral contingency of acts that benefit an actor with the need for an absolute moral maxim if we are to ascribe morality to human endeavor. The obligation to be other-regarding is responsive to the categorical imperative by suggesting that the obligation to think about the well-being of another is not contingent merely because the actor rewards herself for following the appropriate methodology.

For Kant, a person who follows the methodology required by the categorical imperative can never be acting out of self-interest because the categorical imperative rules out self-interest as a basis for choosing a maxim on which to act. Kant's antipathy to goal-driven reasoning is pervasive. Even when Kant disparaged action taken out of instinct or sentiment, and thus challenged Hume's appeal to social instinct, he based his criticisms on the fear that instinct and sentiment would be influenced by the decision makers's interests. That is why for Kant a moral decision must be directed only at its own goal – the goal of identifying a universal maxim – and not at some other goal. It is not the moral maxim that must be directed at its own goal but the way we think about the moral maxim that must be directed at the goal of universality.

We can therefore understand what Kant had in mind when he talked about a universal maxim. He was not referring to a maxim that was true no matter what the context. He was referring to a maxim that would be true in a particular context to everyone who thought in the appropriate way about what the maxim should be. He had in mind a maxim that would garner universal assent by all those who thought in the appropriate way about the maxim. And it is the quality of universal assent that makes the categorical imperative a cornerstone concept of social cohesion.

Although Kant only used the word *universal* to describe the maxim that a moral person should search for, it is clear that a universal principle must also be a neutral principle – one that fairly balances obligations under the principle by not unfairly privileging the interests of one person over the interests of another. Under the principle of neutrality, each person must search for a maxim when making decisions that does not unduly favor that person's interest and that the decision maker would assent to if the decision maker's circumstances were different. A maxim that is unduly influenced by the existing status, idiosyncratic circumstances, or power of the decision maker cannot be universal because it cannot be one that others would ascribe to if they faced a different status, idiosyncratic circumstance, or power. Only a maxim that is neutral – one that is appropriate without regard to the status, idiosyncratic circumstance, or power of the person making the decision – can aspire to be universal.

4.4. KANT'S CONSEQUENTIALISM

Kant established that to be moral the goal of finding and following a neutral and universal maxim must be consequence-neutral. The search for the neutral/universal maxim may not be undertaken with a view toward endorsing a particular consequence or guided in a way that would take into account or achieve consequences that would be in the decision maker's interest. That means that the desire to search for the neutral/universal maxim must be undertaken without any goal in mind other than the desire to find a maxim that is moral because it is neutral and universal. The requirement that the goal be a maxim that was neutral/universal in the way I have described ensures that consequences that uniquely favor the decision maker are not involved in the decision of whether to search for the universal maxim and how to identify it.

It would be a mistake, however, to believe that in determining which maxim meets the requirements of universality and neutrality, the consequences of the maxim are irrelevant. The categorical requirement is to search for the appropriate maxim, but the inquirer must necessarily evaluate a number of potential maxims as candidates for the one maxim to follow. And while determining which maxim from among a number of maxims fits the neutrality and universality criteria, the consequences of a maxim must be taken into account. The categorical imperative is to find a maxim that does not depend on having any object other than that of finding the universal maxim, but exactly which maxim emerges from the required rational thought must depend on which maxim has the consequences that meet the criteria of universality and neutrality. Consequences are to be ignored when deciding whether to make decisions according to a universal and neutral maxim, but consequences are not to be ignored when deciding what that maxim must be.

The distinction between the obligation to choose a maxim that is universal (an obligation that is categorical and does not depend on consequences) and the choice of a maxim that meets those criteria (which depends on the consequences of various proposed maxims) is crucial. It is, of course, the distinction between the deontic and the consequential. The categorical command, "Kill only in accordance with a maxim that can be a universal maxim," does not determine when one is entitled to kill. One could imagine a maxim that says one can kill in self-defense, but in deciding whether that maxim is universal and neutral – indeed, to apply the maxim at all – one would have to take the consequences of the maxim into account.

What Kant essentially does is to rule out consequences as a reason for thinking about how to act by centering duty on the obligation to find and follow a universal maxim, but he then allows the decision maker to take some consequences into account in determining which maxim is likely to be neutral and universal. This filters out self-interest at two levels: first by filtering out self-interest when the question is whether one has a duty, and second by filtering out self-interest when one determines what maxim describes that duty. By making the search for a universal maxim consequence-free but making the choice of a maxim turn on the consequences that would allow the maxim to be called universal, Kant is narrowing the range of (self-interested) considerations that one may take into account in determining how to act morally without being blind either to the consequences of picking one maxim over another or to the fact that the maxim will have consequences for people in the community.

Kant does not focus on the distinction between consequences that matter and those that may not be taken into account, but Kant himself understood that consequences matter when a person is evaluating various maxims to see which ones might be counted as universal. Right after his first announcement of the categorical imperative, Kant gave a series of illustrations of maxims that could not meet the concept of a universal maxim. Each of the illustrations turned on the consequences of the maxim. Thus, if a person in need borrows money knowing that he will not pay it back, the maxim that might govern that decision is this: "When I think myself in want of money, I will borrow money and promise to repay it, although I know that I never can do so." This, for Kant, cannot be justified under a universal law for a consequential reason: "the promise itself would become impossible, as well as the end that one might have in view of it, since no one would consider that anything was promised to him, but would ridicule all such statements as vain pretenses."[21] We must, in other words, reject as a universal law the proposed maxim precisely because of its consequences.

As another example of Kant's awareness that consequences matter, Kant said that the search for a universal maxim is the search for a maxim that would not contradict itself. What he meant was that if, in practice, the decision maker could envision a set of circumstances in which she would not follow her own maxim, the maxim could not be universal. This requires the decision maker to test her proposed maxim under various states of the world to determine whether the maxim would still hold, and to adjust the maxim if it would not hold (i.e., if the maxim would contradict itself). But this search for a maxim that is not self-contradictory requires one to understand the consequences of each proposed maxim, for it requires that the decision maker specify a maxim that would hold in various states of the world (in which case it would be followed despite different consequences in different circumstances).

[21] *Id.* at 180.

That is why Kant conceded that human experience is an essential part of morality. Early in the *Metaphysics of Morals*, while extolling the virtues of pure moral philosophy, Kant concedes that:

> No doubt these laws [laws given humans a priori from pure reason] require a judgment sharpened by experience, in order on the one hand to distinguish in what cases they are applicable, and on the other to procure for them access to the will of man [the ability to reason above instinct], and effectual influence on conduct; since man is acted on by so many inclinations that, capable of the idea of a practical pure reason, he is not so easily able to make it effective *in concerto* with his life.[22]

Once we admit that experience matters when a decision maker mediates between the maxim development and application (even if it is not so easy to make it effective *in concerto* with one's life), we are admitting that we cannot develop or apply the maxim separately from how we experience the maxim as human beings.

In his basic views on the relation between natural and moral philosophy, Kant also acknowledges that the consequences matter. He first classifies ethics as a discipline that is material rather than formal, which means that ethics has an object. Further, he says that its object is freedom, which we can understand to be the consideration of how we exercise our freedom – that is, how we make decisions. Moral laws can therefore have "their empirical part" just as natural laws do. Natural philosophy "has to determine the laws of nature as an object of experience; [moral philosophy] the laws of the human will, so far as it is affected by nature; [natural philosophy]…being laws according to which everything does happen; [moral philosophy] laws according to which everything ought to happen. Ethics, however, must also consider the conditions under which what ought to happen frequently does not."[23]

In other words, experience (and thus consequences) must teach us how to think for ourselves about the circumstances in which various maxims are applicable and what conduct the maxim wants us to take. Kant was aware that consequences matter to morals and that morals evolve over time.

4.5. KANT AND HUMANS AS A RESOURCE

In the Kantian scheme of morals, therefore, the question is not whether consequences matter but which consequences matter and how they are to be taken into account. In particular, we need a scheme for taking account of

---

[22] *Id.* at 147–8.
[23] *Id.* at 146.

consequences that are relevant for developing maxims that are neutral and universal in the two ways that we have come to understand universal maxims: They must be unaffected by the self-interest of the person developing the maxim (or people similarly situated) and they must be subject to universal assent (by those who would be moral).

Yet this approach seems to drive a wedge between moral philosophy and economic philosophy. Economists suggest that human beings ought to be perceived to be a resource for society and that the maxim that is universal is one that makes society better off by taking maximum advantage of human beings as resources. I have endorsed that approach by saying that, because people have different projects and preferences, people have conflicting claims on society's resources, including the resources of other people. The resource viewpoint has much to commend it. From a community standpoint, public streets and highways are public commons, and tort law recognizes rules governing the commons by requiring each person to be reasonable in the claims they make on the common resource. But people also make claims against each other as a resource, making one person a resource for the projects and preferences of another in the sense that one person must accept burdens so that others need not be burdened.[24]

This economic characterization of tort law seems to run afoul of the Kantian maxim that humans should "so act as to treat humanity, whether in thine own person or in the person of any other, in every case as an end withal and never as a means only."[25] This injunction would, on its face, seem to bar an actor from inflicting injury on another without an overriding justification, for that might be understood to use the other as a means to an actor's end.[26]

As the many examples from tort law show, when deciding between injurer and victim, the law is always deciding whose projects and preferences must give way to another's projects and preferences, and therefore which actor may use another as a means to the actor's end. Similarly, Kant understood that not

[24] Viewing tort law as a system for reconciling conflicting claims to resources, including the resources that other people bring to the community, seemed somewhat crude when Judge Posner first presented it as the cornerstone of economic analysis in 1971. Linguistically, however, it is no different from the more common but less descriptive claim that tort law must reconcile the conflicting interests (or rights) of injurer and victim. And it has the advantage of stating an important truth: that human beings – their capacity and their ingenuity – are a resource for the community and therefore a resource for other people in the community. As each member of the community adds to the community, the community and its members draw strength from other individuals.

[25] *Id.* at 186.

[26] This position is implicit in the literature that disputes the relevance of the Hand formula to the determination of negligence. See, e.g., Richard W. Wright, *Justice and Reasonable Care in Negligence Law*, 47 AM. J. JURIS. 143 (2002).

all human ends could be achieved simultaneously. He referred to the "maxim that humanity and generally every rational nature is an end in itself (which is the extreme limiting condition of every man's freedom of action)."[27] We can treat this to mean that the need to take every human being as an end in itself actually limits one's freedom of action (and thus one's ability to achieve one's own ends), indicating that treating every person as an end and not as a means must be understood in a restricted way. In this section, I argue that Kant fully understood his means-end maxim to allow society to choose between individuals when people have conflicting projects and preferences. I also argue that his view is fully compatible with the vision of tort law that I present.

Kant used the means-end maxim not as a standalone principle but as part of the proof that the categorical imperative – the obligation to search for a neutral/universal law – exists. Consider the context of the means-end discussion. Kant first offered a proof that if there is a moral duty it is a duty that is categorical in that it does not get its moral force from the objectives it aims to achieve. This categorical imperative is a necessary condition for morality. He then proceeded to demonstrate that it is also a sufficient condition – that is, the principle he has advanced as the categorical imperative really exists and is a moral duty by which we can evaluate human decisions.

Kant offers the following proof. He posits that the ends of humans – what I have called their projects and preferences – serve as the sole objective of being human. Being human means to view one's life as an end in itself, one that is self-directed and self-guided. Because a human life is an end in itself, the decisions a human makes must be the means to human's chosen ends. Otherwise, the human would be denying that she is an end in herself. Because the categorical imperative is *also* an end in itself – that is, the categorical imperative is its own object – the end of each human is to make decisions in accordance with the end of the categorical imperative. Each person is an end in itself and each person who would act morally should use the same end (the categorical imperative) as the means to that person's own end. Because the categorical imperative calls for a means to an end that is also an end, and because the categorical imperative calls for an end that is universal, every moral person must be adopting the same means to his or her own end. If that is true, then the categorical imperative must exist because no moral person can get to his or her end without using it. Because every moral person gets to his or her end, and because the categorical imperative must be the end to get to that end, the categorical imperative must exist. That is why Kant can repeat the categorical imperative in the following form: "So act in regard to every rational being

[27] Immanuel Kant, FUNDAMENTAL PRINCIPLES OF METAPHYSICS 188.

(thyself and others) that he may always have place in thy maxim as an end in himself." That can be understood to say that decisions should always be made in accordance with a maxim that views the interests of all people to be the end toward which the maxim is aimed.[28]

However, because the ends chosen by different people present conflicting claims to resources, they cannot all be satisfied at once. They can exist together only if each individual end is understood in the context of the maxim that takes the ends of the other people into account. The categorical imperative gives this in terms of the assent of the other to be used in this way.[29] For a maxim that guides conduct to be universal, it must be one that every person would hold under the same circumstances, as well as one in which every person understands himself, and the decisions he makes, as an end in itself. Because the goal of every person is to honor herself and every other person as an end in itself, every person must act according to a maxim that reconciles people as ends. A person, "being an end in himself must be able to regard himself as also legislating universally in respect of these same laws, since it is just this fitness of his maxims for universal legislation that distinguishes him as an end in himself."[30] Because of this, he must always take his maxims from the point of view which regards him, and likewise every rational being, as lawgiving beings (on which account they are called persons).

To put it more succinctly, universal laws are the ends and the means to moral decisions for every person, and because universal laws are the ends of the will, it must be that every person is treated as an end (not a means to an end) if every person finds and follows the universal maxim in the categorical imperative.[31] That is the way, and the only way, by which everyone can act

---

[28] It is worth noting that Kant also addressed the question of how a rational person could be reasonable. To view one's life as an end in itself, self-directed and self-guided, does not excuse a person from acting according to a maxim that serves as an end in itself. A moral person will therefore guide decisions by a maxim that all end-seeking persons must use in order to be moral. The rational person must be reasonable if he is to seek his ends by means that are also an end.

[29] In evaluating the universal maxim that could govern lying, he says: "For he whom I propose by such a promise to use for my own purpose cannot possibly assent to my mode of acting towards him, and therefore cannot himself contain the end of his action." *Id.* at 187.

[30] *Id.* at 195.

[31] Jean-Jacques Rousseau made the same point with less precision but more romanticism by saying:

> The passing from the state of nature to the civil society produces a remarkable change in man; it puts justice as a rule of conduct in place of instinct, and gives his actions the moral quality they previously lacked. It is only then, when the voice of duty has taken the place of physical impulse, and right that of desire, that man, who has hitherto thought only of himself, finds himself compelled to act on other principles, and to consult his reason rather than study his inclinations. And although in civil society man surrenders some

according to a universal law. The only possibility of a universal law – to have the duty that is the end of human enterprise – is if every person treats every other person as an end when they reason toward a maxim that would be neutral and universal.

The important text is in a footnote. My paraphrase follows:

We humans make decisions based on the conception of some universal maxim that guides the decision. Only human beings have that faculty. All human beings make decisions with some universal maxim in mind – and the maxim is the end of the decision – and the end must therefore hold for all rational beings. The end must be something other than the possibility of attaining something, for that is a means to an end – a means to what is sought to be attained. That is, the ends must be something other than an objective or purpose or goal. The end must be to think according to a maxim that can be universalized. The goals that people seek to achieve as a means give rise to a maxim that depends on the goal and this is contingent or hypothetical only. For the human being to be an end in itself the human being must reconcile his ends with those of everyone else.[32]

In other words, each person must define his own ends in terms of the ends of others. That means that one person cannot define his own ends by himself

of the advantages that belong to the same state of nature, he gains in return far greater ones; his faculties are so exercised and developed, his mind so enlarged, his sentiments so ennobled, and his whole spirit so elevated that, if the abuse of his new condition did not in many cases lower him to something worse than what he had left, he should constantly bless the happy hour that lifted him forever from the state of nature and from a stupid, limited animal made a creature of intelligence and a man....To be governed by the appetite alone is slavery, while obedience to a law one prescribes to oneself is freedom."

Jean-Jacques Rousseau, THE SOCIAL CONTRACT 64–5 (1762) Penguin Classics (Maurice Cranston, ed., 1968).

[32] "The will is conceived as a faculty of determining oneself to action in *accordance with the conception of certain laws.* And such a faculty can be found only in rational beings. Now that which serves the will as the objective ground of its self-determination is the *end* and if this is assigned by reason alone, it must hold for all rational beings. On the other hand, that which merely contains the ground of possibility of the action of which the effect is the end, this is called the *means.*....Hence all these relative ends can give rise only to hypothetical imperatives.....Now I say: man and generally any rational being *exists* as an end in himself, *not merely as a means* to be arbitrarily used by this or that will, but in all his actions, whether they concern himself or other rational beings, must be always regarded at the same time as an end....If then there is a supreme practical principle or, in respect of the human will, a categorical imperative, it must be one which being drawn from the conception of that which is necessarily an end for every one because it is *an end in itself,* constitutes an *objective* principle of will, and can therefore serve as a universal practical law....But every other rational being regards its existence similarly, just on the same rational principle that holds for me: so that it is at the same time an objective principle, from which as a supreme practical law all laws of the will must be capable of being deduced." Immanuel Kant, FUNDAMENTAL PRINCIPLES OF METAPHYSICS 184–6.

but only in terms of the ends that would be chosen if one followed a neutral/ universal maxim. That requires the actor to take into account the ends of others. Kant then extended the analysis to posit that if every person treated others as an end and not as a means to an end there would be a "kingdom of ends." When he did so, he was positing the possibility of stable relations that we have come to think of as social cohesion. But he is necessarily admitting that not all ends can be simultaneously achieved and that some ends must be sacrificed for others. All that Kant required to avoid using another as an end is that the ends be reconciled in a way that each person would fairly reconcile his ends with the ends of other humans. In this way, the economic account is not at odds with the Kantian account. An actor can use another as a resource as long as that use fairly reconciles his resource use with the resource use of other humans.

4.6. CONCLUSION

Kant's great contribution was to develop a theory of morality that focused not on examining how humans behave, but on how humans think about their decisions that implicate the well-being of other people. By focusing on the unique ability of humans to reason toward a neutral and universal principle that would take into account the well-being of others and then to subjugate their own interests and passions to the community interests defined by that principle, Kant identified an obligation that elevates humans from their narrow self-interest and allows them to reason toward mutual and reciprocal cooperation with other humans that does not depend on hierarchy, external commands, or animal instinct. By developing a theory of morality that centers on the ability of humans to reason toward a reconciliation of competing projects and preferences in a way that promotes the interests of the individual by promoting the interests of the individual in a community, Kant opened both philosophical and behavior sciences to an examination of how people make decisions and what moral decisions look like. It was not long before tort law would adopt this orientation as it explored the requirements of the reasonable person in a community of persons.

The Kantian project is not complete, however, until we specify the nature of the decision-making process that can be said to be moral. This process cannot ignore the consequences of an actor's decisions, and Kant did not claim that it should. Nor can the thought process avoid subjecting some people's interests to the interests of others, for the interests inevitably clash. We turn then to an assessment of Rawls's veil of ignorance to examine the ways by which a moral person will determine which consequences of a decision matter and how the consequences are to be valued and balanced against each other.

5   Rawlsian Consequentialism

Rawls and Social Cohesion

To summarize the discussions in Chapter Four, Kantian philosophy establishes the standards one should use when thinking about one's projects and preferences in the context of the well-being of others: One should decide according to a maxim that is neutral and universal. If an actor makes a decision with sufficient neutrality and universality, the actor will be acting morally (and, I argue, the collective decisions made by all actors will lead to an efficient, fair, and stable society). When deciding *whether* to decide in terms of maxims that are neutral and universal, an actor may not think about the consequences of that decision; the actor's decision may depend only on the actor's desire to fulfill her duty to the social community. On the other hand, once an actor makes the decision to search for maxims that meet the tests of neutrality and universality, deliberation about such a maxim does not ignore the consequences of the various maxims from which the actor is choosing. The actor who would act morally must surely take consequences into account, for a prerequisite for moral thought is to take into account the consequences of one's decisions for the well-being of others. On the other hand, not all consequences of a decision count or are given equal weight. If the actor were to honor all consequences, the actor could well privilege consequences that affect his well-being in a way that would violate the standards of neutrality and universality.

In this way, the standards of neutrality and universality guide the decision maker in determining which consequences matter and how they matter, for the actor may only take consequences into account in a way that will lead to a maxim that is neutral and universal. The actor's view of the empirical world must be melded with the actor's duty to make decisions in accordance with a maxim that is neutral and universal, and the actor therefore needs a methodology of assessing and choosing among the consequences of various kinds of decisions – a methodology of consequences – that leads the actor/decision maker to a maxim that is neutral and universal.

Rawls offered the veil of ignorance as a way of thinking about social contracts.[1] We can appropriate the veil of ignorance to help us understand the deliberation that a moral person is required to use when sifting through different consequences to find a maxim that meets the requirements of neutrality and universality – a methodology of consequences that does not allow the consequences of various options to distort the decision away from a neutral and universal maxim. Although Rawls developed and defended the veil of ignorance in the context of decisions about major structural divisions of power and resources within a social community, I believe the device of the veil of ignorance helps us understand the moral way of addressing the coordination problems with which tort law deals. I undertake a defense of the veil of ignorance in the context of how actors morally solve coordination problems in Section 5.1.[2]

The central task of tort law, however, is to choose between various kinds of consequences when the consequences fall differently on different people. Either one person must drive more slowly or another person must accept more risk than the person would like. Either the freedom of a person with epilepsy must be curtailed or the risk that others thereby face must be tolerated. Therefore, if an actor is to act according to a maxim that is neutral and universal, he must compare the consequences of the decision for himself and others and respond by considering the consequence that would be chosen under a neutral and universal maxim. The actor is therefore required to compare states of the world and undertake a social comparison of consequences between the actor and the victim. This interpersonal comparison is an essential element of tort law and a central object of the device of the veil of ignorance.

But it is not, I argue, an interpersonal comparison of well-being or welfare. It is instead a comparison that shows what is best for the social community. This aspect of Rawlsian consequentialism is defined and defended in Section 5.2. In Section 5.3, I conclude by briefly relating the theory of morality developed here to the law's role in advancing social cohesion.

---

[1]   The account here draws especially from John Rawls, A THEORY OF JUSTICE 11–22 and 136–40, Harvard University Press (1971) (Rawls, *Theory of Justice*).

[2]   I do not seek to situate tort theory within the context of the broader political and moral theory of John Rawls. Rather, I seek to import one aspect of Rawlsian theory, the veil of ignorance, into tort theory. On the broader issue of integrating corrective justice into Rawlsian theory, see Stephen Perry, *Ripstein, Rawls, and Responsibility*, 72 FORD. L. REV. 1845 (2004).

5.1. THE VEIL OF IGNORANCE IN TORT THEORY

By and large, scholars have not taken advantage of the device of the veil of ignorance when thinking about tort theory. That is, perhaps, because they believe the device concerns distributive not corrective justice, imagining that they have to contend with the difference principle if they are to use Rawls and his social contract theory. Or it is because they do not want to admit that some consequences matter. But their skepticism seems to miss the adaptability of the veil of ignorance and its value to our understanding of tort law.

The most sustained skepticism about Rawls and tort law comes from Arthur Ripstein, who suggests that the "contract argument is poorly suited to understanding the doctrinal details of the law."[3] But his objections seem to uncompelling. He wrote in the context of the choice of liability regime, strict liability or negligence, rather than, as I do, in terms of the details of the negligence regime. He correctly points out that the veil of ignorance is "merely" an expository device, not an algorithm, and that "the specification of the interests and concerns of the parties cannot be derived from it, but must instead be brought to it, and defended on independent grounds."[4] And he repeats Thomas Pogge's argument that the contract argument cannot take into account the relational nature of tort law.[5] I hope to meet these objections by offering the veil of ignorance as a way of understanding how people normally think about the fair division of rights and responsibilities when dealing with interpersonal conflicts. The "specification of interests and concerns" that must be brought to it are, as I stressed in Chapter Two, based on the values that people normally use and expect others to use when making decisions. The fact that analysis from behind the veil of ignorance is expository (and therefore subject to debate) is an asset for justificatory analysis because it helps us understand the refinements that are important for our understanding of the evolving nature of the reasonableness concept.

Ultimately, skepticism about the veil of ignorance seems to be grounded on the fact that it is consequential and, it is thought, violates the deontological structure of tort law. But the social contract approach I advocate is wrapped within, and constrained by, the deontological structure of tort law. It is subservient to the responsibility of one person for the well-being of another, while at the same time being an essential part of working out what that means. Only the most die-hard conceptualist would deny that at some point in applying

---

[3] Arthur Ripstein, *The Division of Responsibility and the Law of Tort* 72 Ford. L. Rev. 1811, 1816 (2004).

[4] *Id.*

[5] *Id.* at 1817.

concepts like duty and due care consequences matter; I offer the veil of igno-rance as a device for determining which consequences must matter and why. In this light, it is difficult to understand the force of Ripstein's argument that "because [parties] are concerned only with outcomes, [they] must be prepared to trade liberty off against security in whatever way will best protect their interests"[6] or that "the distinction between harms I suffer in general and those harms that are brought about through wrongdoing of others is invisible."[7] To the contrary, as I show below, the veil of ignorance is the perfect way to think about a person's interests as a member of a community, and people are per-fectly able to distinguish between misfortune they must bear and misfortune for which others are responsible. In particular, writing on this subject seems to suggest that choices are dichotomous – freedom versus security – and that people cannot reason toward a scheme of responsibility for the well-being of others that melds the two. In this chapter, I describe and defend the use of the veil of ignorance; in later chapters I show how it justifies the contours of duty, proximate cause, and the choice of liability regimes.

5.2. THE VEIL OF IGNORANCE

The device of the veil of ignorance invites the actor/decision maker to simul-taneously consider the conditions of decision that will allow the actor to rea-son toward a maxim that is neutral and universal and also to consider the appropriate maxim itself. The actor is required to strip from the decision any information relating to factors that ought not be taken into account in that kind of decision so that the actor can reason from only permissible factors. At the same time, the actor must choose between different maxims that might be posited based on permissible factors. The veil of ignorance invites the actor to engage in the following thought process: If I were looking for a neutral and universal maxim to guide my decision, what factors (or considerations or consequences) would I have to rule out in order to develop a neutral and universal maxim and what maxim would be neutral and universal given the permissible factors? By separating reasoning about the conditions of decision and reasoning about the decision maxim to guide the decision, the actor is invited to move between the methodology of decision making and the result-ing decision until both the methodology and the decision meet the standards of neutrality and universality.

---

[6]   *Id.* at 1822.
[7]   *Id.* at 1823.

The idea of the veil of ignorance also links the decision of the individual with decisions of other individuals in the community. The idea is to ask each actor in a community to make decisions under conditions of equality and under constraints that forbid the actor from taking into account considerations that would keep the actor from finding a maxim that is neutral and universal. When a decision is thus constrained, the actor will be forced to identify those consequences of a decision that are acceptable under the standards of neutrality and universality and that are not unacceptably influenced by the inequality that exists in society or by the status or goals of the decision maker. At the same time, the decision maker is forced to ignore information about which people would differ because of their station in life. As Rawls said, the idea of the original position [that lies behind the veil of ignorance] "is to rule out principles that would be rational to propose for acceptance....only if one knew certain things that are irrelevant from the standpoint of justice"[8] in our inquiry under the standards of neutrality and universality.

Although Rawls developed the device of the veil of ignorance to help us understand the concept of distributive justice – that is, the division of primary goods among people and the institutions that a community would adopt to make distributive decisions – the device is equally useful for decisions of the kind that corrective justice addresses. The device of the veil of ignorance works because it forces the decision maker to eliminate reasons or reasoning that would bias the decision in his or her favor. The device therefore addresses the central concern of corrective justice – to find the appropriate balance of rights and responsibilities of one member of the community to others – by making sure that the decision represents a neutral and nonidiosyncratic assessment of competing interests.

The justification for using the veil of ignorance as a thought-device that determines what maxims an actor ought to follow is that the veil of ignorance allows the actor/decision maker to reason toward a decision that rules out any considerations that might keep the decision from being called neutral and universal. The device of the veil of ignorance therefore legitimizes the decision by meeting standards of transparency (we know the basis on which the decision was reached and can challenge the decision by questioning the basis on which it was reached), legitimacy (the decision is one that meets the tests of acceptability and proportionality), and reciprocity (the decision is one that the injurer would make if the injurer were in the victim's shoes and that the injurer would expect the victim to make were the victim in the injurer's shoes). Decisions made behind the veil of ignorance are decisions to which we would

---

[8] Rawls, *Theory of Justice.*

expect all people to assent if their reasoning followed the same methodology. When each person follows that methodology, the resulting decisions are fair, efficient, and stable.

Moreover, decisions behind the veil of ignorance are self-justifying: People would choose the veil of ignorance as a basis for making decisions if they were behind the veil of ignorance. If people did not know their station and personal circumstances and had to make a decision, they would choose to reason from a position of ignorance because that would give them the best possibility of reasoning toward a position they would want to be in once they knew their station and circumstances. A person behind the veil of ignorance would understand that if he knew whether he were the injurer, he would make a different decision than if he knew that he were the victim, but he would not seek to guess whether he was injurer or victim because a decision supported by that guess could make him worse off. This is not a matter of being risk averse. The person who makes a decision knowing that he cannot know its effect would make the decision in a way that even an unwelcome result would be one he could justify and live with under the circumstances.

Within this framework, we can make some reasonable assertions about the application of the device of the veil of ignorance in helping individuals solve coordination problems. We can assert, for example, following Rawls, that certain kinds of information would be excluded from the actor/decision maker's knowledge behind the veil of ignorance:

(a) The actor/decision maker would have no knowledge of whether she was injurer or victim. The connection between the decision of the actor/injurer and the effect on the victim is often a matter of luck. If an actor is driving at an unreasonable speed, what connects the actor to the victim is luck. Good luck on the part of the driver means no injury; the bad luck of the driver is transferred to the victim. Once we know whether the accident happened, we know whether the actor and victim were lucky. By denying the decision maker knowledge of whether she is actor or victim, we deny her the ability to make assumptions about whether she would be lucky if she were the injurer. Constraining the decision maker so that she does not know if she is the injurer or the victim induces her to assume that luck is irrelevant to the choice, because luck can fall on either the injurer or the victim.

(b) The actor/decision maker would not know his place in society, class position, or social status, or about the distribution of natural assets and abilities, his intelligence, strength, and the like. Those factors influence what one has to gain from the distribution of rights and responsibilities, but they do not determine how rights and responsibilities *ought* to be distributed. By eliminating such knowledge, the decision of which maxim to follow would not be influenced by what a person had to gain or lose that was extraneous to the choice being made. It would also signify that choices are being made on the basis of equality.

(c) The actor/decision maker would make no judgments about the goals that others seek to achieve (their projects) or the means they use to achieve them (their preferences). This is disallowed because an actor who would make judgments about the ends others seek or their means of seeking them could do so only by using judgments based on the ends and means that he himself holds, and this would introduce an impermissible bias into decisions. This is the requirement of empathy.

(d) The actor would be denied knowledge of how many people were in various classes. The veil of ignorance does not invite the actor/decision maker to guess as to what group (injurer or victim) the person would belong or the likelihood that the actor would have this or that personal characteristic that might influence the degree of risk the person presents to the community. We are not asking the decision maker behind the veil of ignorance to decide what percentage of people are likely to be in one group rather than another – say in the group of epileptics or nonepileptics – and then determine a maxim that reflects the probability of being in that group. If we were, those in small groups would be systematically disadvantaged; decisions would be skewed against people with epilepsy because people would know that their chance of having epilepsy would not be great. Instead, we are assuming that the decision maker behind the veil of ignorance would have an even chance of being in one class or the other and we are asking the decision maker what the appropriate rule would be if she did not know which class she were in.

At the same time, the actor/decision maker behind the veil of ignorance would be equipped with important information that was necessary to create the relevant maxim but that did not skew the thought process by introducing information that would prejudice the result. The decision maker would be required to know the range of beliefs and fears that people generally bring to their affairs (what Rawls called general laws of human psychology), general principles of human behavior (including principles of economic behavior), the way that people work out coordination problems in other contexts (as a reflection of the adjustments people normally make to the interests of others), the alternatives available to reconcile claims to resources, the way that people generally think about such conflicting claims, and general causal knowledge. And the decision maker would understand that he stood in a position of equality with respect to every other decision maker.

The device of reasoning from behind a veil of ignorance allows us to understand the relationship between how people act and the kinds of decisions people would make if they were to make moral decisions. The law can only judge people's conduct, but the appraisal of a person's conduct depends on the relationship between their conduct and the conduct they would have undertaken if they had been thinking appropriately about the well-being of others. When we evaluate a person's conduct, we are asking whether a person would have acted that way if he or she had to make choices behind a veil of ignorance. When we conclude that the person would not have acted that way had the choices been made behind the veil of ignorance, we conclude that the conduct was unreasonable. On the other hand, if a person reasoning from behind a veil of ignorance would have undertaken the conduct, then the conduct is reasonable, even if the person did not reason from behind the veil or did not reason at all. A person who is wrong in her reasoning but right in her actions cannot be held responsible for injury that results; it is the conduct that a reasonable person would have undertaken had the person used the appropriate reasoning to determine her conduct.

The device of the veil of ignorance does not put too many informational requirements on the decision maker. Not only does the device abstract from the decision maker's actual knowledge in order to reach an unbiased decision – thereby reducing information requirements – the device is not foreign to people. It is, in fact, the kind of reasoning that people in a community use every day when coordinating their activities with other members of the community. People are used to reasoning in the following fashion: "if I step to one side on an escalator to allow someone to pass me, that follows a norm that allows all people on the escalator to move at their preferred speed and I know that my sacrifice this time is worth it for the community and for me when I am in a hurry. It is the behavior that we would all choose if we did not know whether we were the walker or the stander." All the device of the veil of ignorance requires is that the decision maker drop her ego and blend her own ideas of projects and preferences with those of other members of the community. People do that all the time in communities that are healthy because people blend their own personalities with those of others for the sake of community. It is in those moments when Hume's appeal to social instinct can work alongside Kant's appeal to reason; as long as the instinct to which one appeals is the community instinct rather than the individual instinct, Hume and Kant work together.

Finally, the device of the veil of ignorance allows us to distinguish the *is* from the *ought*. Norms often reflect the other-regarding behavior called for by reasoning behind the veil of ignorance. That is why social norms are often a good indication of the way people ought to behave. But norms can be evaluated using the device of the veil of ignorance. The question is whether the norms that guide human behavior are those that a community would have chosen behind a veil of ignorance, for it is only those norms that have the social morality that is required to become law. If, on the other hand, the norm reflects some preexisting power or inequality within a community, then it would not be endorsed behind a veil of ignorance and ought not be adopted as a reasonable standard.

5.3. INTERPERSONAL COMPARISONS

Inevitably, because the projects and preferences chosen by free and equal persons clash, the projects and preferences of one person must give way to those of another. This presents a tricky problem of valuation. If, as we have seen, a person with epilepsy has a seizure while driving, tort law must compare the victim's freedom from physical injury with the injurer's freedom to drive. How are we to deal with these incommensurate values when we determine the rights and obligations of people in a community? We need a basis for understanding how an actor/decision maker would compare his projects and preferences with those of different persons when they cannot all be satisfied and when they are not easily valued under a common metric. The device of the veil of ignorance helps us, but not in the way that is usually understood.

Comparisons of these kinds are often thought of as interpersonal comparisons of welfare or well-being, as if the task was to determine how much welfare one person would have to give up to preserve or increase the welfare of another person. The comparison, in fact, is not so lavish, for in tort law we are dealing with corrective, not distributive justice. Rawls developed the device of the veil of ignorance to understand the requirements of justice that would allow society to compare claims to society's resources across people when the claims are not based on the interaction between people – that is, claims that are based on need or benefit or on distributional fairness. A comparison based on relative gains or losses in welfare works when the issue is essentially a zero-sum game, for such distributions take from one person and distribute to another without increasing the total of rights or privileges to be distributed. That comparison therefore requires some metric of comparison that relates the resources to be divided (basic liberties or wealth) to the worthiness of the individual who claims those resources, which requires an allocation based on some measure of welfare – either comparative benefit, comparative need, or aggregate well-being. That is why it is often thought that comparisons of this type are comparisons in individual welfare or well-being.

It would be a mistake, however, to believe that comparisons made for the purposes of corrective justice are the same kind of comparisons. Superficially, it can be asked whether the rights associated with the projects and preferences of the injurer or the rights associated with the projects and preferences of the victim are more important. This leads to the implication that we are comparing the welfare of the injurer and victim, as if we should find a way of expressing the loss each would feel under various arrangements in metrics that would then be compared. But this similarity is only superficial, and it is important to distinguish the comparisons being made in the context of corrective justice from the comparisons being made in the context of distributive justice.

The interpersonal comparison we are making in tort law is unique. In tort law (as in private law generally) we are asking which party must bear burdens so that the other party can benefit by being able to undertake her projects and preferences without burdens. Here, what we are distributing is the burdens of being a member of the community, not the general welfare or well-being of the two parties to the dispute. As a result, this is not a free-flowing inquiry into the well-being of the injurer and the victim, which is why we can rule out some of the ways that have been advanced to address interpersonal comparisons in the distributive context. Tort law does not require, or ask for, a comparison of the well-being of the victim and the injurer before the accident and after the accident. Nor does it require an inquiry into the welfare of injurer and victim in some abstract way. We do not decide which party needs, or can benefit from, an increase in welfare the most. Nor does the comparison seek to compare the utility of the freedom from burdens to the actor and victim. We ought not to think of this in traditional utilitarian terms, as if we were comparing the total utils that result from one outcome with the total utils that result from another outcome. And for these comparisons we do not need a definition of the good life that is independent of the way people actually define it.

Indeed, we are not really asking about the well-being of this or that individual at all, except to ask which of the two parties should bear the burdens of being a citizen in a community of citizens. Instead, the decision is about social utility; it is about the benefit of the trade-off for society given the way the community normally values these things. Under this view, people operate from an implicit social index – an index of values that allows them to compare the burdens they must accept in order to coordinate their projects and preferences with the burdens that others would otherwise be compelled to assume. We can understand this as an index of shared values. It is the social index that suggests, for example, that when it starts snowing and the roads get icy, one should burden one's projects and preferences by slowing down rather than imposing burdens on others by accepting the risk of an accident.

As I indicted earlier, the social index is worked out through human interaction and is evolutionary. Its success at avoiding conflict and minimizing interference between the projects and preferences of different people is rewarded by becoming implanted in people in a way that reinforces the successful and induces the community to revise the comparative social indexes that are, or become, unsuccessful. But the relevant social index is also capable of being worked out from behind the veil of ignorance. The veil of ignorance does this by requiring the decision maker to remain neutral toward both injurer and victim except as an appeal to social values, and priorities favors one set of interests over others. This usage captures the central notion of reciprocity – the notion that if I were in the place of the other, I would want to be treated in this way – or at least I think now that I would want to be treated in this way. All problems of torts (and private law generally) are reciprocal in the sense that the problems exist only when the projects and preferences of two or more people clash. Therefore all require some degree of empathetic imagination. In situations of reciprocal experience, where an actor is both a driver and a pedestrian, the actor can empathize directly. Where the actor plays only one general role – say as a person with epilepsy or a person without epilepsy – the veil of ignorance requires more empathetic imagination to determine what it would be like to walk in the other's shoes. In either case, reasoning from behind the veil of ignorance allows the decision maker to compare projects and preferences in a way that reflects a socially constructed index of burdens and benefits.

5.4. CONCLUSION: THE METAPHYSICS OF SOCIAL COHESION

We are now equipped to relate the moral philosophy of Kant and Rawls to the concept of social cohesion developed here. When each person in a community makes decisions following a methodology that would lead to a maxim that is neutral and universal, each person is incorporating the well-being of another into the actor's projects and preferences in an appropriate way. When an actor does this, others have no cause for resentment or envy, for others have been treated with the equal dignity afforded to all people in the community. And we can understand that decisions made under these constraints will improve the well-being of the community. Any decision that is made in accordance with the values of the community and is also sustainable behind the veil of ignorance improves the community. Improvement is measured by the values of the community, not by some external factor, and any decision that follows values the community normally uses, or normally should use, will improve social cohesion.

PART III

THE THEORY APPLIED

In this part, I show how the main doctrines of tort law reflect the theory of other-regarding behavior and how tort doctrine can be made more coherent if it is interpreted in light of that theory. I seek to do so in a way that leaves room for debate about the requirements of the other-regarding person, providing my own conclusions but suggesting a framework that allows others to advocate for an expanded or contracted scope of responsibility within that framework.

Chapter Six addresses duty, providing an analytical framework for understanding the content of an actor's obligation to take into account the well-being of others and its limits, including the normative justification for no-duty rules. Chapter Seven shows that proximate cause cases are an important limitation on one person's responsibility for the well-being of others and that they combine with duty and breach to form a coherent and unified theory of responsibility. The chapter also explains the normative justification for the proximate cause limitation on responsibility and provides a single analytical lens for determining whether that limitation should be recognized. Chapter Eight takes up strict liability for abnormally dangerous activities, arguing that such liability ought to be absorbed within the negligence regime, showing that the cases in which liability has been justly imposed are all cases in which the defendant made an unreasonable decision about the location, timing, method, or frequency of an activity, and arguing that the negligence regime easily encompasses those cases. It also argues that strict liability ought not be imposed if the defendant has not made unreasonable decisions.

The next three chapters address outcomes that look superficially like strict liability, but are really applications of other-regarding fault principles. Chapter Nine takes up the *Vincent* case, arguing that the concept of fault revealed by the theory of other-regarding behavior shows why the defendant in that case was required to compensate the plaintiff even though the defendant's conduct was not faulty. Chapter Ten then addresses product liability, showing how it, too, reflects the theory of other-regarding behavior and advocating that product liability be reunited with service liability under one doctrine of expanded responsibility for suppliers. Chapter Eleven explains that a group of specialized cases, symbolized by the McDonald's hot coffee case, stand for the limited version of enterprise liability by requiring an enterprise to compensate those customers who are hurt by an attribute of the product that benefits customers as a group. Finally, Chapter Twelve shows that even intentional torts embody the theory of other-regarding behavior.

6 Social Cohesion and Autonomy

The Justificational Boundary of Duty

The Hand formula expresses the foundational duty of all actors: to take into account the well-being of others when making certain decisions. But this is not a general obligation of beneficence and it does not give others a free-standing claim on an actor's projects and preferences. Tort law understands that giving others an open-ended claim on the actor's resources would violate the actor's autonomy. In tort law's famous and brutal hypothetical, an actor has no obligation to pick up a baby from the tracks (even if a train is speeding toward the baby), unless the actor has a relationship to the event that requires the actor to take the well-being of the baby into account when deciding how to act. Because tort law draws a distinction between the duty to be other-regarding and the duty to be altruistic (affirming the former but leaving the latter to the actor's free choice), tort law needs an analytical and normative basis for distinguishing duty from no-duty; it must distinguish the obligation to take into account the well-being of others from instances in which the well-being of others is a matter of choice. Ideally, such a theory would provide a consistent view of responsibility that explains the scope of an actor's duty and addresses, without artificial distinctions, one of the fundamental mysteries of negligence law: If picking up a baby from the tracks is easy, why would it not be the reasonable thing to do, and why does the law not require it? How can tort law simultaneously say, with coherence, that the duty to be reasonable runs to the world and also that sometimes an actor has no duty to consider the well-being of another? Given the unworkable distinction between nonfeasance and misfeasance,[1] how are we to understand the justification for, and analytical content of, tort law's duty and no-duty concepts?

---

[1] Saul Levmore, FOUNDATIONS OF TORT LAW 225, Foundation Press (1994). The characterization of a particular choice as nonfeasance or misfeasance depends on whether the defendant had a duty to act, which depends on the scope of the defendant's responsibility over the risk. The distinction therefore depends on, but cannot determine, one's duty. Compare *Johnson*

In this chapter, we will see that an actor's obligation to take into account the well-being of others does not exist until the actor has made a choice that puts the actor in the position of accepting responsibility for reasonably controlling the risk another faces.[2] The actor must take dominion over the risk another faces as part of the actor's projects and preferences before being required to account for the well-being of others. Most often, an actor has dominion over a risk because the actor has created the risk; the act of creating the risk is a choice to accept responsibility for how the risk might affect the well-being of others. It is a duty that runs to the world. But even if the actor has not created the risk, the actor may take dominion over the risk that another faces (and therefore over the other's well-being) if the actor has chosen to make that risk a part of the actor's projects and preferences. The actor's choice of an activity that implies the acceptance of dominion over another's well-being creates the "special relationship" that gives an actor the duty to reasonably consider the well-being of another. But when the actor creates no risk and has no relationship with the risk another faces, the actor's autonomy protects the actor from having a duty to another.

6.1. THE DUTY WARS

A justificational analysis of the concept of duty is badly needed. Given the focus of existing theory, it is not surprising that the concept "remains in turmoil."[3] Current scholarship concentrates primarily on the form and use of the concept of duty, not on its justificational content. The function of duty is well debated. Duty is said to perform four functions[4] (or is it six?[5]). The form of duty is well debated. It is understood as a reflection of the relationship that is inherent in corrective justice, as a gauge to control the standard of care, or as a "policy decision" that recognizes exceptions to the general standard of

---

   v. State, 553 N.W. 2d 40 (Minn 1996) (halfway house not responsible for failure to make a
   phone call to warn police of parole violations) with Dan Dobbs, The Law of Torts at 875,
   West Hornbook Series (2000) (placing the phone call could be construed to be part of the
   enterprise of running a halfway house, making the failure to act misfeasance).
[2] Arthur Ripstein uses the concept of "risk ownership" to tie together questions of duty of care,
   remoteness, and standard of care. Arthur Ripstein, Equality, Responsibility, and the Law
   53–60, Cambridge University Press (1999). The theory here uses the concept of "risk ownership" or "dominion over risk" to explain the existence and scope of an actor's duty.
[3] W. Jonathan Cardi & Michael D. Green, *Duty Wars*, 81 S. Cal. L. Rev. 671 (2008).
[4] John C.P. Goldberg & Benjamin C. Zipursky, *The Restatement (Third) and the Place of Duty
   in Negligence Law*, 54 Vand. L. Rev. 657 (2001) (Goldberg & Zipursky, *The Place of Duty*).
[5] Dilan A. Esper. & Gregory C. Keating, *Putting "Duty" In Its Place: A Reply to Professor's
   Goldberg and Zipursky*, 41 Loy. L.A. L. Rev. 1225 (2008) (Esper & Keating, *Putting Duty in
   Its Place*).

care. But the current literature does not address the analytical content of the concept of duty. It does not tell us the circumstances, factors, and values that are relevant to determining whether an actor has a duty in a particular situation and how one thinks about the scope of that duty.

One reason for the lack of justificational content in the current literature may be strategic. Our understanding of the concept of duty would be advanced if we understood duty to implicate two questions: one is the obligation to think of the well-being of another (its existence or nonexistence) and the other is the scope of that obligation, thought of as the circumstances, factors, and values that would tell us the kinds of behavior that would fulfill the obligation. Duty champions appear to be afraid to distinguish between these two aspects of duty because they are afraid that the scope of the duty inquiry would fold the concept of duty into the concept of breach.[6] But, as I argue below, that is not the necessary implication of recognizing an independent inquiry into the scope of the duty, for the scope of an actor's duty folds into the concept of breach in some cases but not in others. When it does not, the scope of the duty inquiry retains independent conceptual and justificational force.

This can be understood in Kantian terms. Sometimes the obligation to find a universal maxim leads to no obligation to another. The Kantian obligation is categorical in two senses. First, it is the obligation to reason toward a maxim that determines whether the well-being of another must be taken into account. That, of course, requires a division between duty and no-duty rules – a principled basis for apprehending the existence of the obligation to take into account the well-being of others. Then, the categorical imperative has a second obligation – the obligation to take into account the well-being of another by thinking about the conflicting projects in a way that is resolved by a neutral and universal maxim. The obligation to think in a certain way – which is also categorical – implicates the scope of the duty – that is, the range of factors that must be taken into account in determining how to behave toward another. The second obligation suggests that the scope of the content of the

---

[6] John Goldberg and Ben Zipursky try to separate duty from breach by suggesting that duty is operable when it is fairly clear what is prudent but the court must decide whether the defendant had an obligation to act prudently. This turns every duty case into a baby-on-the-tracks case, but it assumes that the prudent course is clear if one has an obligation. It assumes, for example, that if the psychiatrist in *Tarasoff* had an obligation to be prudent, we know what he should have done. In the view presented here, duty and breach are not so easily bifurcated, for the prudent course is never obvious. I posit instead a three-step process: (1) does the actor have an obligation to consider the well-being of another; (2) what circumstances, factors, and values control the behavioral scope of that obligation; and (3) if the behavior requested by the plaintiff is within the scope of the obligation, has the actor breached the obligation? As the text explains, the first two inquiries are for the judge, the final one for the jury.

concept of duty must be understood in an analytical, justificational way that Kant requires.

My belief is that underneath the current debate about the form and function of the duty concept lies an implicit theory of obligation that has not yet been adequately articulated. I seek to make that theory explicit. Once we do, the duty wars will be seen to be far less controversial than the combatants suppose. In this chapter, I present a justificational analysis of the concept of duty and show how it informs our understanding of the duty wars.

6.2. THE HAND FORMULA AND THE LIMITS OF RESPONSIBILITY

Although the Hand formula does not tell us when it applies, the foundation of a theory of duty is inherent in the concept of the reasonable person. When an actor has the obligation to be other-regarding, others have a legitimate claim on the actor's projects and preferences – a legitimate claim that the actor should invest reasonable resources to ensure the victim's well-being. An automobile driver must burden his projects and preferences by adopting a reasonable speed; those injured if the driver does not do so have a claim on the actor's resources. But the potential victim's claim against the actor is only to the reasonable expenditure of resources, not a claim to guaranteed well-being. If the actor behaves reasonably, the victim has no claim on the actor's resources; the negligence standard leaves the victim with the risks that are not eliminated if the actor takes due care (the residual risks of the actor's activity).

This limitation on an actor's responsibility occurs when no decision of the actor could improve the well-being of the victim in a socially appropriate way, either because the decision would sacrifice the socially overriding interest of the actor or because no decision of the actor would make a difference to the victim's well-being. The actor is not responsible when harm is traced to matters that are effectively or socially beyond human control. Thus, harm inflicted by sudden and unanticipated seizures, like harm attributable to lightening, are seen to be acts of nature and therefore not a source of responsibility for the well-being of the victim.[7] The limitation on responsibility also occurs

---

[7] *Rodgers v. Central Pac. R. R Co.*, 8 P. 377, 377(Cal. 1885) ("if the accident was attributable to a 'superhuman or irresistible' cause – to an 'act of God' – the defendant would not be liable; that as a general principle no man shall be responsible for that which no man can control"). See also, *Cohen v. Petty*, 65 F. 2d. 820,821 (D.C. Cir. 1993) ("It is undoubtedly the law that one who is suddenly stricken by an illness, which he had no reason to anticipate, while driving an automobile, which renders it impossible for him to control the car, is not chargeable with negligence").

when the actor effectively loses control of the well-being of the victim because the actor would have to sacrifice more of her own projects and preferences than is socially warranted or because the techniques of protecting the victim's well-being are beyond the actor's control. The dividing line that distinguishes an actor's responsibility for the well-being of another from nonresponsibility therefore turns on the actor's ability to affect acceptable change by making different decisions. If the actor cannot make a decision that would affect change at acceptable social costs, the actor is not responsible for the harm that results.

In other words, under the negligence rule, the potential victim must assume the burden of risk that an actor need not assume, and this is the risk of citizenship in a community. The negligence rule is both a statement of the right of the potential victim to have the actor account for the victim's projects and preferences and a statement of the extent to which the potential victim must accept the projects and preferences of the actor as preeminent. This is a form of other-regarding behavior of the victim – the victim's acceptance of the social ranking of projects and preferences that privilege the actor's projects and preferences over the victim's projects and preferences. If the actor acts reasonably, the actor has a right to avoid having her projects and preferences called into question. This gives the actor freedom and autonomy to pursue her projects and preferences without burdens.

In this way, the negligence rule both constrains and affirms an actor's right to choose. Responsibility ends where no choice an actor *should or could* make would improve the well-being of the victim. As Holmes said, the "moral element" of making a choice is to "make the power of avoiding the evil complained of a condition of liability."[8] The negligence rule embodies a concept of autonomy that marks the border beyond which one person has no responsibility for the well-being of another. As the next section shows, the same concept of autonomy determines whether one has the obligation to take into account the well-being of another in the first place.

6.3. CHOICE AND THE REQUIREMENTS OF SOCIAL COHESION

Autonomy to choose is an important element of social cohesion. Autonomy empowers individuals by making them responsible for the consequences of their choices, and it also empowers individuals by protecting them from claims of others.[9]

---

[8] Holmes, The Common Law 94–6, Little, Brown & Co. (1881).
[9] As the reader will recognize, this is a constrained form of the libertarianism of Richard Epstein. Richard A. Epstein, *A Theory of Strict Liability*, 2 J. Legal Studies 151, 198–200

In interpersonal affairs, the law advances social cohesion by allowing each person to exercise maximum freedom to make choices, consistent with the equal freedom of others to make choices.[10] The freedom to choose (although constrained by the reasonableness requirement) gives each actor a sense of control and purpose. If individuals are to fulfill their potential as human beings, they must be free to develop their talents in directions they find to be important, toward goals they value, and by means that enhance their journey. An essential part of personhood is the freedom to choose one's projects and preferences, a reciprocal right shared by all that governs how individuals think about each other's well-being. By making each person responsible for his own well-being, autonomy gives each person an incentive to make choices that lead to things the person values. Because a person cannot depend on, and has no legal right to, beneficence from others, the person makes decisions knowing that he or she bears the consequences of those decisions.

By limiting the extent to which others can make a legal claim on the actor's projects and preferences, tort law advances social cohesion by facilitating participation in society.[11] By minimizing the claims that others can make, autonomy allows the actor to enjoy the rewards of good choices. Autonomy thereby allows society to harness the energies of each person by protecting the person's ability to lead a life that she finds to be fulfilling. The social cohesion that autonomy creates allows each person in the community to work within her projects and preferences to the maximum extent possible, given the equal need for all others to do the same. Because a person's projects and preferences reflect the decisions that the person makes, social cohesion maximizes each person's capacity set (given their innate abilities and resources), subject (again) to the requirement that the person integrate the well-being of others into her choice set in reasonable ways.

In this way, social cohesion is advanced by a respect for human capacity that implicates not only the obligation to leave others alone (in order to protect their autonomy) but also the right to be left alone. We would not expect a person who has chosen to cut herself off from the community to be subject to

---

(1973). It is constrained by the obligations an actor takes on by her choice of activities. The actor is free to avoid activities that require him to take into account the well-being of others, but the actor is not free to get the benefits of activities that implicate the well-being of others without also accepting their burdens. This constraint puts considerable distance between my position and the libertarian position.

[10] The reader understands that I am referring only to the private claims of one person against another. Claims that are made through public law, distributive mechanisms also contribute to social cohesion, but they are not implicated in this discussion.

[11] By contrast, giving another a claim on an actor's resources when the actor has not made a choice that validates that claim might make people less other-regarding.

the interpersonal, private law claim by another, for that would give society a claim on that person's resources and reduce that person's right to choose a life she finds to be fulfilling. We would expect, instead, that the claim that one legitimately makes on the life of another must flow from the other's choice that implicates the well-being of the person making the claim.

This view of a constituent element of social cohesion advances social cohesion in another way: when an actor altruistically comes to another's aid without demand or legal compulsion, looking out for the well-being of others by choice, rather than by legal obligation, the actor both recognizes and supports social cohesion. Such behavior recognizes social cohesion because the choice reflects a bond between donor and recipient that would not be possible in the absence of a sense of community. And it spurs social cohesion because the choice to aid another strengthens the sense of community.[12]

For these reasons, it seems sensible to believe that people setting up a system of interpersonal rights and responsibilities behind the veil of ignorance would choose a view of autonomous choice that would restrict the claims a person could make on the resources of an actor to those claims that could be traced to an actor's choice that makes the actor open to the claim. After all, behind a veil of ignorance each person would not know whether he or she was favored with life's resources. A sensible rule for each person to adopt – and one that would be consistent with minimizing conflicts with others – would be to limit a person's claim against an actor to situations in which the actor had made a choice, expressly or impliedly, to accept responsibility for the well-being of that person. Without such a rule, claims of one person over another would be governed by one person's power over another, and power would be the basis on which resources would be distributed. By choosing a rule that restricts the claims that one person makes on another, each actor is free of the power of another except to the extent that the actor has consented to be subject to that power. Moreover, behind the veil of ignorance, we can conjecture that people would endorse a concept of responsibility that would depend on an actor's choice to get involved in another's life because this concept matches the burdens and benefits of being a member of society. Under this concept, an actor is allowed to decide the benefits the actor receives as a member of society in the context of the burdens that are associated with those benefits.[13]

---

[12] Of course, the law also encourages beneficence by shielding an actor from responsibility when the actor does choose to come to the rescue and acts reasonably under the circumstances.

[13] We must be precise about the question we are asking behind the veil of ignorance. The question is not "Would you pick up the baby from the tracks?" We would expect most people to answer that question in the affirmative once they were assured that rescue was easy. The relevant question behind the veil of ignorance is whether a person would favor a legal system

An actor's general attitude toward the well-being of others is therefore shaped by the actor's freedom to choose her projects and preferences without undue interference from others and by her reciprocal duty to avoid interfering unnecessarily in the projects and preferences of another. An actor must respect another's freedom to be left alone just as the actor expects others to respect her freedom to be left alone. The right to be left alone links an individual with society, for the interest in being left alone – an interest that is shared and reciprocal with every other member of society – marks both an actor's boundary that others should not cross and a respect for the boundaries of others that an actor will not cross. It is both a protection of an actor's interests and a limitation on an actor's interest in the affairs of others.

Moreover, practical reasons explain why actors are hesitant to interfere in the projects and preferences of others and why the law is reluctant to make inaction a source of responsibility. Interestingly, the baby-on-the-tracks hypothetical is just a hypothetical. Perhaps when rescue is easy and important, people generally do the right thing, even when not compelled to do so by law. In real-world cases, the ease and benefit of rescue are ambiguous. When an actor is not associated with the risk in some meaningful way, the risks, to the actor/outsider, are usually ambiguous. When an actor played no role in creating, augmenting, or evaluating the risk another faces, the risk is not the actor's risk, it is another's, and the actor's unfamiliarity with the risk makes it hard for the actor to act in the face of the risk. An actor who sees another struggling in the water might be rightly frozen into inaction by ambiguity about the degree of risk or the ability of the other to cope. Without more knowledge, the actor will have trouble discerning whether or how to act, which means that failure to act may well be reasonable. An actor may also be unsure of the choices that led to the risk and the consequences of intervention. Anyone who has experienced a parent reprimanding a child in a public place understands the ambiguity of intervening (in all but the most clear signs of imminent danger to the child) because one does not know the origins of the parent's anger or the consequences to the child of intervening.

Risk is also ambiguous because of our belief that sometimes risks should be followed by consequences. When we see someone undertaking risky behavior, we understand that suffering the consequences is an important way by which people learn to control or avoid risks. We are reluctant to get involved because getting involved may reduce the incentive of a person who created the risk to be more careful in the future.

The ambiguities of risk are heightened by the ambiguities of rescue. The notion of "easy rescue" is itself an analytical construct, for no rescue is without effort. The actor must divert himself from other tasks in order to undertake the rescue and this diversion is a source of ambiguity; the rescuer may not know how long the rescue will last or what its continuing implications will be. Additional ambiguity of rescue is introduced when more than one person is a potential rescuer. An actor may reasonably assume that another is in a better position to undertake the rescue and may defer to the other to take over. Or the rescuer may fear that his intervention will deter another who is in a better position to effectuate the rescue, and may choose inaction for that reason. The ambiguities of risk and rescue serve as a natural barrier to the intervention of an actor into the lives of others when the actor is not associated with the risk in any way except to perceive it. This explains why the law is wary of giving a victim a general claim to the protection of a stranger.

For the reasons just given, an actor's choice to get involved in an activity that implicates the well-being of others is the moral springboard for legal responsibility. Choice implies that the actor voluntarily put herself in a position that implicates the obligation to think of the well-being of another. Without a choice of that kind, the other has no basis for making a claim on the actor and the actor has no obligation to consider the well-being of the other.

Justice Cardozo explained this in the *Moch* case.[14] The choice that is implicated after duty is established is the choice to reasonably integrate the well-being of another with one's own. "Given a relation involving in its existence a duty of care ... a tort may result as well from acts of omission as of commissions in the fulfillment of the duty thus recognized by law."[15] But the choice to do or refrain from doing something is not even raised until there is a prior choice to take responsibility for the risk that another faces. As Cardozo explained, what we "need to know [to determine duty] is not so much the conduct to be avoided when the relation and its attendant duty are established as existing. What we need to know is the conduct that engenders the relation."[16] We need, in other words, to know the choices that give one person some level of responsibility for the well-being of another person. Cardozo continued: "The query always is whether the putative wrongdoer has advanced to such a point as to have launched a force or instrument of harm, or has stopped where inaction is at most a refusal to become an instrument of good."[17]

---

that imposed an obligation to compensate the baby if the actor did not pick up the baby on the tracks. For the reasons given in the text, an affirmative answer to that question is not assured.

[14] *H.R. Moch Co. v. Rensselaer Water Co.*, 159 N.E. 896 (N.Y. 1928).
[15] *Id* at 898.
[16] *Id*.
[17] *Id*.

In other words, before the actor has any obligation to think of another's well-being, the actor must choose to get involved with the risk another faces. Under this view, an actor is not responsible for the well-being of others unless the actor has chosen an activity that implies that the actor has accepted another's well-being as part of the actor's projects and preferences. If an actor makes no prior choice to get involved in the victim's world, then to force the actor to look out for the well-being of the victim would be to conscript the projects and preferences of the actor and make the actor a means to the victim's ends. It is a choice taken with respect to the risk another faces that signifies an actor's willingness to consider the risk another faces in the context of the actor's projects and preferences.

6.4. CHOICE OF ACTIVITIES AND RISK; TWO KINDS OF NEGLIGENCE CASES

To operationalize this concept of duty, I present an analytical framework for evaluating the relationship between an actor and the risk. It is helpful to distinguish, as the *Restatement Third* does,[18] between an actor's activities that create a risk to others and activities that do not create a risk to others.[19] It is therefore analytically helpful to distinguish two types of negligence cases.

When the defendant engages in an activity that is the source of the risk – that is, where the risk would not exist apart from the choices the defendant has made – the obligation of the defendant to think about the well-being of others arises from the creation of the risk. This is because when the actor has created the risk the actor has altered the state of the world for others and that change requires the actor to think about how that alteration will affect others. An actor who rearranges the world in a way that subjects others to increased risk must accept responsibility for thinking of other's well-being; doing so becomes a part of the actor's projects and preferences. The act of creating a risk signifies

[18] Section 7(a) provides: "An actor ordinarily has a duty to exercise reasonable care when the actor's conduct creates a risk of physical harm." This applies when the actor is the source of the risk. On the other hand, Section 37 provides: "An actor whose conduct has not created a risk of physical harm to another has no duty of care to the other unless a court determines that one of the affirmative duties … is applicable." This approach was further described, although not justified, in Cardi & Green, *Duty Wars* at 676.

[19] The distinction was first recognized by Ernest Weinrib in *The Case for a Duty to Rescue* 90 YALE L.J. 247 (1980). It should replace the unhelpful distinction between acts of nonfeasance and misfeasance. An actor who creates a risk (driving a car) can be negligent by acts of misfeasance (driving too fast) or nonfeasance (failing to put on the brakes). And an actor who has not created the risk can violate a duty by acts of misfeasance (entrusting a car to a known drunk) or nonfeasance (having inadequate lighting in a parking lot that is known to attract muggers).

that the actor has chosen to put herself in a position to accept responsibility for the risk and therefore creates the duty to think reasonably about the well-being of others.

An actor who creates a risk also knows about, and has agency over, that risk. She possesses unique and specific information about the risk that is practicably unavailable to others. The actor knows the ends for which the risk is being taken, the burdens of protecting others against the risk, and the ways that the risk might combine with other circumstances to produce harm. When an actor engages in an activity that creates a risk, the actor faces none of the ambiguity of risk that occurs when another is the source of the risk.[20] In this type of negligence case, duty plays no analytical role because the choice to create a risk also creates responsibility for that risk. The duty to be other-regarding is therefore automatic and can be merged analytically into the issue of the scope of the risk (breach). This is the duty to the world that Andrews wrote about in *Palsgraf*[21] and that is affirmed in many cases.[22]

---

[20] An actor who creates a risk faces no ambiguity about preserving the boundaries of another's autonomy. That actor has already intervened in the world of the potential victims and will not face ambiguity about whether further intervention will be unwelcome. When an actor creates a risk, the potential victims expect the risk to be reasonably addressed (and are entitled to that expectation) and they therefore give the actor implied permission to further intervene in their lives. As we will see later, the situation is different when the defendant is not the source of the risk.

[21] *Palsgraf v. Long Island Ry. Co.*, 162 N.E. 99 (N.Y. 1928) (Andrews, J., dissenting). The duty is only to think about the well-being of those who might be adversely affected by the risk and to act reasonably with respect to that risk. The actor need not take more than reasonable precautions. Nor is the actor responsible if the actor cannot reasonably foresee the circumstances that might link the risk to a victim's harm. And even when the actor acts unreasonably, the actor is not responsible if the circumstances that link the actor's unreasonable act and the victim's harm are ones that a reasonable person would not take into account. This, the proximate cause concept, is explained in Chapter Seven. The duty can be fulfilled by making reasonable choices and when those choices are made, the obligation to think about the well-being of another is fulfilled. The current draft of the restatement confuses matters by stating, in Section 7 that even when the defendant has created the risk a court may make a "no duty" finding "in exceptional cases," on a categorical basis, by articulating a relevant policy or principle. The no-duty exception in this class of cases is sensible, but its rationale has nothing to do with the concept of duty as obligation, and the restatement ought to make this clear. The exception ought to relate to a problem different from the problem of obligation, one illustrated by *Strauss v. Belle Realty Co.*,482 N.E. 2d 34 (N.Y. 1985). Where an actor has an obligation to different classes of plaintiffs, some of whom have an injury that is derived from injury to others, it may make sense to cut off liability to those whose claims are derivative. The best understanding of this kind of case is to admit that the obligation exists but to limit liability in order to ensure that the primary victim can recover. This is not a no-obligation rationale; it is the pragmatic cutting off of liability. Because this limitation on liability does not involve a limitation on an actor's obligations, the fact that the limitation is pragmatic and instrumental does not introduce a nonmoral element into the theory of obligation.

[22] See, e.g., *Heaven v. Pender*, 11 Q.B.D. 503 (1883).

In a second type of negligence case, however, the defendant is not the source of the risk; the risk would exist quite apart from anything the defendant did or did not do. When an actor walks by and sees the baby on the tracks, the actor bears no relationship to the risk or its creation; the risk would exist even if the actor had stayed at home. The risk is created by the person who put the baby on the tracks. The actor has not altered the baby's world by choosing to go for a walk, and the obligation to think of the well-being of the baby, if there is to be one, must come from an obligation that exists quite apart from having created a risk. Similarly, nature creates health risks; doctors are not the source of those risks. Muggers are the source of risks; landlords, universities, and retailers are not the source of the risk, even though their customers might be hurt by the mugger. They are responsible, if at all, only for addressing the risk that others present.

When the actor is not the source of the risk, duty is contingent, not automatic, for an actor's duty to attend to the risk does not attach automatically from the fact that the victim faces a risk. The existence of the risk, and even the actor's knowledge of it, does not, in itself, create a duty to think of the well-being of others, for the actor may have made no choice that implicates the obligation to think about the well-being of the other. As I have said, to find a duty simply from knowledge of the risk would create a duty of beneficence – that is, a duty to others that transcends any individual responsibility for the state of the world the other faces. Creating duty would deny the actor the choice of whether to make the well-being of another a part of the actor's projects and preferences.[23] In these cases, the concept of duty must be given analytical content by determining whether the actor's activity implies that the actor has agreed to take the well-being of the victim into account when undertaking the activity. The duty to think about the well-being of another must be derived from the actor's choice to engage in an activity that implies the defendant's obligation to consider the victim's well-being as a part of the defendant's activities. In other words, in this second kind of negligence case, the law does not impose a duty to think of the well-being of others until the law finds a reason to think, from the nature of the actor's activities, that the actor has chosen to assume that obligation.[24]

---

[23] Moreover, if a duty for the well-being of another existed whenever an actor knew that another faced a risk, an actor might be tempted to intervene in the life of another without the other's authority. It is easy to assume that the baby on the tracks would give implied authority to intervene by rescue, but if knowledge signifies authority in that case, why would duty not imply that a person who knows of the dangers of smoking may (or must) warn others of those dangers?

[24] Informatively, the distinction between the two types of negligence cases is implicit (but not drawn out) in the concept of duty rendered by Goldberg and Zipursky in their primary article

In short, because the duty to think of the well-being of others arises automatically when an actor is the source of the risk, there is no need to analyze duty. The issue of duty as obligation is merged into, and incorporated into, the issue of breach (scope of duty), and has no separate analytical content. The question of duty arises as a separate analytical matter only when the actor is not the source of the risk. It is in this type of negligence case that the relationship between the actor and the risk is not automatic, for the risk is not initially the risk of the actor; it is the risk of the mugger or of nature. It does not become the risk of the actor until the relationship between the actor and the risk provides a sufficient basis for concluding that the actor has taken dominion over the risk in a way that requires the actor to consider the well-being of others. The issue of the existence and scope of the obligation must be addressed analytically.

Although the two types of negligence cases are analytically separate, they are normatively identical. Duty – the obligation to think appropriately of the well-being of others – arises either from the creation of a risk or from choosing to engage in an activity that a reasonable person would understand to necessarily involve thinking about the way risks might ripen into harm for others. The impulse behind this obligation stems from a common normative source – the obligation to think reasonably about the well-being of another – but it manifests itself differently depending on whether the defendant has created the risk or is simply in a position to protect the victim from risks that arise from other sources. Duty is an analytically important concept in the second kind of negligence case, even if it springs from the same normative impulse (the obligation to think of the well-being of others) that governs the obligation of one who has created a risk.[25]

---

on duty, *The Place of Duty*. Each time they want to illustrate the concept of duty they rely on a case where the defendant was not the one who created a risk. They never felt compelled to understand duty in the context of cases where the actor had created the risk (where duty plays no analytical role). Their account is nonjustificational because they explain neither the reason duty is sometimes *not* an issue nor why it sometimes *is* an issue. In addition, they provide no consistent normative ground for linking together these two types of negligence cases.

[25] Courts do not generally recognize explicitly the distinction between defendants who create a risk and defendants who are in a position to protect the victim from risks that flow from another source. Instead, courts generally assume, correctly, that a reasonable landlord should reasonably protect her tenants from muggers, and courts therefore do not separately analyze why the landlord has put herself in a position to accept responsibility for that risk and has control over it. They merge the analysis of duty into the issue of whether the landlord has acted reasonably with respect to the risk of mugging. This tendency reflects the fact that once we find that the defendant is attached to the risk in a meaningful way – that is, once we find a "special relationship" that gives rise to an "affirmative duty" – this second kind of negligence case looks as if the defendant is the source of the risk and we treat it as if the defendant were

In summary, duty is the obligation to take into account the well-being of another, but duty manifests itself differently in the two kinds of negligence cases. The relevant analytical distinction is between cases in which an actor is the source of the risk and cases in which the actor is not the source of the risk but has chosen an activity that implies the obligation to protect the victim from risks that arise from other sources.[26] When an actor creates a risk, for example by driving, digging a hole in the sidewalk, or lifting a stick to separate dogs, the actor has immediate dominion over the risk. We can then understand the relation in Diagram 6.1a.

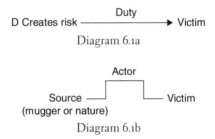

Diagram 6.1a

Diagram 6.1b

Where the source of the risk is independent of the actor, say a mugger or nature, the relationship can be understood in Diagram 6.1b.

The issue is whether and under what circumstance the actor has an obligation to invest in the victim's well-being. Often, duty comes in the relationship between actor and victim. At other times it comes in the relationship between the actor and the source of the risk.[27] In all cases, the actor must have chosen an activity that implies the obligation to think of the well-being of the victim.[28]

the source. Once we determine that the defendant owes the victim a duty, the scope of that duty is to be reasonable in the circumstances and the second type of negligence case merges with the first type of negligence case. A theory of duty, however, must explain, in this second type of negligence case, why there is a special relationship and the scope of the duty implied by the relationship.

[26] Had Esper and Keating understood this, they would have endorsed, rather than criticized, courts that affirm a general duty of railroads to passengers, but no duty to an inebriated passenger (who created the risk of his own harm) and general duties of businesses to customers but no duty to an assailant (who created the risk of harm to the customer). Esper & Keating, *Putting "Duty" in Its Place*, at 1222–7.

[27] It is conventional to believe that duty is about relationships between people. In the approach developed here, the relation between victim and defendant is through the defendant's relationship to the risk the defendant has accepted and must consider. Therefore, we should understand duty not by looking at relationships between people but by looking at relationships between people with respect to risks over which the defendant has taken dominion. As I will argue later, the Long Island Railroad had a duty to Mrs. Palsgraf, but not with respect to the risk of the explosion that occurred.

[28] I have presented the distinction between the two types of negligence case as an analytical way of exploring the concept of duty. The distinction is also relevant, as the subsequent text

6.5. ACTIVITIES THAT IMPLY ACCEPTING RISKS

When an actor has not created the risk another faces, the court must determine both (1) whether the actor's chosen activity implicates the obligation to think of the well-being of the victim and, if so, (2) whether the particular risk the victim faced was one that is within the scope of the risk for which the defendant was responsible. The defendant is in a position to protect the victim from the risk that the other source presents – the landlord might protect the tenant from a mugging, a doctor might protect the victim from the spread of gangrene, or a school might protect its students from harms caused by scoliosis. A court must determine – consistent with the theory of responsibility for other-regarding behavior – whether the defendant, by choosing the activity, has accepted responsibility for the victim's well-being. The court must also determine the scope of those obligations – that is, how intensively the defendant must invest in the well-being of the victim in order to fulfill his duty. This makes the determination of risk in this type of case a three-stage process: the existence of the duty, the scope of the duty, and whether the defendant has breached the duty.

This typology of duty – separately identifying the existence of the duty and its scope – implicates the role of the judge and jury. When the defendant has created the risk, the jury determines the scope of the risk for which the defendant is responsible by deciding whether the defendant has breached the standard of care. In this type of case, the issue of duty as obligation disappears and the issue of the scope of the risk for which the defendant is responsible merges with the question of whether the defendant breached the duty. But when the defendant has not created the risk, defining the scope of the risk for which the defendant is responsible is different from determining whether the defendant has breached the standard of care. Not only do scope of the risk and breach embody different analytical justifications; they are decided in different

indicates, in thinking about cause-in-fact, proximate cause, and comparative fault concepts. If a mugger attacks the victim in an apartment, what does it mean to ask whether the landlord *caused* the harm by failing to have a reasonably adequate lock on the door? If the doctor is presented with a case of gangrene, what does it mean to say that the negligence of the doctor in failing to use the standards of the profession to diagnose the gangrene *caused* the leg to be amputated? Evidently, the concept of "cause" has to be finely tuned when the mugger causes the harm and the landlord simply fails to protect against it. And more than one court has been confused by trying to figure out whether the mugger or the landlord (the gangrene or the doctor) was the proximate cause of the harm. Finally, the distinction between the two types of negligence cases shows that we need to pay more analytical attention to the issue of comparative fault (or comparative causation) if the mugger and the landlord are both defendants.

institutional settings – the first by the judge and the second by the jury. Any theory of duty must adequately address this dichotomy.

In this second kind of negligence case, duty arises when an actor engages in an activity that implies the actor should know that the victim is relying on the actor to address the risk. These cases make up the bulk of the "special relationships" that give rise to "affirmative duties." Suppliers have an obligation to think of the well-being of those who buy their products or services and to those who might be adversely affected by their products or services.[29] One who has promised another to address the risk must reasonably execute that promise. Actors engaged in a co-adventure have implicitly accepted the obligation to think of the other's well-being. In these cases, the duty arises because the relationship between the actor and the victim indicates that the actor has voluntarily assumed dominion over risks the victim faces; the risks that are the subject of the duty arise from the nature of that relationship. The defendant has a relevant relationship to the risk because of an implicit contract between the actor and the victim that the actor, because of the victim's justified reliance, will use his relatively greater knowledge and ability to protect the victim.

But an actor's choice to accept responsibility for the risk does not depend only on the relationship between the actor and the victim. The relevant relationship is between the actor and the risk – not necessarily the actor and the victim – and it can arise whenever the actor has chosen to take dominion over the risk as part of the actor's activity. This concept explains the controversial *Tarasoff* notion that psychiatrists have a duty to warn potential victims of the threats made by their clients.[30] When a psychiatrist accepts a patient, the psychiatrist is taking on the risk that comes with that patient. This is the voluntary acceptance of risk that is clearly a part of the enterprise of the psychiatrist. The California Supreme Court is clear (almost) on this point, for it placed its determination of duty on ground that the "defendant bears some special relationship to the dangerous person…the person whose conduct needs to be controlled." The significant characteristic of the psychiatrist–patient relationship is that the psychiatrist has voluntarily taken on the risk that the patient faces, including the risks that the patient poses to himself and the victim. Because that risk is central to the psychiatrist's enterprise, the psychiatrist's dominion over the risk – which is the very risk the victim faces – gives the psychiatrist an obligation to incorporate the well-being of the victim into the choices the psychiatrist makes.

Similarly, when a school district is writing a recommendation for an employee who has been accused of molesting children, the school district

---

[29]   This duty is explored at greater length in Chapter Ten.
[30]   *Tarasoff v. Regents of University of California*, 17 Cal. 3d 425 (1976).

has a duty to a child at another school district who is later molested by the employee.[31] This duty arises neither from the relationship between the school district and the victim (for there is no relationship) nor from the school district's knowledge that the employee posed a risk to students. Duty arises instead from the relationship between the school district that writes a letter and the school district that receives the letter. The activity of writing a letter of recommendation knowing that the recipient school district will rely on the letter to fulfill its duty to *its* children is a choice to take dominion over the risk that the recipient is trying to address. The school district writing the letter – a voluntary act of choice clearly within the activity of running a school district – therefore knows that it is associated with the risk about which it writes. The school district's relationship to the risk and voluntary acceptance of that relationship in writing the letter gives the school district the responsibility to act reasonably with respect to that risk.[32]

In the enabling torts, an actor accepts responsibility for the risk by supplying resources that knowingly heighten a preexisting risk or make it possible for the risk to continue.[33] An actor who unreasonably entrusts a car to one whom the actor knows to be either intoxicated or unlicensed and incompetent has taken dominion over a risk by making a choice to let another use the car under circumstances where the risk is clear.[34] Similarly, an actor who unreasonably leaves her keys in the car in a neighborhood where she can anticipate a theft has made a choice to embrace the risk that a thief will steal the car and injure another.[35] In cases such as these, courts are determining

---

[31] *Randi W. v. Muroc Joint Unified School District*, 14 Cal. 4th 1066 (1997).

[32] The California Supreme Court knew that school administrators who must deal with an employee charged with sexual misconduct might try to fulfill the duty to *their* students by getting the employee out of the school district, which often means passing the problem on to other school districts (the most likely employer of the man charged with misconduct). The duty the court created recognizes that the relationship between school districts is such that when one school district voluntarily discloses something good about that employee, the recipient is likely to rely on that information to fulfill its duty to *its* students. The school district writing the letter must therefore give the recipient school district fair notice that the employee presents a risk of physical and emotional harm. The defendant school district clearly has dominion over the risk of a dangerous employee, and its activity includes the obligation to respond to letters of inquiry about the employee (because it depends on receiving such letters as a part of its enterprise). Under these circumstances, a duty of honesty in writing the letter is implied by the relationship with other school districts.

[33] Robert L. Rabin, *Enabling Torts*, 49 DePaul L. Rev. 435 (1999).

[34] See, e.g., *Lombardo v. Hoag*, 566 A. 2d 1185 (N.J. Super. Ct, 1989) (entrusting an auto to an intoxicated friend).

[35] See, e.g., *Cruz v. Middlekauf Lincoln-Mercury, Inc.*, 909 P. 2d 1252 (Utah 1996) (defendant car dealer left keys in car on the auto sales lot and an auto thief hit plaintiff while trying to allude the police).

whether an actor has chosen, as part of its activity, to take dominion over a risk that another faces.

When an actor in this type of case has taken dominion over a risk, the actor has a duty to think reasonably about the well-being of others and to act accordingly. Initially, this is not a question of breach. Courts must first determine the scope of the risks for which the actor is responsible. When the actor is not the source of the risk, a judge determines the extent to which the actor's activity implicates the obligation to think of the well-being of another, and also whether in that activity the omitted precaution is one that the jury is allowed to find to be unreasonable. The scope of the risks for which the defendant is responsible is determined first by the judge, as to the activity in general, and then by the jury, as to the conduct of that particular actor in a particular context.

The reason the judge initially determines an actor's scope of responsibility when the actor is not the source of the risk is that the actor has not necessarily accepted dominion, as part of the actor's activities, over every aspect of the other's well-being or every risk that might affect the other. A psychiatrist has not impliedly agreed to take on all the risks that patients bring her, nor to warn potential victims of the client under any and all circumstances. A retail seller has a duty to his customers, but that does not necessarily mean that the actor must consider every aspect of the well-being of its customers. The duty might encompass protecting customers from a mugger in the store, but not in the parking lot, and not a block away. A judge must decide which risks are an inherent part of the actor's activities and which risks lie outside the scope of those activities, and this determination is a prelude to the jury deciding whether the actor has acted unreasonably in a particular context.

For these reasons, when the actor is not the source of the risk, courts necessarily approach the definition of the scope of the risk as a two-stage process – the first (given to the judge) to determine the general scope of risks inherent in the actor's activities, and the second (given to the jury) to determine whether the particular defendant breached that standard. This occurs because courts but not juries understand that if the law puts too many responsibilities on an actor to invest in the well-being of others when the actor is not the source of the risk, the law could detract from the actor's activity. A court may say that a psychiatrist has taken dominion over the patient's risks by virtue of being a psychiatrist, but courts are also conscious that if they impose too much responsibility on the psychiatrist for the well-being of third parties they may well adversely affect the activity – the doctor–patient relationship – that is the source of the duty. And it is easy enough to say that a retailer has a duty to look out for the well-being of its customers, but if the law were to impose too many requirements to protect customers from muggers, the law would be in danger of changing the nature of the activity itself. If a low-price store is required to hire security guards and take other precautions, it may stop being a low-price store.

When an actor is not the source of the risk, the relevant scope-of-the-risk inquiry is whether protecting the victim in the way the victim requests is so likely to detract from the activity as to reduce the value of the activity to society. Because the actor's activity is not creating the risk, the activity serves some other social purpose; adding resource burdens to the activity could detract from that purpose. This requires courts to determine which aspects of risk are a natural part of an actor's activity and which would so divert the resources of the actor that the actor would be unable to pursue her activity effectively. A school district naturally has a duty to its students on educational matters, but it would not naturally be expected to take dominion over the risk of scoliosis.[36] A duty to test for scoliosis would divert the energies of the school district from its educational missions and might imply a duty to protect its students from other health risks. And if a school district's duty to its students extended to protecting them against health risks, should not the school also address other social risks the children face? A Sam's Club store has a duty to its customers, but that duty may not encompass putting a security guard in the parking lot if a court concludes that the benefits of the security guard are not worth the cost of changing the low-cost character of the Sam's Club store.[37]

Courts undertake a kind of Hand formula review to determine whether adding the burden of protecting against particular kinds of risks will be detrimental to the actor's activity. Where the expected benefits of burdening an activity with a particular investment are outweighed by the investment's adverse effects on the activity, a court will not allow juries to determine whether it was unreasonable to omit the investment, for we do not trust juries to understand the balance between burdens and benefits of activities. A determination that a particular precaution is outside the scope of the defendant's duty is a determination that the decision to omit the precaution is reasonable as a matter of law. *Tarasoff* illustrates the trade-off courts make. The court, in determining whether to impose a duty on a psychiatrist to warn a third party of a patient's death threats, carefully considered whether imposing such a duty to warn would have an adverse impact on the doctor–patient relationship. It was only after concluding that the doctor–patient relationship would not be unduly burdened (or that the benefits of the duty to warn in some class

---

[36] *Uhr v. East Greenbush Central School District*, 94 N.Y. 2d 32 (N.Y. Ct. App. 1999).
[37] *Posecai v. Wal-Mart Stores Inc.*, 752 So. 2d 762 (La. 1999).

of cases outweighed the burden on the doctor–patient relationship) that the court allowed the jury to determine whether the doctor in that case had acted unreasonably in light of the duty. By contrast, in determining the responsibility of a Sam's Club store, where the victim's risks of being mugged appeared, from the historical record, to be low, the court felt that the burden on the store (and its other customers) of hiring a security guard for the parking lot outweighed the potential benefit to the customers. It ruled that Sam's Club had, as a matter of law, no duty to hire a security guard.

This judicial constraint on the scope of duty is necessary to ensure that the resources of the activity are not unduly diverted from the activity's central purpose just to address risks that the actor is not responsible for creating. When an actor creates a risk, we expect the actor to have the resources to address the risks, for we do not want actors to engage in an activity that creates risk if they cannot reasonably control the risk. But where the actor has not created a risk, the law does not want the activity in which the resources are invested to be unduly burdened, for to do so would reduce the benefits of the activity.[38]

The resource concern is augmented because an actor who has not created a risk may be unlikely to have information about, and control over, the risk and is therefore more likely to have to invest resources in gathering information and controlling the risk, which drives up the costs of protecting the victim. In this class of cases – where the actor is not the source of the risk – the actor may not naturally have information about the risk and how it might be addressed. As a result, the scope of an actor's duty when the actor has not created the risk is likely to be highly influenced by the relationship between the information needed to protect the victim and the information normally gathered as part of the activity. Educators, for example, are not in the health business and will not naturally acquire information about the health risks of their students. An actor may be uncertain about a particular risk because that risk is not the kind the actor normally considers in her activity, and the actor may have no incentive to get information about a risk because the information is not otherwise relevant to the actor's activity.

On the other hand, where an actor receives information about specific risks as a normal part of its activity, courts are more inclined to find a duty. Manufacturers generally receive information about the safety of their products

---

[38] Consider the close analogy to the inquiry judges make in product liability cases. When courts determine whether the manufacturer had a reasonable alternative design, they focus on the design of products in the same class, for they do not want the burdens of an alternative design to take away the benefits of that class of goods. Not all automobiles are required to have the safety features of the safest car, for that would deprive customers of the benefits of a variety of price ranges from which to choose.

as part of their activity and are able to understand the implications of that information, so it is not particularly burdensome to expect them to use that information to make their products reasonably crashworthy. And a psychiatrist receives, and is able to analyze, specialized information about the risks her patients pose to others in the course of her activity.

Moreover, when an actor has not created the risk, the actor's control over the risk implicates significant resource issues. In this class of cases, the risk is something outside the actor's direct control. Although it is sometimes easy to say that if an actor had invested more resources, the harm would not have occurred, in most cases the issues of causation and prevention are sufficiently ambiguous to make the resource requirements also ambiguous. A landlord has a duty to invest reasonable resources to protect her tenants from a mugger, but what level of protection is likely to be effective? If added protection would not have prevented the harm – if the mugger would have gotten into the apartment building anyway – then the failure to have added protection could not have caused the harm. And this causal question implicates another resource question. The more the actor invests, the greater the chance of protecting the victim but the further that investment takes the actor away from her original activity. In theory, it is possible to make landlords the insurers of the safety of their tenants – perhaps by asking them to form neighborhood watches, or to install electronic surveillance equipment, or to undertake social service projects in their community – but there are limits to which the activity can bear these expenses without losing the activity's central focus. Courts must balance the costs and benefits of investing additional resources, taking into account their likely effectiveness, and their effect on the landlord's central activities.

6.6. CONCLUSION

The concept of duty is poorly understood because theorists have not recognized two categories of negligence cases: the category in which actors have created a risk (and thereby take on the obligation to think appropriately about the well-being of others) and the category of actors who did not create the risk but are in a position to protect the victim from risks that arise from other sources. In the first category, duty as obligation arises from creating the risk and the scope of the duty is determined by asking the finder of fact whether the defendant breached the duty. The second category is the one that is analytically relevant to whether the actor has a primary obligation and to the scope of that obligation. The second category requires judges to determine the scope of an actor's duty before the jury determines whether the duty has been breached, and it requires us to reconceive the concept of causation.

Despite the analytically relevant distinction between actors who create risks and those who do not, a single theory of duty underlies tort law. Tort law draws a distinction between obligations that an actor has chosen because of the actor's activities (either the activity of creating a risk or an activity from which it can fairly be implied that the actor has accepted responsibility for the risk another faces) and obligations that are voluntary and therefore not legally required. This focus on an actor's choice is an important element of social cohesion because choice protects the actor's freedom of action and prevents others from making open-ended claims on the actor's resources. However, the focus on choice also allows the law to impose responsibilities on those who choose activities that put others in a position of relying on the actor, for those activities imply the obligation to be other-regarding that is expected in an interdependent world. In this way, tort law creates an analytically and normatively defensible line between duty and no-duty without petrifying the law as social conditions and values change.

7 Social Cohesion and Moral Agency

The Justification for Proximate Cause

If an actor has dominion over a risk (as understood in the last chapter) and acts unreasonably, why would the actor *not* be responsible for the harm that results? The law's response is that the actor is legally responsible *only* if the actor is the "proximate cause" of the other's harm. But what, exactly, does proximate cause mean and what is the justification for this restricted scope of responsibility?

7.1. NONJUSTIFICATIONAL APPROACHES

Conventional approaches to proximate cause center on rules, principles, or tests. None are sufficiently justificational.

As a rule-based approach, the *Restatement Third* has narrowed the range of rules to eight: a general rule (limiting an actor's liability to "physical harms that result from risks that made the actor's conduct tortious"),[1] and then special rules for the speeding trolley case (no liability),[2] the thin-skull cases (liability),[3] liability to rescuers,[4] intentional and reckless tortfeasors,[5] intervening acts and superseding causes,[6] enhanced harm from medical aid to the victim,[7] and, finally, trivial contributions to multiple sufficient causes.[8] Substantial incoherence remains.

---

[1] Restatement of the Law Torts: Liability for Physical Harm, Proposed Final Draft No. 1, American TAW Institute (April 6, 2005) (*Restatement Third*) § 29, at 575.
[2] *Id.* § 30, at 633.
[3] *Id.* § 31, at 638.
[4] *Id.* § 32, at 648.
[5] *Id.* § 33, at 658.
[6] *Id.* § 34, at 667.
[7] *Id.* § 35, at 693.
[8] *Id.* § 36, at 700.

What, for example, is the relationship between the general rule and the thin-skull rule? If the thin-skull rule is only an application of the general rule, what theory explains why a preexisting condition is the kind of harm that makes the actor's conduct tortious, and why do we need a special rule if we understand that explanatory theory? On the other hand, if the thin-skull rule is an exception to the general rule, then the general rule really reads as follows: "an actor is not liable for harm different from the harms whose risks made the actor's conduct tortious, unless the victim's harm was from a preexisting condition, in which case the actor is responsible for the harm." But that robs the general rule of its generality; it is simply a rule to be applied unless it is not to be.

Moreover, even if the application of the thin-skull rule is clear – as it is in many instances – the outer edges of the "rule" still need to be defined. Are we sure that we know which characteristics of a person qualify for the rule? If the victim knows of her preexisting condition, knows that it can be addressed with medication, and yet fails to take the medication, we would not want the defendant to be responsible for the harm that the victim could have reasonably prevented. Yet is that instance within the rule because the harm results from a preexisting condition or is it outside the rule because the condition could not "reasonably be expected" (it being reasonable to expect the victim to self-protect)? In a case like that, a court is likely to ignore the thin-skull rule altogether, deciding the case instead under the related doctrines of avoidable consequences or contributory negligence. But that simply means that we apply the rule in cases where it applies and not in cases where it does not apply, which keeps the rule from being determinate.[9] Viewing law in terms of *what* the law does, does not explain *why* it does what it does.

Approaches to proximate cause that rely on principles can be workable with the appropriate analytical justification, but their mere statement lacks justificational content. We understand, with Warren Seavey, that "[p]rima facie, at least, the reasons for creating liability should limit it."[10] But this principle,

---

[9] The *Restatement Third* applies only to preexisting physical or mental conditions, but a similar issue arises with respect to property damage. Say a victim leaves her Ming vase in the backseat of her car without reasonably protecting it, and the defendant negligently runs into the car, ruining the vase. Here we have a preexisting condition (the vase in the back seat) and the question is whether the defendant should be responsible for that damage. I assume that all would agree that defendant should not be responsible (notwithstanding the literal preexisting condition) because the victim could have so easily self-protected. But this outcome cannot be found in the logic of preexisting conditions as it is presently articulated.

[10] Warren Seavey, *Mr. Justice Cardozo and the Law of Torts*, 34 COLUM. L. R. 20, 34 (1939). See e.g., Dan B. Dobbs, TORT LAW 446, West Publishing Co. (2000) ("proximate cause cases seek to limit liability to the reasons for imposing liability in the first place").

like the *Restatement Third's* "harm within the risk rule," requires a theory of responsibility that imposes liability for some unreasonable conduct but withholds liability for other unreasonable conduct. What is the justification for these outcomes that responds to the theory or function of negligence? We can agree with Jules Coleman that the "harm must be connected in an appropriate way with respect to that aspect of the actor's conduct that is at fault," but that requires us to determine which aspect of the conduct is at fault.[11] Before we can apply a legal conception, we must understand the wisdom that is shaping it. It is easy enough to say that the risk of a negligently made vacuum cleaner does not include the risk that the owner will be hurt in an auto accident when he takes the vacuum cleaner to be repaired. But why, exactly, is that so? What is it that takes that harm out of the risks that makes the defendant's conduct tortious? Why do we not say the opposite? And what do we do in a closer case?

In this connection, consider the *Restatement Third's* illustration 6.[12] The defendant negligently ran Parker's car off the road, and Deborah, the victim, stops her car to observe the accident. While she is stopped, another driver negligently hits Deborah, and the law must decide whether the defendant is responsible for this harm (perhaps in conjunction with the other negligent driver). Under the *Restatement Third* approach, we need to determine whether the risks of injury to a bystander like Deborah are among the risks that made the act of running a car off the road tortious. Under Coleman's approach, how are we to determine whether the harm is "appropriately connected to the conduct that is at fault?"

We can see the difficulties with the *Restatement* test if we consider how juries would decide cases under the rule. The *Restatement Third* sees the difficulties,[13] but its approach does not solve them. Under the *Restatement Third*, the jury would be told

> that in deciding whether plaintiff's harm is within the scope of liability, it should go back to the reasons for finding the defendant engaged in negligence or other tortious conduct. If the harms risked by that tortious conduct include the general sort of harm suffered by the plaintiff, the defendant is subject to liability for the plaintiff's harm.[14]

It is not clear what the jury will understand from this instruction. How does the jury decide what "general sort of harm" it had in mind when it found the

---

[11] Jules L. Coleman, Risk and Wrongs 346, Cambridge University Press (1992).
[12] *Restatement Third* at 582–3.
[13] See Reporter's notes to § 29, at 609.
[14] *Id.*, cmt d, at 6.

defendant to be negligent, or whether that "general sort of harm" was properly considered in the "negligence" phase of the case because it was one of the harms risked? Not only are those concepts not defined, but whether the defendant *should* be responsible for this harm must surely depend on a host of factors that are not even alluded to in the test. The jury, it seems to me, would want to consider factors like the following:

- Whether the road was lightly or heavily traveled (in order to think about the likelihood that bystanders would appear).
- The kinds of risks that bystanders would expose themselves to if they did stop (given, for example, the width of the highway's shoulder), and whether the bystanders could take steps to minimize those risks.
- The general hazards to bystanders that are generated by the nature of the traffic on the highway.

One can well imagine that a jury might find the defendant not responsible for this harm if the highway were not congested, if bystanders could safely pull off the highway, or if the traffic was slow. The jury might come to the opposite conclusion if traffic were congested, the highway's shoulder were narrow, or the drivers erratic – all of which make the risk to bystanders greater and therefore require the actor to think about how his behavior might affect the bystanders' well-being. Yet none of this is hinted at in the test of the *Restatement Third* and, without more, the jury would be left to guess as to what the test meant in practice.

Aside from rules and principles, other commentators take refuge in tests based on "foreseeability" or "directness," the two standard doctrines that are used to understand proximate cause.[15] These approaches, however, are not justificational. For one thing, the tests themselves require so many qualifications and elaborations that they offer little guidance in deciding cases and no hope for finding unity in the proximate cause concept. The problems are well known. How do we know whether to use a foreseeability approach or a directness approach? If one "works" when the other does not, how are we to know which one to use? And what does it mean to say that a test "works"?

---

[15] See, e.g., Jane Stapleton, *Legal Cause: Cause in Fact and the Scope of Liability for Consequences*, 54 VAND. L. REV. 941 (2001). (commenting on the difference between the direct test and the foreseeable test); Mark F. Grady, *Proximate Cause and the Law of Negligence*, 69 IOWA L. REV. 363 (1984) (dividing proximate cause into two situations – multiple-risk situations and concurrent efficient cause situations – to be governed by two tests – the reasonable foresight doctrine and the direct consequences doctrine); and Mark F. Grady, *Proximate Cause Decoded*, 50 U.C.L.A. L. REV. 293 (2002) (identifying five direct consequences paradigms and five reasonable foresight paradigms).

The concept of *directness* has no known content and the term *foreseeabil-ity* is ambiguous. As Arthur Ripstein has shown, foreseeability could be an epistemic concept, an ideal concept, or a description of how the reasonable person ought to think about the world.[16] The term *foreseeability* is too mallea-ble to be justificatory.[17] After all, in the famous *Wagon Mound* pair of cases,[18] a defendant spilled bunkering oil that later caught fire and burned a dry dock. Yet for this single act, the defendant was held liable as to one plaintiff (the owner of the ship in the dry dock) on the ground that the fire was foreseeable and was held not liable to another plaintiff (the owner of the dry dock) on the ground that the fire was not foreseeable. One fire was said to be both foresee-able and unforeseeable.

We should not confuse a "test" that describes the outcome of a case with a justification that explains why the case was decided one way rather than another. As a statement of what a court concluded in a particular case (an output), a statement about foreseeability is serviceable, but as a statement of the basis on which the court made its decision (an input), the statement is vacuous.

Justifications for proximate cause have, of course, been advanced. The *Restatement Third* offers two: crushing liability[19] and the fairness rationale.[20] The first, crushing liability rationale, provides a partial rationale for those few cases in which liability is found as to some victims but is cut off for victims that are further removed from the conduct in question.[21] However, that rationale does not explain most proximate cause cases.

[16] Arthur Ripstein, Equality, Responsibility and the Law 105, Cambridge University Press (1999).
[17] Consider also the familiar problem of dealing with thin-skull cases in terms of foreseeability. An actor cannot know whether potential victims have a preexisting thin-skull condition; in that sense, a preexisting condition is not foreseeable. If that kind of foreseeability is what matters, then an actor should not be responsible for harm from preexisting conditions. Yet it *is* foreseeable that some percentage of the population will be particularly susceptible to physi-cal harm, and if that kind of foreseeability is what matters, then the actor would be liable under a foreseeability test. Because of this ambiguity, a foreseeability test does not work until we know what kind of foreseeability matters and why it matters.
[18] *Overseas Tankship (U.K.) Ltd. v. Mort's Dock & Engineering Co. (Wagon Mound I)*, [1961] A.C. 388 (P.C.) (appeal taken from Austl.) (owner of dry dock may not recover) and *Overseas Tankship (U.K.) Ltd. v. The Miller Steamship Co. (Wagon Mound II)*, [1967] 1 A.C. 617 (P.C.) (appeal taken from Austl.) (damage to the ship being repaired in the dry dock was the defen-dant's responsibility).
[19] See e.g., *Restatement Third*, at 579.
[20] *Id.* at 585. See also, Grady, *Proximate Cause Decoded*, at 294 (2002) (suggesting that because some negligence is inadvertent, limiting liability is necessary to avoid making people overly cautious and to put pressure on others to intervene to protect risk from becoming harm).
[21] See e.g., *Strauss v. Belle Realty Co.*, 482 N.E. 2d 34 (N.Y. 1985) (applying duty to deny recov-ery to a victim who was injured in a blackout caused by defendant's unreasonable conduct,

The fairness rationale, of course, has no normative appeal unless the justificatory basis of the unfairness label is revealed, and the *Restatement Third* makes no attempt to do that. The *Restatement Third* says that "[t]he risk standard appeals to intuitive notions of fairness and proportionality by limiting liability to harms that result from the risks created by the actor's wrongful conduct, but for no others." But this "rationale" simply repeats the conclusion that harms must be related to the actor's wrongs. Its appeal to "intuitive notions of fairness and proportionality" supplies neither justification nor content for the conclusion, except to say that it feels right.

Proximate cause cases are so difficult to justify that some have abandoned the search for a justification. Law professors love proximate cause cases because the cases lead to endless mind games. Agnostics believe that we cannot know the mysteries of proximate cause. Under this view, proximate cause is a residual category of cases that bear the inscrutable content of justice, a kind of justice-cocktail.[22] And those who believe that law is politics fear that proximate cause has been used to limit liability for political purposes.[23]

Other justificatory analysis is evocative but, in my view, incomplete. Some analysts have emphasized the fortuity or luck that comes into play when unreasonable conduct ripens into harm.[24] Sometimes a specific act causes a great

recognizing that those who purchased electricity directly from the defendant could sue for their injuries); *Homac Corp. v. Sun Oil Co.*, 258 N.Y. 462, 180 N.E. 172 (1932) (limiting responsibility for negligently started fire to first person and cutting off responsibility to others injured by the fire); *Petition of Kinsman Transit Co.*, 338 f.20 708 (2D Cir. 1964) (*Kinsman II*) (although property owners could recover for negligent collisions on the Buffalo River, plaintiffs suffering economic harm could not). The justification is only "partial" because the real concern in these cases is not the amount of damages the defendant must pay, but the possibility that liability to victims whose harm was derivative or represented a less important interest would impair the ability of other, more deserving plaintiffs to recover. The class of cases is what Justice Andrews must have had in mind in his dissent in *Palsgraf.* This class of cases is not addressed in the theory presented in this book.

[22] See, e.g., William L. Prosser, HANDBOOK OF THE LAW OF TORTS, 158 West Publishing Co. (4th ed. 1971). ("The term 'proximate cause' is applied by the courts to those more or less undefined considerations which limit liability even where the fact of causation is clearly established.") *Zaza v. Marquess & Nell, Inc.*, 144 N.J. 34 675 A.2d 620 (1996) (proximate cause doctrine "is an instrument of fairness and policy…. The determination of proximate cause by a court is to be based upon mixed considerations of logic, common sense, justice, policy, and precedent.")

[23] See Morton Horwitz, THE TRANSFORMATION OF AMERICAN LAW, Harvard University Press (1977).

[24] The *Restatement Third*, at 633 refers to harm that is "merely serendipitous or coincidental." See also, Grady, *Proximate Cause Decoded* (because negligence standard is relatively harsh, many people cannot meet it, despite best efforts; proximate cause relieves of liability when the "only connection between [defendant's] lapse and the plaintiff's injury was the purest chance, a total coincidence."), Michael L. Wells, *Proximate Cause and the American Law Institute: The False Dichotomy Between the "Direct-Consequences" Test and the "Risk*

deal of harm; at other times little harm. Proximate cause cases seem to relieve the defendant of liability when harm is merely a fortuitous outcome of conduct. These luck-based theories, however, fail to tell us why luck matters, or what luck has to do with responsibility. And they do not explain why a defendant is sometimes responsible for his bad luck (hitting a plaintiff who has a preexisting heart condition) and sometimes not (driving the trolley so fast that it arrives at a point in the tracks where a tree is falling). At bottom, the luck-based theories still lack a convincing account of the normative basis for proximate cause.

Law and economics scholars face a unique justificatory challenge. If the goal of negligence law is to deter unreasonable conduct, why not hold the defendant responsible for all harm the defendant negligently causes? The responses that have been supplied by law and economics scholars also seem to be incomplete. Of course, we do not want to overdeter risky activity that prom-ises benefits for society,[25] but why is the connection between the risks and harm that the proximate cause doctrine explores relevant for that purpose? And, of course, we want to induce those who, by intervening, can prevent harm to do so,[26] but why is relieving the defendant who created the risk from responsibility necessary to that end? Would not an apportionment of damages between two wrongdoers induce both wrongdoers to do better? And, while some proximate cause outcomes may simply reflect a desire to conserve the administrative costs of a detailed inquiry,[27] does that provide a general theory, and if it does, how do we know when and why to apply it?

Our search for a normative justification for these proximate cause cases is still in its infancy.

7.2. A FAULT-BASED THEORY

The foundation for the theory developed here was laid by Arthur Ripstein. For him, the foreseeability of harm (and therefore the scope of responsibility) is definable only as a constituent part of defining the fair terms of interac-tion between persons.[28] Under this reading, determining what an actor should

---

Standard," 37 U. Rich. L. Rev. 389, 391 (2002) (advocating a "magnitude of the harm approach" in order to "save the defendant from the unfairness of paying huge damages for small departures from due care.").

[25] See, e.g., Grady, *Proximate Cause Decoded*, at 294.

[26] See, e.g., Grady, *Proximate Cause and Negligence*, at 416.

[27] See e.g., William Landes & Richard Posner, The Economic Structure of Tort Law 245, Harvard University Press (1987) (arguing that where the administrative cost of identifying a risky situation is high and is not likely to influence the defendant's behavior, the benefit of imposing liability to deter bad conduct may be outweighed by the high administrative cost).

[28] Ripstein, *Equality and Responsibility* 94–5.

have foreseen (and therefore what an actor should have reasonably done) is an integral part of determining how a reasonable actor should act in those circumstances. He (and I) would therefore situate the concept of proximate cause not as a limitation on liability otherwise established but as an integral part of determining whether the actor is responsible for addressing the risk of harm that occurred in the first place.[29] This is an important analytical and conceptual insight, for it means that the proximate cause concept is not at war with the reasonable person concept, but is united with it. It means that in any restatement of tort doctrine, proximate cause ought *not* to be placed after duty, breach, and cause in fact. It ought to be integrated with duty, breach, and cause in fact.[30]

I take this central insight and develop it analytically, normatively, and conceptually. Ripstein understood that proximate cause is an important normative limit on an actor's responsibility for the well-being of another. My account more fully integrates a theory of the limits of human cognition into the notion of the fair terms of interaction between people. I take Ripstein's central insight and specify precisely the kind of questions that allow us to analyze whether the connection between the actor's conduct and the victim's harm is enough to establish the actor's responsibility for the harm. I deliberately avoid the traditional language of proximate cause (although Ripstein's foreseeability concept is never far from the surface). Strategically, I hope this allows us to reconceptualize the analysis of proximate cause cases. Methodologically, I shift away from terms such as foreseeability in the belief that such terms have been used to describe the output of particular cases, but do not specify the

---

[29] There is an important distinction between limiting responsibility and limiting liability. *Limiting responsibility* means that an actor has no responsibility for the well-being of another (because of some factor that breaks the connection between the actor and the victim). When we *limit liability*, we assume that an actor is responsible for the well-being of another and has breached that responsibility, but we have chosen to cut off the obligation to correct the wrong for some reason. Cases like those in footnote 21 limit liability. The cases discussed in this chapter limit responsibility.

[30] Arthur Ripstein is not alone in considering proximate cause to be a constituent part of a theory of responsibility. Other scholars have suggested, without explanation, that we should understand proximate cause in terms of a theory of responsibility. Jules L. Coleman, RISKS AND WRONGS 346, Oxford University Press (1992). See also, John C.P. Goldberg, *Rethinking Injury and Proximate Cause*, 40 SAN. L. REV. 1315, 1332–39 (2003) (positing that an actor who commits a wrong [in the sense of unreasonable behavior] is responsible for resulting harm only if the behavior is also wrongdoing, and positing that proximate cause plays the role of determining when unreasonable conduct is not wrongdoing toward the plaintiff); and Richard W. Wright, *The Efficiency Theory of Causation and Responsibility: Unscientific Formalism and False Semantics*, 63 CHI. KENT L. REV. 553, 555 (1987) (responsibility, not causation, changes as the causal chain lengthens).

analytical inputs relevant to determining whether an actor is responsible for the connection between her acts and the victim's harm.

Here again, the focus on unreasonable conduct seems to have led us astray. Coleman and the *Restatement Third* both emphasize the relationship between the injurer's conduct and the victim's harm, but that begs the issue of how we know what relationship is normatively required as a basis for responsibility. If a trolley driver is speeding, and a tree falls on the trolley, how are we to know whether the falling tree is connected in an appropriate way with the speeding or whether the risk of the falling tree is a risk that made the speeding tortious? We can only address these questions if we seek to understand the relationship between the actor's conduct and the decision making that a reasonable actor would have undertaken in those circumstances. A reasonable actor would not have been speeding, but as long as we believe that a reasonable actor would not have thought about a tree falling when deciding how fast to go, the actor is not responsible for the consequences of his decision. We can assess the relationship between the conduct and the harm only by assessing the range of considerations that a reasonable person would have had in mind when deciding how to act, and determining whether an actor who accounted for a relevant consideration would have avoided the harm.

For these reasons, the crucial issue in determining proximate cause is whether the circumstances that link the conduct to the harm are ones that a reasonable person would take into account in a particular context. As this chapter shows, the ideal of social cohesion suggests that an actor should *not* be responsible for another's well-being when the circumstances that connect the actor's decision to the victim's harm are circumstances that an actor – even one who is appropriately other-regarding – would not be expected to take into account in the accident's setting. This occurs when the circumstances that link the defendant's decisions to the victim's harm are either irrelevant to the actor's decisions or are beyond the ability of the actor to understand and evaluate. Thus, an actor who is deciding how fast to drive a trolley need not consider the possibility that the trolley will, by virtue of the chosen speed, come to a spot on the tracks where a tree is falling[31]; that consideration is beyond the range of circumstances that a reasonable trolley driver would consider when deciding how fast to go. And a tugboat captain, when deciding how careful to be, need not consider the possibility that employees of a barge the tugboat hits would fail to reasonably protect the barge against further damage[32]; the captain is permitted to believe, in those circumstances, that the barge employees

---

[31] *Berry v. Sugar Notch Borough*, 191 Pa. 345 (1989).
[32] *Sinram. v. Pennsylvania Ry. Co.*, 61 F. 2d 767 (2d Cir. 1932).

would mitigate the damage. Even an other-regarding actor would not take the circumstance of a falling tree or a negligent bargeman into account in those settings and an actor is therefore not responsible for the resulting harm. The circumstances that a reasonable person would ignore remove the obligation to be other-regarding with respect to those circumstances, even if the actor fails to be other-regarding with respect to other circumstances that connect the actor's conduct to *other* potential victims.

The justification for this restricted scope of responsibility is related to the concept of duty discussed in the last chapter. There, the theory of other-regarding behavior emphasized the importance to social cohesion of preserving an actor's autonomy by making sure that the well-being of another was appropriately within the actor's chosen activity. Another limitation on the responsibility of one person for the well-being of another reflects the importance of human moral agency – the ability of actors to effectuate a different result in another's well-being. As developed in the next section, the law does not expect people to make decisions that are beyond the mental capacity of a reasonable person, for social cohesion would not be advanced by expecting more of humans than they are capable of delivering.

7.3. MORAL AGENCY AND THE REASONABLENESS CONCEPT

The negligence standard attends to circumstances that limit an actor's responsibility for the consequences of her conduct. In order to be reasonable, the defendant must take into account most circumstances that link her decisions to the plaintiff's harm, but the actor is entitled to ignore circumstances that a reasonable person would ignore. This is the responsibility of moral agency. Agency is the ability to make a difference in another's life by making a different decision. An actor's moral agency is an important determinant of an actor's responsibility for the well-being of another because it implies that the actor could have brought about a different outcome by making a different decision. The actor is not responsible if the actor injures the victim but the harm was not, for one reason or another, traceable to the actor's agency.

The concept of moral agency is inherent in the but-for test for determining cause in fact. Under the but-for test, an actor is not responsible unless the actor's decision was necessary for the harm; the actor is therefore not responsible if the harm would have occurred even had the actor been reasonable. This is a matter of moral agency. A minimum requirement for legal responsibility is that the actor could have effectuated a different outcome by making a different decision. The harm must have been within the actor's effective control. If the defendant's unreasonable choice was not necessary to the result, the actor is not responsible for the result. Consider the hypothetical in which an actor unreasonably fails to sound his horn when going around a danger-ous bend on a one-lane road. If the driver of the oncoming car is deaf, the actor's failure to sound his horn is not the but-for (necessary) cause of the actor hitting the oncoming car. The harm would have happened anyway. In this event, the actor is not the moral agent of the harm (even though the actor acted unreasonably and "caused" the harm) because the actor was powerless to do anything about the harm. The actor is not responsible that the other driver was deaf and could not control the risk by making a more reasonable decision. The responsibility of an actor is limited to circumstances that reflect the actor's moral agency.

Moral agency is also an important foundation of the reasonable person standard. An actor deciding how deeply to bury a pipe must consider circum-stances that determine whether the pipe will freeze, but the actor is entitled to ignore circumstances that a reasonable person would ignore – such as the circumstance of an unpredictably severe frost.[33] Reasonable decisions address normal frosts but an actor is not responsible if the frost is one that a reason-able person would not contemplate; such a frost is *not* one of the circum-stances a reasonable person must consider and is therefore beyond the actor's moral agency. Similarly, because a reasonable person is not expected to have prevision,[34] a reasonable person may be unable to imagine circumstances that will link the actor's decisions with the victim's harm. An actor may assume, for example, that an ordinary package can safely be opened with a chisel; if it turns out that the package contains nitroglycerine, the actor is not responsible for the resulting harm because the content of the package is not a circum-stance the actor had to consider when deciding how to open the package.[35] And a trolley company that maintains exposed wires above its tracks is not responsible if a twelve-year-old boy walks over a bridge twirling an eight-foot wire and is electrocuted when *his* wire comes in contact with the trolley wire.[36]

---

[33] *Blyth v. Birmingham Waterworks Co.*, 11 Exch. 781 (1856).
[34] Judge Cardozo reminded us in *Palsgraf*: "Life would have to be made over, and human nature transformed, before prevision so extravagant can be accepted as the norm of conduct, the customary standard to which behavior must conform." 248 N.Y. 2d at 341.
[35] *Parrott v. Wells-Fargo*, 15 Wall [U.S.] 524 (1872). See also *Van Skike v. Zussman*, 318 N.E. 2d 244, 247 (Ill. App. Ct. 1974) (defendant placed a gumball machine that dispensed toy lighters in a store that also sold lighter fluid, but was not responsible when a boy filled the toy with lighter fluid and was burned); and *Cunis v. Brennan*, 308 N.E. 2d 617, 619 (Ill. 1974) (defendant left a drain pipe protruding from a parkway and a victim who was thrown from the car had his leg impaled on it; "the risk, although recognizable, would commonly be disregarded.").
[36] *Adams v. Bullock*, 227 N.Y. 208 (1919).

That occurrence was so beyond what could be predicted reasonably that it fails to provide a source of responsibility for the trolley company.

These cases recognize that when the circumstances that connect an actor's decision to a victim's harm are ones the actor need not consider, the harm is outside the actor's moral agency and therefore outside of the actor's responsibility. The actor has not acted negligently with respect to that harm.

7.4. THE JUSTIFICATION FOR MORAL AGENCY LIMITATIONS ON RESPONSIBILITY

The requirement that the victim's harm be within the actor's moral agency represents a limitation on individual responsibility that is important to social cohesion. Even when an actor takes seriously the obligation to be other-regarding, the actor may not be able to see how a decision might adversely affect the other's well-being. Because it is a fact of life, the law understands that people make decisions facing uncertainty and bounded rationality,[37] with limited abilities to acquire, assimilate, and evaluate information. The law therefore understands that even mistaken choices can be reasonable. The concept of moral agency does not require that humans be superhuman, and it would be a disservice to human agency to require more of humans than they are capable of doing. Just as the theory of other-regarding behavior recognizes the normative necessity of taking into account the well-being of others, it also recognizes the normative necessity of not imposing more expectations on human cognitive processes than humans can be expected to fulfill. The law cannot command what humans find impossible to accomplish. If people cannot reasonably get the information they need to understand the circumstances that will connect their acts to harm, it would be wrong for the law to punish them for their failure.

Accordingly, if an actor cannot know, even with the exercise of reasonable cognitive capacities, how her decisions (even unreasonable ones), in combination with other circumstances, will result in harm, the actor should not be responsible for the resulting harm because the well-being of others is effectively out of the reasonable person's control. An actor should not be responsible for another's misfortune unless the actor had a fair chance at ameliorating or addressing the misfortune without unduly limiting the actor's own freedom of

---

[37] Herbert A. Simon, *A Behavioral Model of Rational Choice*, 69 Q. J. Econ. 99 (1955), Herbert H. Simon, Models of Man, John Wiley (1957). The subsequent literature is large, having unified fields such as behavioral studies, sociology, and anthropology.

action. The theory of responsibility inherent in the reasonable person concept is justified by the belief that human responsibility should end when reasonable human control ends.[38]

This justificatory foundation for limitations on an actor's responsibility for the well-being of another reflects corrective justice's insistence that the wrong to which negligence law is aimed is always a wrong between the defendant and a victim, not just a general wrong to society. The essential connection between actor and victim is the actor's reasonable ability to comprehend the circumstances that connect the injurer and victim. Where an actor of reasonable cognitive capabilities should have thought about the circumstances more reasonably, justice commands that that lapse be corrected when harm occurs. On the other hand, when an actor could not, with reasonable cognitive abilities, have anticipated how her actions would ripen into harm (i.e., what other circumstances would contribute to the harm), the actor has not failed to think of the well-being of another in a way that needs to be corrected, and corrective justice does not require that responsibility be assigned to the actor.

Any broader concept of responsibility would also do violence to moral agency in consequential terms. If the social contract were to hold people responsible for effects that are beyond their cognitive capabilities, people would become unduly cautious in the decisions they make. They would systematically overestimate the possibility that unimaginable external circumstances would combine with their own decisions to render them liable for acting, even when they had done the best they could to make sure that their decisions took into account the effect of their behavior on others. Trolleys would run more slowly and tugboats would be unduly cautious. Holding people to a higher standard of cognitive ability than people can possibly meet would overdeter socially beneficial conduct and society would be the loser.

In short, if the circumstances connecting an actor's decisions to another's harm are beyond the capacity of the defendant to address, the defendant does not bear responsibility for that harm in a suit by the victim, for imposing responsibility for matters beyond human capacity would detract from our sense of human potential. By properly analyzing the circumstances that connect the injurer's conduct to the victim's harm, we can understand the justificational basis for proximate cause.

---

[38] As Arthur Ripstein says, an account of why one person must correct the harm to another "can only apply to agents who are capable of moderating their activities in light of the interests of others." Ripstein, EQUALITY, RESPONSIBILITY AND LAW at 94.

7.5. THE ANALYTICS OF CIRCUMSTANCES

In each of the proximate cause cases, there is a reason to say that the defendant should have acted differently, but it is not clear whether the defendant is responsible for circumstances that connected the defendant's act to the victim's harm. A court must determine whether the actor is responsible for factoring the circumstances into the actor's decisions or whether the actor's failure to consider the circumstances is justifiable. The actor's consideration of the circumstances is what determines whether a victim's loss "is connected in an appropriate way with respect to that aspect of [the actor's] conduct that is at fault."[39] When the defendant's decisions are connected to the victim's harm only by circumstances for which the actor is not responsible, the actor has not been inappropriately other-regarding. In the words of the *Restatement Third*, the actor is responsible for "risks [circumstances] that made the actor's conduct tortious," but not for risks [circumstances] that the defendant is justified in ignoring.[40]

When we focus on the defendant's responsibility for the circumstances that connect the defendant's decision to the victim's harm, we have a straightforward way of assessing whether the defendant was thinking appropriately about the victim's well-being. With this analytical focus, the proximate cause cases merge into a consistent pattern of normative responses to the question of whether it was reasonable to ignore the circumstances that led to the harm.

7.5.1. *The* Palsgraf *Example*

Cardozo's brilliance was to recognize that an actor's responsibility for the well-being of others responds to a view of moral agency that appreciates which circumstances an actor must take into account and which the actor may ignore.

In *Palsgraf*,[41] the Long Island Railroad took an unreasonable risk when it tried to help two passengers onto the train. Accordingly, it was responsible for the harms associated with that risk. Moreover, the railroad had a duty to Helen Palsgraf, its passenger, perhaps even a duty of utmost care. But what risk did the railroad take when it helped the passengers, and when the risk resulted in an explosion, what does that tell us about whether the railroad breached its duty to Mrs. Palsgraf (by thinking inappropriately about her well-being)? Two factors stand out. First, the railroad did not create the risk of explosion; had the passenger's package contained bagels there would have been risk of neither an

---

[39] Coleman, RISKS AND WRONGS at 346.
[40] *Restatement Third*, §30.
[41] *Palsgraf v. Long Island Ry. Co.*, 162 N.E. 99 (N.Y. 1928).

explosion nor of harm to Mrs. Palsgraf. The railroad took the risk of an explosion only if it should have known about the possibility of the explosion – that is, only if it was chargeable with recognizing that the package contained an explosive (e.g., had the package been so marked). Second, the decision they made – their project – was to assist the two passengers getting on the train – to keep them from suffering greater harm from possibly falling.[42]

Under these circumstances, Cardozo saw that to impose responsibility on the railroad for the harm to Mrs. Palsgraf would be inconsistent with the theory of responsibility that underlies the negligence concept. When deciding what level of care to exert on behalf of the passengers, the railroad was not required to consider the circumstance that the package might contain fireworks. When making a quick decision that seemingly implicated only the well-being of the two passengers, where the only risk that was apparently at stake was risk to the package or to the passengers, it was not unreasonable for the railroad to fail to consider the fact that the package might be more dangerous than it appeared. Thinking about the well-being of Mrs. Palsgraf when making that decision was not within the scope of considerations that the railroad had to consider and the explosion was therefore not a source of responsibility toward Mrs. Palsgraf.

In terms of moral agency, when making the decision about what level of care to use as they helped the passengers, the railroad could permissibly ignore the possibility that the package might contain fireworks. That was a circumstance that a reasonable person, in the context of that case, need not consider, making the explosion outside the effective moral agency of the railroad.

7.5.2. *Relevance and Reasonable Assumptions*

An actor's decisions rest on information about circumstances and potential consequences. The question is what information an appropriately other-regarding actor ought to gather before making a decision. Sometimes information about the circumstances that connect the defendant's decision to the plaintiff's harm is so outside the scope of the actor's decision that an actor is excused from considering that information. When a trolley driver is deciding how fast to go, the trolley driver can foresee that a tree might fall on the track. But the driver cannot know (without more) which tree might fall or what

---

[42] Under this reading of the case, the scale that supposedly fell on Mrs. Palsgraf plays no role in the analysis, it being assumed that even a reasonably maintained scale would have fallen in the concussion that actually occurred. If, on the other hand, the scale was negligently maintained, the case was wrongly decided, for the railroad clearly had an obligation to reasonably secure the scale from reasonably anticipated explosions.

circumstances might cause the tree to fall, and finding out would be unduly expensive (given the low probability of the occurrence).[43] Without knowledge of a particularized sort (e.g., knowledge about which tree will fall), the driver need not think about whether a tree might fall when deciding how fast to go; that circumstance is irrelevant to the decision the driver is making. The knowledge that a tree *might* fall does not increase the risks that are associated with driving a trolley at an unreasonable speed[44] and is not the kind of circumstance that a reasonable person would take into account when deciding how fast to go.

Under other circumstances, however, the knowledge that an event might occur is relevant to an actor's decision of how careful to be. Under the thin-skull rule, an actor deciding how carefully to drive must factor into the decision the fact that some percentage of drivers have preexisting conditions that will make the result of an accident greater than normal. The inability to foresee *which* driver will have a preexisting condition does not excuse an actor from considering the known fact that some drivers do have preexisting conditions. The decision about how careful to be influences whether an accident will occur and the exacerbated harm from a preexisting condition is sure to occur if the accident occurs. We therefore want the driver to factor that into her decision about how careful to be. The speeding trolley case is different because the trolley driver does not increase his risk of getting hit by a falling tree when he decides how fast to go; the knowledge that a tree might fall is therefore not relevant to the decision.

Even unlikely events are circumstances an actor must consider. For example, when a company omits protective barriers for employees who work near oncoming traffic, the company is responsible when a car hits an employee, even though the accident occurred because the driver had a seizure.[45] The risk to which the defendant exposed its employees was the risk of injury from errant drivers of whatever kind, whether drunk, inattentive, or even non-

---

[43] *Berry v. Sugar Notch Borough*, 191 Pa. 345 (1889). See also, *Texas and Pacific Ry. v. McCleery*, 418 S.2d 494 (Tex. 1967) (railroad whose train is speeding is not responsible for harm to passenger in a car that ran into the train when the driver of the car would not have observed or averted the train even if the train had been going a reasonable speed), *Mahone v. Birmingham Electric Co.*, 73 So. 2d 378 (Ala. 1954) (bus company that let the passenger out on the street rather than at the bus stop is not responsible when passenger slipped on a banana peel, which could have happened even if the passenger has been let out at the bus stop).
[44] As the *Restatement Third* explains, "greater care would not reduce the frequency of such accidents" (in which a tree falls on a trolley only because the trolley was speeding). *Restatement Third*, at 633.
[45] *Derdiarian v. Felix Contracting*, 51 N.Y. 2d 308 (1980). See also, *Tise v. Yates Construction Co., Inc.*, 345 N.C. 456 (1997).

negligent. The fact that the accident occurred in an unexpected way does not excuse the defendant because the circumstance of an errant driver was relevant to the defendant's decision. On the other hand, even if a defendant fails to reasonably protect an unguarded hole, the defendant is not responsible if a mugger intentionally pushes the victim into the hole. The risk of an unguarded hole is the risk of accidental, not intentional, injury, for an actor digging a hole does not generally increase the risk of a mugging and the barriers that would protect against accidental injury would not protect against the mugging. The mugger could injure the victim just as much if the hole were reasonably guarded or even had no hole existed. Accordingly, the risk of mugging is not one of the circumstances that a person digging a hole must take into account when deciding how to protect others against its risks.[46]

A defendant is permitted to make reasonable assumptions about how others will reduce the risks of harm. Where a manufacturer of a heat block negligently failed to include an effective written warning that users should wrap the heat block before using it, the defendant was nonetheless not responsible in a case where the defendant *had* trained a fireman who oversaw use of the heat block.[47] The failure of the fireman to warn the nurse was, the court said, a superseding, intervening cause, but the case is better understood as one where the defendant was not responsible for the circumstance that led to *this* harm (the defendant being reasonable in assuming that the well-informed fireman would protect the victim). The defendant "could not be expected to foresee that its demonstrations to the fireman would callously be disregarded by a member of the department."[48] This is tantamount to saying that a verbal warning to users of this heat block was reasonable and therefore not a source of responsibility to this victim, even though the absence of the direct or reasonably written warning would have been inadequate as to a different victim. As long as it was reasonable to rely on direct training of the fireman to address the risk, the fact that the defendant did not reasonably warn other users of the heat block is relevant only to other victims, not to this one.

Similarly, a defendant who negligently discards live blasting caps is allowed to assume that parents of the child who finds them will recognize the danger

---

[46] If the circumstances change, the actor's responsibility to take them into account might change as well. Where the defendant knows of the risk of a mugging and the mugging might not otherwise occur, a court may well include harm from that circumstance within the risk for which the defendant is responsible if reasonable precautions would have addressed the possibility.

[47] *McLaughlin v. Mine Safety Appliances Co.*, 11 N.Y. 2d 62 (1962).

[48] *Id.* at 71.

and keep the blasting caps away from the children.[49] This follows from the notion that it is reasonable to assume that others will react reasonably to a risk. When making choices about the disposition of the blasting caps, the defendant must take into account the range of harm that could come from failing to dispose of them properly, but the defendant is allowed to reduce the level of precautions to reflect the reasonable assumption that those who find the caps will be careful with them. If that is true, then the expected harm from the carelessness is less because the defendant is not responsible for the subsequent failure of others to protect against the risk.

As other examples, an electric power company that negligently allows a live wire to fall to the sidewalk is not responsible when a police officer mishandles the wire and a bystander is injured.[50] And a railroad that negligently permitted its platform to become saturated with flammable oil was not responsible when someone, knowing of the danger, threw a match on the platform, igniting it.[51] But prison guards are responsible when imprisoned boys escape and steal a yacht, crashing it into, and damaging, plaintiff's yacht.[52] The theft of the yacht is well within the contemplation of the guards when they decided how careful to be.

7.5.3. Information About Victim's Behavior

Cases of the type we are discussing frequently chart the line between an injurer's and a victim's responsibility. Ordinarily, an actor is permitted to assume that others will take reasonable precautions to protect themselves; an actor's failure to protect another is then not inappropriate behavior.[53] Without

---

49 *Pittsburgh Reduction Co., v. Horton*, 113 S.W. 647 (Ark. 1908).
50 *Seith v. Commonwealth Electric Co.*, 89 N.E. 425 (Ill. 1909). The court foreshadowed the theory here when it said that "it seems inconceivable that the defendant ought to have anticipated that a policeman would throw the wire upon the plaintiff by striking it with his club when it was lying where no injury would be done by it either to a person on the sidewalk or on the roadway." *Id.* at 429.
51 *Stone v. Boston & Albany Ry*, 51 N.E. 1 (Mass. 1989).
52 *Home Office v. Dorset Yacht Co.* [1970] 2 A.C. 1004 (appeal taken from England). See also, *Elgin, Aurora and Southern Traction Co. v. Wilson*, 75 N.E. 436 (Ill. 1905) (negligent railroad guard is responsible for allowing boys to turn the switch, diverting a train to a line where plaintiff was hurt in a crash).
53 Every contributory or comparative negligence case could be termed a "proximate cause" case. To the extent that the victim is responsible for the harm under principles of comparative or contributory negligence, the defendant was not the "proximate cause" of the harm. Both types of cases require a court to sort through the contributions of both plaintiff and defendant to the harm, which can best be done by considering whether the circumstance of the plaintiff's risky behavior is one of the circumstances that should have influenced the defendant's decision making.

specific information to the contrary, an actor may assume that a victim will mitigate the harm from an accident and is therefore not responsible for the harm that could have been mitigated.[54] Similarly, an actor who creates a hazard may assume that others will react reasonably with respect to the hazard.[55] But the other-regarding actor is also charged with understanding human nature enough to know when a victim is not likely to self-protect and to anticipate that possibility and protect against it. An actor is required, for example, to understand that "danger invites rescue,"[56] and that those whom an actor entices to drive unreasonably may do so,[57] making the other- regarding actor responsible for those injured during a reasonable rescue and to those whom the actor induces to act unreasonably.

The contributory negligence underpinnings of the proximate cause concept explain the mysteries of the *Wagon Mound* cases. The defendant negligently spilled bunkering oil in the Sidney harbor. In addition to damaging the environment, the bunkering oil caught fire and burned a dry dock (whose owner was the plaintiff in *Wagon Mound I*) and a ship that was in the dry dock (whose owner was the plaintiff in *Wagon Mound II*). Although the bunkering oil could be ignited only at a very high temperature, making a fire improbable, the possibility that the bunkering oil would burn under certain circumstances was foreseeable, as *Wagon Mound II* held. The defendant was not sufficiently other-regarding because the damage to the ship by fire was one of low probability but high damage, consequences the defendant should have thought about when deciding how careful to be with the bunkering oil.

But *Wagon Mound I* held, on the ground of unforeseeability, that the same defendant in the same accident was not responsible for the fire-damaged dry dock. Although the defendant knew of the risk of fire, the defendant was allowed to assume that the potential victim of the oil spill would act reasonably with respect to the spill. The defendant was therefore entitled to assume that the dry dock owner, knowing of the presence of the bunkering oil and the risk of fire, would exercise caution to make sure that the fire did not occur. Yet the owner of the dry dock had gone on welding in the face of the spill, believing

---

[54] *Sinram v. Pennsylvania Ry. Co.*, 61 F 2d 767 (2d Cir. 1932), and *Williams v. Bright*, 658 N.Y. 2d 910 (App. Div. 1997) (avoidable consequences). Although the thin-skull rule is often presented as an absolute rule, this is misleading; the victim is required to reasonably protect against the preexisting condition. See, e.g., *Smith v. Edwards*, 195 S. E 236 (S.C. 1938) (plaintiff with diabetes may not recover from beauty shop for accidental injury where plaintiff unreasonably failed to tell defendant of the preexisting condition).

[55] *Seith v. Commonwealth Elec. Co.*, 89 N.E. 425 (Ill. 1909); *Stone v. Boston & Albany Ry.*, 51 N.E. 1 (Mass. 1889).

[56] *Wagner v. Int'l Ry. Co.*, 133 N.E. 437 (N.Y. 1921).

[57] *Weirum v. RKO General Inc.*, 15 Cal. 3d 40 (1975).

(mistakenly) that he could keep its sparks from igniting the oil.[58] Under these circumstances, the defendant was entitled to assume that the owner of the dry dock would act reasonably with respect to the risk and was therefore not responsible for the harm. In terms of foreseeability, the dry dock owner's lack of care was not foreseeable. *Wagon Mound II* was different, of course, because the owner of the ship in the dry dock had no chance to avoid the risk.

7.5.4. *Multiple Effects*

Torts cases sometimes present situations in which a decision will have several possible effects, depending on the circumstances, and not all effects will be in the contemplation of the actor making the decision that leads to harm. We have already seen two such cases. In *Palsgraf*, the decision about the level of care in handling the passengers risked both a dropped package and an explosion of the fireworks in the package. In *Wagon Mound*, the decision about the level of care to use in loading bunkering oil risked environmental damage, and a fire that burned both a dry dock and a ship in the dry dock. In *Palsgraf*, the defendant was not responsible for contemplating that the package contained fireworks and was therefore not responsible for the explosion. In *Wagon Mound* the defendant was not responsible for the damage to the dry dock because the defendant was not responsible for contemplating that the owner of the dry dock might allow the fire to start. In both of these cases, the defendant was responsible for some effects but not for effects that were unconnected to the harm in an appropriate way. The defendant acted unreasonably but not as to the harm that occurred.

In other cases of multiple effects, however, the relationship between the effect that was understood and the effect that was not understood becomes a basis for imposing liability. Because courts are examining the defendant's decisions to see whether the decision appropriately took into account the well-being of the victim, in some cases the negligence itself may be proof that the defendant failed to adequately consider the well-being of the victim, even if the harm came about because of unexpected circumstances.

In *Polemis*,[59] for example, workmen loading a ship carelessly let a plank fall into the ship's hold, which could have injured workmen or property in the hold, or the ship itself. Instead, the falling plank caused a spark that ignited benzene vapors in the hold, and the ship was destroyed. The question was

---

[58] Apparently, the dry dock owner was correct, insofar as a mere spark could not have ignited the oil. Yet when the spark started a fire in some oily rags floating beneath the dry dock, the fire reached the bunkering oil's flash point.

[59] *In re Polemis* [1921] 3 K.B. 560, [1921] ALL. E.R. 40 (Ct. App. 1921).

whether the defendant should be responsible for damage from the fire even though the circumstances that led to the fire were, as the court viewed it, not ones the defendant needed to consider when deciding how carefully to handle the plank. In this case, the risk of harm that occurred (the risk of explosion and fire) was less than the risk of harm that could have occurred (had a workman been standing below). In such cases of lesser-included expected harm, the court is justified in imposing liability because a defendant who risks foreseeable bodily injury must also accept responsibility for the fire on the ship (unforeseeable property damage). Proof that the actor took an undue risk with respect to one circumstance leading to harm is sufficient proof that the actor would have taken an undue risk with respect to a less foreseeable but also less dangerous type of harm, for proof that the actor thought insufficiently about the well-being of workers in the hold (proven by the negligence) is good evidence that the defendant would have thought insufficiently about the well-being of those affected by the fire had it known of that possibility.

In this type of case, the court must determine what it can infer about the defendant's willingness to accept risks of unforeseeable expected harm from the risk of foreseeable expected harm the defendant did accept. If the defendant was unwilling to invest in reasonable precautions with respect to some of the circumstances – thereby showing a willingness to ignore the well-being of others in one respect – the court can conclude that the defendant would have taken inadequate precautions even with respect to lesser expected harms had the defendant understood them. This is the theory of the lesser-included expected harm. The unreasonable behavior as to one effect is evidence of the defendant's failure to think appropriately of the well-being of others with respect to a different, but lesser, effect.

This theory supports the decision in *Hughes v. Lord Advocate.*[60] When men working in a manhole took a break, they left paraffin lamps behind as a warning to passers-by, but negligently failed to sufficiently guard the manhole. A boy was burned when, as he was exploring the manhole, one of the lamps fell into the manhole and exploded. Because the workmen were required to think about the possibility that boys would be attracted to the manhole and fall in, the precautions they would have taken to avoid the consequences they understood (a guard at the manhole) would have avoided the harm that actually occurred. Because the defendants made an unreasonable decision with respect to the possibility that boys would fall into the manhole, it is not hard to say that that they should be responsible for the lesser possibility that the boys would be burned.

[60] [1963] 1 All E.R. 705 (H.L.).

In *Hynes v. New York Central Railroad Co.*,[61] the defendant railroad allowed overhead wires to deteriorate and fall down on a boy who was diving from railroad property that extended over the public waterway. The falling wires swept the boy into the water, where he drowned. Justice Cardozo rejected the argument that because the boy was trespassing on railroad property the railroad owed him no duty. To the contrary, because the same harm would have occurred if the wires had fallen on him while he was in the water, and because the railroad clearly breached its duty to make sure that the wires did not create that kind of risk, the railroad was responsible for the harm. Proof that the railroad was not thinking adequately about the boy's well-being had he been in the water was enough to allow the trespassing boy to recover. As Cardozo put it, the use of the defendant's property to dive into the water was not the abandonment of the boy's rights as a bather.[62]

Palsgraf presents a nice contrast to these cases. For reasons discussed earlier, the railroad was not expected to have taken into account the risk of explosion, only the risk of a dropped package of normal contents. We cannot infer, from the risk that the railroad took, what the railroad personnel would have done if they had known of the risk of explosion. The risk that the railroad did not foresee, the risk of explosion, is not a lesser-included risk of the risk that they did take, because expected harm from dropped fireworks is greater than the risk of an ordinary package falling. Indeed, had the railroad known of the risk of explosion, the railroad might well have stayed away from the package altogether, or would have handled the passengers more carefully. The explosion was the responsibility of the two men who brought the fireworks onto the platform, not the railroad.[63]

---

[61] 131 N.E. 898 (N.Y. 1921).

[62] *Id.* at 899.

[63] Similarly, in *Doughty v. Turner Manufacturing Co.* [1968] 1 Q.B. 518 (C.A. 1963), a worker negligently knocked a cover into a cauldron of molten cyanide. The resulting splash – one of the risks of this negligence – did not injure anyone. However, a minute or two later an explosion occurred when the chemical hit the asbestos cover. A person standing near the caldron was hurt by molten drops in the explosion, but was not allowed to recover. Apparently, the risk of an explosion was unforeseeable in the sense that even had the company thought about the possibility for some time they would not have understood that it could happen. Accordingly, the risk that their negligence did impose – the risk of being hurt by a splash – did not encompass the risk that actually occurred – the risk of an explosion. Under the analysis here, the circumstances for which the defendant was responsible – the possibility that a victim would be close enough to be hurt by a splash when the cover was knocked in – was less risky than the circumstance – the risk of explosion – that the defendant is not responsible for appreciating. Accordingly, proof of the negligence does not make the defendant responsible for the greater expected harm.

7.6. CONCLUSION

The proximate cause cases reflect the theory of other-regarding behavior by identifying instances in which an actor is excused from thinking about the well-being of another because to do so is irrelevant to the actor's decision or is beyond a reasonable actor's normal cognitive capacity. This limitation on the scope of one person's responsibility for the well-being of others is necessary for social cohesion. If the law made an actor responsible for another's well-being when an actor could not affect that well-being with a different decision, the law would weaken rather than strengthen the coordination of projects and preferences of different people. Telling people that they are responsible for matters that are alien to the decisions they are making would deaden initiative and disrupt relationships. Making people responsible only when their moral agency is linked to the harm gives people freedom of action and a sense of responsibility over circumstances that *do* link them to the victim.

8   Social Cohesion and Strict Liability

Although tort law centers on the negligence concept, it is accepted that "pockets" of strict liability provide an alternative to the negligence regime. This belief is fueled by cases in which responsibility for the well-being of others appears to be based on causing harm rather than on committing a wrong that causes harm, and by the proliferation of definitions of "strict liability" to cover situations in which "fault" is thought to be absent. Accordingly, tort theory not only assesses the relative merits of strict liability and negligence liability, it seeks to justify their simultaneous implementation within tort law. In this chapter, I question the success of this venture as it applies to abnormally dangerous activities, and I offer a new interpretation.[1] Strict liability of the kind addressed in this chapter puts the focus on an actor's activity. It makes the defendant responsible for causing harm and thereby induces an actor either to set aside money for victims or, if it is cheaper, to make better choices when engaging in the activity that is subject to strict liability.

Undoubtedly, a system of strict liability applied to all accidental harms, although not without its problems, could be made coherent. Causing harm could be seen as a basis for compelling an actor to correct the harm she caused, whatever the context, with appropriate adjustments for victim error and an appropriate definition of "cause."[2] It might well be thought that other-regarding actors will normally want to make their victims whole when causing

---

[1]   This chapter is drawn from my article, *The Death of Strict Liability*, 50 Buff. L. Rev. 245 (2008). I address other forms of supposed strict liability in other chapters: the *Vincent* problem (using another's property to protect one's own) in Chapter Nine, the problem of an actor's inability to comply with the relevant standard of care in Chapter Two, and strict liability as applied to products in Chapter Ten.

[2]   Richard A. Epstein, *A Theory of Strict Liability*, 2 J. Legal Stud. 151, 152 (1973); and Richard A. Epstein, *Defenses and Subsequent Pleas in a System of Strict Liability*, 3 J. Legal Stud 165 (1974).

the victim to suffer a compensable loss. Although I argue that such a system would be inconsistent with the way people generally think about their responsibility for the well-being of others, it would be a coherent system. What is awkward is not the possibility of a theory of responsibility for causing harm, but the existence of the mixed system we are thought to have – half free and half slave – that tries to impose strict liability on "pockets" of activities but not on activities in general. As I hope to show, the attempts to distinguish abnormally dangerous activities (to which the strict liability regime is applicable) from normally dangerous activities (to which the negligence regime is applicable) is unsuccessful in theory and practice.

Commentators are looking in the wrong place. Rather than identifying and justifying "pockets" of strict liability, we ought to understand that the negligence regime is fully capable of implementing a theory of responsibility that extends the outer limits of a person's responsibility to take into account the well-being of another when that is normatively justified, making the strict liability concept unnecessary. Legitimately imposed liability that now occurs under the label of "strict liability" can be folded easily into other-regarding negligence liability. When an actor *should* be responsible for activity-based harms that affect another's well-being, the actor will be responsible in the negligence regime. That is because an actor who makes unreasonable decisions about the location, timing, frequency, or method of his activity has failed to make reasonable decisions concerning the well-being of others and, properly understood, has acted unreasonably. We ought also to understand, as I argue below that any broader system of responsibility is inconsistent with the requirements of justice.

This is the first of several chapters that seek to dethrone strict liability as an operative concept in tort law by arguing that the justified scope of responsibility for the well-being of others can be imposed under the negligence regime. I also argue that courts or commentators who invoke strict liability too often short circuit the justificational analysis that would allow us to understand and evaluate the concept of responsibility that drives tort law. My skepticism about the role of strict liability as an operative concept in a mixed system is therefore, at bottom, methodological. My overriding concern is that we specify the circumstances, factors, and values that justify the imposition of liability, and my claim is that such justifications can best be understood when they are organized around the fault concept and other-regarding behavior. By contrast, the invocation of strict liability (by invoking liability without fault) authorizes us to avoid the analysis that would otherwise offer real insights into the legitimate scope of one person's responsibility for the well-being of another.

8.1. THE INADEQUACY OF EXISTING THEORY

A striking characteristic of tort theory is how thin is the justification for our mixed system of liability regimes. From the corrective justice side, Ernest Weinrib has presented the detailed case against strict liability under corrective justice theory, an account that I rely on to show that strict liability is inconsistent with the theory of responsibility I advance. Then, bowing to what he perceived to be the reality of the cases, Weinrib provides rather weak arguments for understanding strict liability as incorporating the wrong of corrective justice in isolated cases.[3] For his part, Arthur Ripstein, after firmly defending the division of risks that support the negligence regime, could do no more than admit that strict liability is not required by the theory of risk division, but he concluded (without analysis) that for activities that are "very risky," the relatively greater importance of security interests over liberty interests justify strict liability.[4] In many respects, attention to the mixed system seems to be generated by everyone's belief that we have, indeed, a mixed system.

From the economic perspective, there is not so much a theory of strict liability as a theory of the inadequacy of negligence liability. Generally, economic theorists believe that strict liability is justified when the negligence regime cannot interdict unreasonable activity-level decisions, such as decisions about how frequently to drive, because strict liability will ensure that the actor minimizes costs by investing in reasonable care. For them, unreasonable activity-level decisions are not captured by the negligence regime, and the law is justified in holding the actor responsible for risk that cannot be reasonably avoided in order to induce the actor to make reasonable activity-level decisions. But if unreasonable activity-level decisions can be interdicted in the negligence regime (as shown below), the economic case for strict liability disappears; economists have not advanced an independent justification for making an actor responsible for risk that cannot be avoided with reasonable care.

Three other theories supporting strict liability [the theory of reciprocal risks, the evidentiary theory, and the loss-spreading (or enterprise) theory] seem particularly weak.

3   Ernest J. Weinrib, THE IDEA OF PRIVATE LAW 187–90, Harvard University Press (1995). Weinrib simply concludes that some activities are more dangerous than others and require a heightened standard of care. He does not explain why this is true or attempt to determine for which activities it is true.
4   Arthur Ripstein, EQUALITY, RESPONSIBILITY, AND THE LAW, Cambridge University Press (1999).

8.1.1. Reciprocal Risks

The theory of reciprocal risk, first propounded by George Fletcher[5] and now championed by Mark Geistfeld[6] suggests that the negligence regime applies when actors impose reciprocal risks on each other, but that strict liability applies when the risks are nonreciprocal. This is thought to be a just regime for nonreciprocal risks because it would be unfair to allow one person to control the well-being of another when the other has no control over the person imposing the risk. It is said that automobile drivers impose a reciprocal risk on each other (because each driver is both a potential injurer and a potential victim).[7] The negligence rule is thought to be justified for reciprocal risks because the burden of having to accept the risk of uncompensated injury in non-negligent accidents is offset by the benefit of being free to drive reasonably without having to compensate others if you hurt them reasonably. Blasting, on the other hand, is thought to be a nonreciprocal risk because blasters impose a risk on victims but victims do not impose the same risk on blasters. This is thought to justify strict liability because victims get no benefit from the negligence rule and therefore ought not bear the burdens of uncompensated injury.

The distinction between reciprocal and nonreciprocal risks is chimerical[8] and one would have thought that it was refuted years ago.[9] Whatever the merits of these illustrations, they do not support the distinction between negligence and strict liability because the examples are nongeneralizable. Automobile drivers impose nonreciprocal risks on pedestrians but are not subject to strict liability when they hurt pedestrians. A pedestrian killed by a piece of wood blasted from a tree is just as dead as one hit by a non-negligent driver, but strict liability is thought to apply only to the former, not the latter. It does not do to say that most pedestrians are also sometimes drivers; the rules do not vary for pedestrians who are not drivers and pedestrians pose less risk to drivers than vice versa. Conversely, there are scores of nonreciprocal risks that are not subject to strict liability: dangerous chemicals transported by road or rail, boilers, nuclear power plants, and many others.

---

[5] George Fletcher, *Fairness & Utility in Tort Theory*, 85 Harv. L. Rev. 537 (1972). He later rephrased the test in terms of dominance, Fletcher, *Corrective Justice for Moderns*, 106 Harv. L. Rev. 1658, 1661–2 (1993).

[6] Mark A. Geistfeld, Tort Law Essentials 62–5, Wolters Kluwer (2008).

[7] *Id.* at 62.

[8] For example, George Fletcher characterizes the risk in *Vincent* as nonreciprocal (see Fletcher, *Fairness and Utility* at 546); Geistfeld characterizes the same risk as reciprocal – see Mark A. Geistfeld, "Necessity and the Logic of Strict Liability," *Issues in Legal Scholarship, Vincent v. Lake Erie Transportation Co. and the Doctrine of Necessity* (2005): Article 5. Available at http://www.bepress.com/ils/iss7/art5.

[9] Jules Coleman, Risks and Wrongs 266–9, Oxford University Press (1992).

Moreover, as Ripstein points out,[10] the notion of reciprocal risks puts no upward boundary on an actor's behavior. If all people decided to drive unreasonably fast, they would be imposing reciprocal risks on each other but not violate any reciprocity norm. Moreover, the theory itself does not help us distinguish reasonable risks – that, by definition are reciprocal – from unreasonable – nonreciprocal – risks, and we can support the distinction only by supplying some basis for comparing the risks and benefits of the decisions that were made, which is a fault-based inquiry.[11] As Fletcher himself admitted, when we determine whether a risk is nonreciprocal, we must examine the context in which the defendant made decisions, so that building a reservoir is nonreciprocal when done in coal country but not when done in locations where there are plenty of reservoirs.[12] This implies that something about the choice of location is a source of responsibility, but says nothing about the reciprocity of risks from reservoirs as a general matter.[13]

The concept of reciprocity is not saved by labeling as "nonreciprocal" those risks that are "uncommon or abnormally dangerous."[14] That simply shifts the analytical focus to the relevance of common activities and the degree of dangerousness of the activity. If uncommon activity means "not generally done," then it excludes blasting, which is a common way of getting rid of things. If it means a new activity, then it is consistent with a theory of forcing technology investment, but again does not cover activities like blasting and reservoir building that have settled technologies. If it means an activity in which most people do not engage, or from which they do not benefit,[15] it would have to include transporting dangerous chemicals, and yet that activity is generally subject to negligence, not strict, liability.

In fact, risk is never purely reciprocal or nonreciprocal; it is a mixture. Risk is always bilateral, in the sense that the risk that is relevant to tort law always

---

[10] Ripstein, EQUALITY, RESPONSIBILITY at 55, especially n. 8.
[11] Gregory C. Keating, *Reasonableness and Rationality in Negligence Theory*, 48 STAN. L. REV. 311, 313–21 (1996).
[12] Fletcher, *Fairness & Utility*, at 546.
[13] Fletcher is imagining that building a reservoir in coal country imposes a nonreciprocal risk, whereas building it in textile country (where there are many mills, dams, and reservoirs) makes the risk reciprocal. Yet, under Fletcher's definition, a reservoir over a coal mine in textile country would still be a nonreciprocal risk as to the coal mine, so the existence of other reservoirs in that area would not reduce responsibility to the coal mine under the nonreciprocity theory. The distinction between locating your reservoir in coal country and in textile country is real, but it has to do with the decision about the location of activity. In Fletcher's terminology, locating the reservoir in coal country imposed a nonreciprocal risk because it was an unreasonable location for that activity, while locating the reservoir in textile country was not. This, as I argue below, is a fault-based concept.
[14] Geistfeld, ESSENTIALS at 63.
[15] *Id.*

addresses the activity of injurer and victim. Digging the reservoir in *Rylands v. Fletcher* would not have been risky if there had been no coal mine beneath the surface. The analytical questions is who should bear the risk that the conflicting land or resource uses will in fact result in harm; one cannot address that question by trying to figure out who caused the interference.

8.1.2. The Evidentiary Rationale for Strict Liability

Mark Geistfeld is the chief modern-day proponent of the evidentiary theory of strict liability.[16] Under this theory, strict liability is justified because it induces an actor to engage in cost-justified precautions without putting the plaintiff to the task of proving that the actor was at fault. According to Geistfeld: "Strict liability can serve the purpose of fostering safe behavior and reducing risk when plaintiffs have a hard time proving that certain forms of risky behavior violate the standard of reasonableness."[17] It does this by applying strict liability when the duty-holder might have foregone any of the costly but reasonable precautions due to the plaintiff's inability to prove fault. This serves as a poor justification for strict liability.

For the evidentiary theory to provide a justification for strict liability, one would expect courts to invoke it when deciding between negligence and strict liability. If the evidentiary theory were relevant analytically, we would see courts and commentators analyzing the possibility of false negatives when deciding whether to invoke strict liability – that is, the possibility that the defendant was negligent but the plaintiff would be deterred from pursuing or winning a claim by the cost of proving negligence. We would therefore expect to see opinions talking about why plaintiffs would have a hard time proving that a blaster was negligent in the use of dynamite or that one who built a reservoir was negligent in not protecting against a latent defect in the land. And we would expect a court refusing to invoke strict liability to similarly consider the likelihood and costs of false negatives because of evidentiary problems. Not only does this occur infrequently, but just the opposite occurs. Liability for design defects, which Professor Geistfeld refers to as a kind of "strict liability," often revolves around a "battle of the experts" on highly technical matters that is anything but easing the burden of proving a defect.

Geistfeld attributes the evidentiary view to Holmes, who observed that "as there is a limit to the nicety of inquiry which is possible in a trial, it may be

---

[16] For an earlier account that emphasized the evidentiary simplicity of strict liability, see William K. Jones, *Strict Liability for Hazardous Enterprise*, 92 COLUM. L. REV. 1705, 1778 (1992).

[17] Geistfeld, ESSENTIALS at 57.

considered that the safest way to secure care is to throw the risk upon the person who decides what precautions shall be taken."[18] But Holmes was not talking about strict liability, a term he never used, but about the fact that the negligence regime has a built-in way of adjusting to the possibility of false negatives and problems of proof. It shifts the burden of proof to the defendant, taking into account the presumptions that can justifiably be made and access to relevant evidence. We have already seen this in our consideration of so-called strict liability for an actor's compliance errors. When, in Geistfeld's terms "plaintiffs have a hard time proving that certain forms of risky behavior violate the standard of reasonableness," the negligence standard adjusts to that reality by shifting the burden of proof to the defendant – a matter far different from invoking strict liability. Burden shifting seems to be what Holmes had in mind. True, Holmes uses strict language, referring to the rule against trespass as "a clear case in which public policy establishes a standard of overt acts without regard to fault in any sense,"[19] but Holmes quickly acknowledges exceptions "to the general prohibition against entering another's premises," which seems to indicate a rule subject to a defense. Far from being strict liability, this simply establishes a presumption that shifts the burden of proving the lack of fault to the defendant.[20] Similarly, Holmes cites *Rylands v. Fletcher* in terms that seem to implicate only the burden of proof, as follows:

> When a person brings on his lands, and collects and keeps there, anything likely to do mischief if it escapes, he must keep it at his peril; and if he does not do so, is prima facie answerable for all the damage which is the natural consequence of its escape.[21]

The reference to the prima facie effect of the stringent rule is not a reference to strict liability but to shifting the burden of proof within the negligence regime. Why else would he then argue that the activity of keeping cattle or making a reservoir for water is not a wrong in itself but an opportunity to shift the burden to the defendant: The "safest way to secure care is to throw the risk upon the person who decides what precaution shall be taken." He calls this approach one that lies "on the boundary line between rules based on policy irrespective of fault, and requirements intended to formulate the conduct of the prudent man,"[22] but then he illustrates his focus on the burden of proof

---

[18] O.W. Holmes, Jr., THE COMMON LAW 117, Little Brown & Co. (1881).
[19] *Id.* at 116.
[20] *Id.*
[21] *Id.*
[22] *Id.* at 117.

by recognizing cases in which a trespass to another's land did not lead to liability.[23]

As I will argue at more length below, the negligence standard easily adjusts the burden of proof and the evidentiary standard to account for the importance of avoiding false negatives. Given that reality, problems of proof hardly provide a justification for strict liability.

8.1.3. The Loss Spreading or Enterprise Liability Theory

One of the enduring rationales for strict liability has been the loss-spreading justification, which was first posited as a basis for product liability and then became the basis for a theory of enterprise liability. As law and legal theory have gravitated toward theories of individual moral responsibility, the arc of loss distribution theory has peaked, and loss distribution is no longer generally thought to provide a justification of accident law as it is or as it should be.[24] It remains viable in the form of a theory of enterprise liability advanced by Gregory Keating, who starts from a position similar to that of Ripstein but moves in a different direction. Like Ripstein, Keating develops a theory of social cooperation based on a Rawlsian conception of a just society in which there is "fair cooperation among free and equal persons who are both rational and reasonable." However, he defines fair terms of cooperation differently than Ripstein. Because he views it to be unfair that luck should fall on an individual, he adopts a fairness notion that spreads the burdens to everyone who benefits from the activity.[25] In a way, he is saying that one has the right not to be unduly burdened by bad luck and that all other actors who benefit from an activity have a duty to repair that bad luck. He thus favors a regime of strict enterprise liability (where all who benefit from an enterprise pay for

---

[23] Other support often given for the evidentiary theory of strict liability is addressed at other points in this book. The support either misunderstands the way the negligence concept adjusts to problems of proof or characterizes as strict liability cases that are better understood as negligence cases.

[24] See e.g., Mark A. Geistfeld, PRINCIPLES OF PRODUCTS LIABILITY 51–8, Foundation Press (2006) (explaining why producer responsibility is not justified by insurance considerations). RESTATEMENT OF THE LAW TORTS: LIABILITY FOR PHYSICAL HARM, PROPOSED FINAL DRAFT No. 1 at 285 (April 6, 2005) (*Restatement Third*) ("The appeal of strict liability, it can be noted, does not depend on any notion that the defendant is in a better position than the plaintiff to allocate or distribute risk of harm...."), William K. Jones, *Strict Liability for Hazardous Enterprise*, 92 COLUM. L. REV. 1705, 1778 (1992) ("risk distribution and the dispersion of losses should be given little or no weight in formulating tort policy").

[25] Gregory C. Keating, *Reasonableness and Rationality in Negligence Theory*, 48 STAN. L. REV. 311, 318 (1996).

harms to those hurt by the enterprise) over negligence.[26] This is a distributive notion wrapped in a corrective justice cloak.

We can understand the difference between Ripstein and Keating in the following way: Ripstein would match the benefits and burdens of membership in a community by determining how much burden one person must adopt in order to facilitate the projects and preferences of another, but would do so only on the basis of the interaction between injurer and victim. It is the interaction that requires the correction, not some other aspect of a person's well-being. Keating would distribute the burdens and benefits based not on interpersonal interaction but on membership in a community, a social contract writ large.

Keating's theory provides a justification for legislative intervention to socialize the costs of accidents. It does not provide a basis for private law, which features one person's claim against another for the repair of something the other has done. Keating's matching of burdens and benefits applies to a citizen as a member of the community or enterprise and is a claim against the community, although administered through an enterprise. Ripstein's applies to a citizen vis-à-vis another citizen. Keating's proposal implicates the legislative realm, Ripstein's the judicial realm. Thus, while Keating's theory is commendable for its coherent justification, it does not help us understand the foundations of private law.

8.2. LIABILITY FOR ABNORMALLY DANGEROUS ACTIVITIES

Current understanding is that strict liability is to apply if an activity is "abnormally dangerous" (the *Restatement Third* formulation)[27] or if an actor makes activity-level decisions that might be unreasonable but cannot be interdicted through the negligence regime (the formulation favored by economists).[28] Under the first formulation, an activity such as blasting is thought to be subject to strict liability because even if one blasts carefully the risk of damage remains high. Under the second formulation, the activity of running a nuclear power plant may be subject to strict liability because no matter how carefully one runs a nuclear power plant, if the plant is located too close to a metropolitan area, the costs of harm from the activity ought to be internalized into the activity. The Restatement and economic formulations can be combined by suggesting that an activity is abnormally dangerous when the actor makes unreasonable activity-level decisions that are not subject to the negligence

---

[26] Gregory C. Keating, *Rawlsian Fairness and Regime Choice in the Tort Law of Accidents*, 72 FORDHAM L. REV. 1857 (2004).

[27] *Restatement Third* § 29, at 575.

[28] The distinction between quality-of-care decisions and activity-level decisions was first recognized in Steven Shavell, *Strict Liability Versus Negligence*, 9 J. LEGAL STUD. 1, 2–3 (1980).

cause of action. But neither formulation is necessary, workable, or consistent with the requirements of social cohesion.

The different attitudes toward strict liability can be understood in conjunction with Diagram 8.1. Risk from an activity can be understood to consist of three segments: risk from unreasonable decisions about the level of care used when undertaking the activity; risk from unreasonable decisions about where, when, how, and how often to undertake an activity (called activity-level decisions); and residual risk – the risk that cannot be eliminated by any reasonable decision the actor makes about the activity. Strict liability fills up the entire area of risk; it holds the actor responsible for all the harm from the activity, including that which could have been avoided by more reasonable decisions about due care or activity levels and that which is left over after the actor makes reasonable decisions.

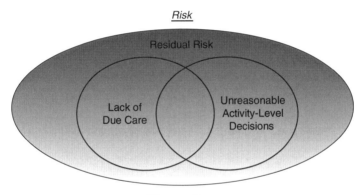

Diagram 8.1

For economists, unreasonable activity-level decisions are not captured by the negligence rule and the law is justified in holding the actor responsible for residual risk in order to make sure that the actor makes reasonable activity-level decisions. But, as mentioned above, if unreasonable activity-level decisions *can* be interdicted in the negligence regime, the economic case for strict liability disappears. The Restatement approach suggests that all risks left over after the actor takes due care should be thought of as residual risk; if it is large enough, the activity should be called "abnormally dangerous" and subjected to strict liability. This approach, however, offers no basis for identifying the size of residual risk, no test for determining which activities are "abnormally dangerous," and no reason that large residual risk should be the source of responsibility while small residual risk need not be.

The theory of other-regarding behavior suggests that abnormally dangerous activity cases ought to be incorporated into negligence liability. An actor who makes an unreasonable activity-level decision is failing to think about the well-being of others in an appropriate way and should be responsible for harm caused by that decision, just as is an actor who makes an unreasonable due care decision. Strict liability is unnecessary, however, because the negligence regime is fully capable of identifying such decisions and making the actor responsible for the harm they cause. Moreover, if the defendant's decisions about due care and activity levels are reasonable (if the only risk is residual), the imposition of liability would wrongfully hold the actor responsible for matters over which the actor has no control, and would therefore violate the actor's autonomy and moral agency. Because it imposes liability even if the actor could not have avoided the harm with a socially responsible decision, strict liability violates the autonomy of the actor and is inconsistent with the theory of justice that animates tort law. Just as the no-duty and proximate cause concepts shield an actor from responsibility when the actor could not have affected a different outcome in a way that society endorses, courts should reject liability for risk left over after an actor makes reasonable decisions.

Appropriate analysis undermines both the assertion that some unreasonable decisions will escape detection under the negligence regime and the assertion that an actor should be responsible for risks that remain after the actor has made reasonable due care and activity-level decisions. The theory of other-regarding behavior thus supports two general propositions: first, that the unreasonable activity-level decisions should subject the actor to liability, which the negligence regime is fully capable of doing, and, second, that an actor ought not be responsible if the actor makes reasonable due care and activity-level decisions. The first proposition is the subject of Section 8.3 and the second the subject of Section 8.4.

8.3. ACTIVITY-LEVEL DECISIONS AND THE NEGLIGENCE RULE

8.3.1. Activity-Level Decisions

Most negligence cases consider an actor's decisions about how much care to take. But an actor also influences the well-being of others by so-called activity-level decisions. Although an actor undertakes an activity with reasonable care, she may create unreasonable risks by undertaking the activity with unreasonable frequency, in an unreasonable location or time, or by an unreasonable method. A driver might drive a truck containing a dangerous explosive through a congested area when a less dangerous, but effective, route is available (unreasonable location or time) or the driver might be able to transport the dangerous explosive by a means – say by rail – that is less dangerous (unreasonable method). Or a manufacturer of industrial wastes might dump the wastes in a particular location so often that the build-up creates a hazard (unreasonable frequency). When such an activity-level decision is unreasonable, the law has an interest in apprehending that unreasonableness, for the decision was not made with an appropriate regard for the well-being of others.

Illustrative are cases that have traditionally been thought of as "strict liability" cases. In *Rylands v. Fletcher*, the defendant constructed a reservoir to use with a cotton mill in a district that had previously been devoted to coal mining.[29] A latent defect under the reservoir caused the water to run through an abandoned mine shaft and into the plaintiff's mine.[30] The defendant was held responsible for the harm even though the defendant was not unreasonable in hiring or supervising the contractor. Although the court seemingly applied strict liability, the fault-based intuition that underlies the decision is easy to discern. The case involved a conflict between potentially incompatible uses of land – coal mining and cotton milling. The coal mines had been there first, making coal mining a background fact that the defendant should have reasonably accounted for in determining where to construct his cotton mill. Moreover, coal mines must, by physical necessity, be where the coal is, while cotton milling can be done in innumerable locations. What the court called defendant's "non-natural" use of the land was a use in which the decision about where to locate had to be reasonably made in light of uses of adjoining land so that interferences were minimized. Liability forced the defendant to internalize all the costs of the chosen location because that is the best way of ensuring that the defendant reasonably considered where to put the reservoir and how intensively to investigate the underlying ground before constructing it. "Strict liability" in *Rylands* simply makes the defendant responsible for not thinking reasonably about his cotton mill's location and how to prevent harm to the underlying mines.

Similarly, although the early blasting cases were written in strict liability language, their outcome would have been the same if the court had focused on the relevant activity-level decision. In the Erie Canal cases,[31] blasting might be done with due care but with unreasonably large quantities of powder. Using less powder per blast would have taken longer, but would also have reduced the risk of harm. Had the court understood this, it could

---

[29] *Rylands v. Fletcher*, 3 L.R.E. & i. App. 330, 331 (H.L. 1868).
[30] We can assume that the defendant knew that this was mining country and therefore knew of the possibility that there might be mines in the area. This knowledge might, under current law, have imposed a duty to reasonably inspect the property to see if there was a latent defect.
[31] *St. Peter v. Denison*, 58 N.Y. 416 (1874); *Hay v. Cohoes Co.*, 2 N.Y. 159 (1849); *Tremain v. Cohoes Co.*, 2 N.Y. 163 (1849).

easily have said that proof that the harm occurred is proof that the defendant used an unreasonable amount of blasting powder; indeed, the opinions suggest that the courts understood that the defendants had made unreasonable decisions.[32] In *Sullivan v. Dunham* the defendant was blasting to remove a 60-foot tree and the blast hurled a piece of wood more than 400 feet, killing the victim.[33] Clearly, there would have been more reasonable means of getting rid of a 60-foot tree; axes and saws suggest themselves. In another early case, *Guille v. Swan*,[34] a hot-air balloonist landed in New York City without intending to, and the crush of people who came to see the balloon damaged the plaintiff's property. Following Judge Posner's analysis,[35] because of the rudimentary technology for controlling hot-air balloons and the low value of the defendant's activity, New York City was an unreasonable location for ballooning and the decision to do the ballooning in the city subjected the defendant to liability.

When an actor makes an unreasonable decision about where, when, how, and how frequently to undertake an activity, the actor is failing to consider appropriately the range of circumstances that might attach the actor's decision to the victim's harm and the actor ought to be found responsible for the harm. This has always been the law, whether it is under the rubric of strict liability or negligence liability.

8.3.2. The Negligence Regime Reaches Unreasonable Activity-Level Decisions

Although economic analysts often assert that negligence law is unable to impose liability when activity-level decisions are unreasonable, that view underestimates the strength of the unreasonableness concept. Relevant activity-level decisions are comparative choices; they are subject to the same analysis that courts use when evaluating an actor's due care decisions. The defendant is faced with at least two options for conducting his activities, one more reasonable than another under comparative cost–benefit analysis – that

---

[32] See, e.g., *Hay v. Cohoes*, 2 N.Y. at 161 ("If [the defendant] cannot construct the work without the adoption of such means, he must abandon that mode of using his property, or be held responsible for all damages resulting therefrom"). The term *such means* could refer either to the amount of blasting powder the defendant used or to the fact that the defendant had other means of removing the rock. *Id.* In the *St. Peter* case, 58 N.Y. at 416, blasting was done to remove frozen earth, suggesting that perhaps waiting until the next thaw might have been a reasonable alternative.

[33] *Sullivan v. Dunham*, 161 N.Y. 290, 290 (1900).

[34] 19 Johns. 381 (N.Y. Sup. Ct. 1822).

[35] *Indiana Inner Harbor Belt Railway Co. v. American Cyanamid Co.* 916 F.2d 1174, 1176–7 (7th Cir. 1990).

is, one that achieves the actor's goals with the least social risk. A defendant might be faced with two routes to get hazardous wastes through a city, two time periods at which it might transport dangerous cargo, or two methods of removing a tree. A reasonable other-regarding person would make the choice that minimizes the expected harm in light of the benefits of each method. Like due care cases, these cases ask what the defendant could have done differently and what effect the alternatives would have had on the victim and the injurer.[36] The choices the defendant made in the care she used and her choices about the frequency, method, timing, or place of the activity are conceptually the same.[37]

In fact, courts regularly assess the reasonableness of activity-level decisions as if they were due care decisions without recognizing it.[38] The appropriate

[36] Professor Hylton has translated the basic insights about due care and activity-based decisions into a sophisticated theory for comparing the external costs and benefits of an activity when the activity is done with reasonable care. Keith N. Hylton, *A Missing Markets Theory of Tort Law*, 90 NW. U.L. REV. 977 (1996); Keith N. Hylton, *The Theory of Tort Doctrine and the Restatement (Third) of Torts*, 54 VAND. L. REV. 1413, 1420–3 (2001). When the external costs and benefits of an activity are roughly equal, and the activity is done with reasonable care, there is no warrant for legal intervention. In that instance, any additional liability will eliminate benefits as well as costs in equal proportion and will therefore produce no net benefits. Where, however, the activity is done carefully, but the external costs are high and the external benefits low, strict liability induces the actor to engage in less activity. This can be understood in roughly the following way: When an actor uses dynamite, the benefit (less effort) may be far less than the expected external costs of using the dynamite; accordingly the activity can be called "abnormally dangerous." Professor Hylton would therefore impose strict liability in order to internalize the costs of using dynamite that are not incurred when using a saw. Because we have no meter for measuring externalities directly, Professor Hylton's analytical approach requires that we compare the costs and benefits of various ways of undertaking activities, and this can best be done by asking whether the defendant's choice of a method, location, or time for the activity was reasonable. External harm is simply a synonym for the additional harm to the victim from one course of action over another, and that can easily be compared with the benefits of one course of action over another. When a method of operation imposes greater external costs than benefits compared to other methods, it is an unreasonable method; accordingly, an inquiry into the reasonableness of the activity is the inquiry that is needed to make Professor Hylton's theory workable. It is precisely the comparative inquiry for which the reasonableness concept was designed.

[37] The Restatement (Second) of Torts recognized as much: "A negligent act may be one which involves an unreasonable risk of harm to another (a) although it is done with all possible care, competence, preparation, and warning, or (b) [if due care is lacking]." RESTATEMENT (SECOND) OF TORTS § 297, American Law Institute (1965). Subsection (a) must be referring to activity-based negligence when due care is taken, because due care negligence is covered in subsection (b).

[38] *Adams v. Bullock*, 125 N.E. 93, 93 (N.Y. 1919) ("The defendant in using an overhead trolley was in the lawful exercise of its franchise. Negligence, therefore, cannot be imputed to it because it used that system and not another.") [citing *Dumphy v. Montreal Light, Heat & Power Co.* [1907] A.C. 454 (P.C.) (U.K.)]; *Tedla v. Ellman*, 19 N.E.2d 987 (N.Y. 1939) (choosing to disobey statutory command to walk in direction of oncoming traffic is excused because volume of traffic made that side of the road an unreasonable location for walking).

level of care often depends on an activity-level decision – as when a driver has been on the road a long time.[39] As another example, take the famous *Escola v. Coca Cola Bottling Co.*[40] Plaintiff sued when a reused soda bottle exploded because of a hairline fracture in the bottle. The court held that because soda bottles should not be reused without a "commercially practicable" test that eliminated the possibility of such hairline fractures, the jury could infer negligence from the explosion. This is an application of the activity-level reasonableness standard. The defendant had to decide between two methods of delivery – used bottles or new bottles – the latter safer than the former. The court concluded that if used bottles could not be shown to be without the fracture, the defendant was obligated to use new bottles.[41] This responds to the common sense notion that the choice between two methods of delivering the beverage – in either new or used bottles – must take into account the relative risks of each method. In the context of that case, if used bottles could not be made safe their use was an unreasonable (or "abnormally dangerous") method (given that the additional cost of new bottles was less than the gain in safety from using them). This activity-level analysis enabled the jury to find that the bottler failed to use due care.[42]

Similarly, we can understand the famous *Bolton v. Stone*[43] case in activity-based terms. The plaintiff was injured when a cricket ball hit her outside the playing field.[44] She lost the case because the risks were so small as to be reasonably disregarded, but the judges went on to speak of the cricket club's general responsibility. After indicating that the substantiality of the harm mattered, Justice Reid said: "I do not think that it would be right to take into account the difficulty of remedial measures,"[45] suggesting a kind of disproportional Hand formula – namely, that if the risks are substantial enough the burden of precautions is not relevant unless the precautions are disproportionately high. He then continued, "If cricket cannot be played on a ground without creating

---

[39] See John J. Donohue, III, *The Law and Economics of Tort Law: The Profound Revolution*, 102 HARV. L. REV. 1047, 1060–2 (1989) (explaining that a truck driver will find the burden of staying awake more difficult the more she drives).

[40] 150 P.2d 436 (Cal. 1944).

[41] *Escola*, 150 P.2d at 439.

[42] Mark Geistfeld misunderstands the appropriate analysis of the case in *Escola v. Coca Cola Bottling Co.: Strict Products Liability Unbound*, TORTS STORIES 223–4 (Robert L. Rabin & Stephen D. Sugarman, eds.) Foundation Press (2003). The point is not that the court was trying to eliminate all risks of used bottles (which the negligence standard is not designed to do). The point is that the risk of used bottles was unreasonable in light of the alternative of new bottles (which offered fewer risks without countervailing costs).

[43] [1951] A.C. 850 (H.L.) (U.K.).

[44] *Id.* at 851.

[45] *Id.* at 867.

a substantial risk, then it should not be played *there* at all!'[46] This has been frequently understood as a negligence test that looks only at the degree of risk, and not at the reasonableness of that risk – much like the test for abnormally dangerous activities.[47] But, on analysis, it means something quite different. It is, in fact, a statement that some cricket games might be in an unreasonable location. As Judge Reid said, if the risks are substantial enough – even after due care is taken – perhaps the game should not be played "there," but somewhere else. If there is a more reasonable location for the game – one where the lower value of the location might be offset by the greater safety of the location, the decision to play "there" (an activity-level decision) is unreasonable.

Those who claim that the negligence standard is inadequate to address activity-level decisions have not fully considered its flexibility. Once courts are free to examine directly the reasonableness of decisions about where, when, how, and how frequently to undertake an activity, that flexibility will become apparent. For example, it has been thought that one advantage of strict liability has been to induce actors to avoid liability by investing in information to reduce accidents, and that the incentive is greater under strict liability than it is under negligence.[48] To the contrary, the negligence standard has proven to be flexible enough to impose responsibility when the relevant actor has failed to get and rely on information that is reasonably available and that would have enabled the actor to reduce the harm.[49]

The essence of the reasonableness standard is that an actor must look out for the well-being of others when the actor has created a risk or stands in such a relation to the victim that a reasonable person in that position would take efforts to consider how the victim might get hurt. Under this general concept, the reasonableness standard has long put pressure on the defendant to reasonably investigate its own activity in order to reduce risks. Indeed, the granddaddy of all product liability cases, *MacPherson v. Buick*,[50] involved the duty to investigate, for the alleged negligence was that the defendant failed to

---

[46] *Id.* (emphasis added).

[47] See Weinrib, *Private Law*, at 148–50.

[48] Kenneth S. Abraham, The Forms and Functions of Tort Law 164–5, Foundation Press (2d. ed., 2002). See also James A. Henderson, Jr., *Coping with the Time Dimension in Products Liability*, 69 Cal. L. Rev. 919, 928–9 (1981); David G. Owen, *Rethinking the Policies of Strict Products Liability*, 33 Vand. L. Rev. 681, 711–13 (1980).

[49] Steven Shavell has shown how a socially beneficial level of investment in information can be induced by either the regime of strict liability or the appropriate negligence regime. Steven Shavell, *Liability and the Incentive to Obtain Information about Risk*, 21 J. Legal Stud. 259, 260–1 (1992). In this chapter, I show that the negligence regime is the appropriate one; an actor is unreasonable if the actor fails to invest in information whenever the expected benefits of the information outweigh the burden of getting the information.

[50] 111 N.E. 1050 (N.Y. 1916).

reasonably find the defect in the wheel that it had purchased from a supplier. The product liability "revolution" has continued to develop an actor's obligation to gather information for suppliers of both services[51] and products.[52]

With hindsight, we can see that the negligence standard has ably performed the function that Guido Calabresi and Jon Hirschoff would have assigned to strict liability 35 years ago – namely, to identify the actor who, at least cost, can acquire and disseminate information that can be used to reduce the costs of accidents. They argued that:

> [When a] producer is in a position to compare the existing accident costs with the costs of avoiding this type of accident by developing either a new product or a test which would serve to identify [those who are at risk from a product]...the producer is the cheapest cost avoider, the party best suited to make the cost–benefit analysis and to act upon it.[53]

That is true, but irrelevant to the function of strict liability. Identifying the least cost avoider does not make the liability strict; it simply makes the failure to incur the cost unreasonable.

Indeed, much misunderstanding is derived from the perception that liability for product defects is strict liability and that the justification for strict liability is to avoid the inadequacies of the negligence regime. Instead, as Chapter Ten shows, the lesson from product liability law is just the opposite. Liability for investigation, warning, and design defects turns on whether the manufacturer's decisions were reasonable, and the adaptability of the negligence concept has substantially increased the responsibility of manufacturers without resort to strict liability.

The reasonableness standard also flexibly allows courts to reduce unnecessary information costs for determining fault. When the harm occurs in a way

---

[51] See, e.g., *McDougald v. Perry*, 716 So. 2d 783, 786–7 (Fla. 1998) (although the defendant did not manufacture the chain that might have been defective, the jury may find the defendant liable for accidental harm because he had control of the chain and inspected it); *Bethel v. N.Y. City Transit Auth.*, 703 N.E. 2d 1214, 1216 (N.Y. 1998) (although common carrier is no longer held to utmost standard of care, the jury may find the defendant's bus company liable for failing to observe a defective seat during routine maintenance).

[52] See, e.g., *Richter v. Limex Int'l., Inc.*, 45 F. 3d 1464, 1471 (10th Cir. 1995) (the defendant seller of trampolines as an exercise device had a duty to find out whether the use of a trampoline for jogging might cause stress fractures); *Wooderson v. Ortho Pharm. Corp.*, 681 P. 2d 1038 (Kan. 1984) (explaining that the defendant had a duty to warn consumers based on research and scientific developments and publications in the field); see also Robert D. Hursh & Henry J. Bailey, AMERICAN LAW OF PRODUCTS LIABILITY § 2:29 at 212 (2d ed., 1974) (duty to make tests and inspections as would be reasonably necessary to make a safe product).

[53] Guido Calabresi & John T. Hirschoff, *Toward a Test for Strict Liability in Torts*, 81 YALE L.J. 1055, 1062 (1972).

that would not have occurred had decisions been reasonably made, *res ipsa loquitur* allows the plaintiff to shift to the defendant the burden of providing evidence or proving that the defendant was reasonable. *Res ipsa loquitur* is applicable to activity-based, as well as due care decisions. When the blast that is used to fell a 60-foot tree sends a portion of the tree 400 feet, it is not hard to conclude that a reasonable person would have used an axe, a saw, or less dynamite.[54] Even beyond formal application of *res ipsa loquitur*, courts in negligence cases frequently rely on presumptions and reduced evidentiary burdens to make sure that plaintiffs are not denied an opportunity to prove fault because of the circumstances in which the fault occurred.

In addition, the negligence standard contains a built-in concept of quasi-strict liability. In professional malpractice settings, courts defer to the standard of care set by the profession while making it a fault not to meet that standard.[55] In products liability settings, courts defer to the producer's manufacturing standard, while making it a fault (or defect) not to meet that standard.[56] More generally, when an actor acts on the basis of specialized knowledge or private information that courts are reluctant to second guess, the law absorbs a private standard as the standard of negligence and holds the defendant to that standard. This gives negligence liability the feel of strict liability without removing the anchor of fault from the finding of responsibility. The negligence standard is fault-based but not toothless.

The law ought to advance with a scalpel, not a blunderbuss. Strict liability represents the law's blunderbuss, scattering shot around in the hope that the law can address unreasonable activity-level decisions that are not interdicted by the reasonableness standard. But strict liability is unnecessary because the negligence standard is fully able to assess which activity-based decisions are relevant to the determination of fault and which have been unreasonably made.

[54] See *Sullivan v. Dunham*, 55 N.E. 923, 926–7 (N.Y. 1900) (imposing strict liability, but referring to the "special method" the defendant used to take down the tree); see also *Berg v. Reaction Motors Div.*, 181 A. 2d 487, 496 (N.J. 1962) (A rocket engine testing facility a thousand feet from the center of a small village is subject to strict liability, but the case could have been decided under a negligence standard. It is hard to imagine that the location was so superior to other locations that it was reasonable to put the testing facility so close to the village. Indeed, before it used the labels "strict liability," the court noted that the defendant could have shown "greater care and diligence, perhaps in the selection and arrangement of the testing sites and stands.")

[55] See *Mitchell v. United States*, 141 F. 3d 8, 13 (1st Cir. 1998); *Complete Family Care v. Sprinkle*, 638 So. 2d 774, 777 (Ala. 1994). See generally 61 AM. JUR. 2D *Physicians, Surgeons, Etc.* § 189 (2002).

[56] RESTATEMENT (THIRD) TORTS: PRODUCTS LIABILITY § 2(c) at 18, American Law Institute (1998) (*Products Liability Restatement*) (defining manufacturing defects).

8.3.3. *Liability for Frequency Decisions*

Analysts sometimes cite frequency decisions as ones that cannot effectively be addressed by the negligence regime.[57] Take the reasonableness of an extra (but reasonably done) trip to the store to get an item that was forgotten on an earlier trip. No court can evaluate that activity-level decision under the reasonableness rule because the court would get mired in a series of debates about the marginal utility of an additional trip to the store and the risks of that trip to others. Under strict liability, however, a driver is responsible for all accidents he causes, so before taking that additional trip, he would weigh the value of one more trip to the store against the risk of an accident while driving with due care. An actor faced with strict liability will automatically forego trips to the store when the benefits of the trip are outweighed by the possibility of having an accident while driving with due care.

Although coherent, this analysis wrongfully assumes that the law *should* care how frequently a person decides to go to the store or that some trips to the store are unreasonable ones. On the contrary, an actor's frequency decisions about whether to drive to the store one more time are consistent with social cohesion, and not generally relevant to the calculus of responsibility. Rather than providing a justification for strict liability, most frequency decisions should not be a source of responsibility, which provides a reason to avoid, not embrace, strict liability. Strict liability would impose liability for frequency decisions that society considers to be reasonable and it is precisely because we do not want people to have to assess the value of their trips to the store that we apply negligence, not strict liability, to automobile driving.

Those who assume that frequency-level decisions are generally relevant to auto accidents have confused the empirical with the normative. Even if auto accidents increase with the frequency of driving, frequency decisions are not necessarily a concern of tort law. Tort law is not designed to reduce harm,

---

[57] Steven Shavell, *Economics and Liability for Accidents*, in NEW PALGRAVE DICTIONARY OF ECONOMICS (Steve N. Durlaf & Lawrence E. Blume, eds., 2d ed.: 2008). Landes and Posner acknowledge that courts can examine activity-based issues when low information costs are offset by the advantages of examining activity-based decisions, but they generally believe that the information costs of examining activity-based decisions are high. William M. Landes & Richard A. Posner, THE ECONOMIC STRUCTURE OF TORT LAW 70–1, Harvard University Press (1987). Guiseppe Dari-Mattiacci & Francesco Parisi, *The Economics of Tort Law: A Précis*, in THE ELGAR COMPANION TO LAW AND ECONOMICS (Jürgen Parisi & G. Backhaus eds., 2d. ed. 2005). Available at http://ssrn.com/abstract=458701. ("Although courts may occasionally take into account the frequency of an activity in their assessment of negligence, often no threshold of 'optimal frequency' can be easily utilized by legal rules as a liability allocation mechanism, given the difficulty of pinpointing a critical value to separate efficient from excessive activity.")

but to reduce unreasonable harm – that is, harm that can be controlled by reasonable human effort.[58] Tort law provides a normative basis for determining when to intervene in social arrangements to require an actor to think in more socially appropriate ways about how the actor's decisions affect the risk another faces. As I have already argued, when a court determines whether a person is required to think of the well-being of others, the court is asking whether the actor prefers her own projects and preferences over the projects and preferences of others in a way that unreasonably ignores the social norms that allow a community to function. This is necessarily a qualitative determination about the interests of the defendant and those whom the defendant might potentially injure. The assessment of comparative well-being is a normative – not an empirical – inquiry, for it requires a determination of the values that are important to society. If social norms determine that one need not think about the well-being of others when deciding how frequently to drive, then that decision should not be the source of legal responsibility.

In fact, society does not generally expect people to think about the well-being of others when they decide whether to drive an extra mile. Consider an actor who has a choice between two places to shop, one preferred but farther away, and the other closer but less desirable. Society does not expect the actor to factor into that decision the risk of being on the road; society operates under an implicit and reciprocal social agreement that precludes one member of the community from questioning such decisions. Behind a veil of ignorance, most people are likely to choose a standard of behavior that prohibits one member of the community from questioning decisions of that kind – decisions

---

[58] The argument in the text can be framed in terms of externalities. Choices about how frequently to drive impose external costs on others – because the more miles on the road, the greater the likelihood of an accident. But these external costs are offset by the external benefits of the freedom to drive – a universal and reciprocal benefit – so that frequency decisions do not clearly impose net costs on society. Professor Hylton has made a similar point by recognizing that when the external benefits and costs of an activity are relatively equal, the law has no interest in intervening to change frequency-level decisions. Hylton, *Restatement Third* 1420, and Hylton, *Missing Markets*, 984–6. The relative balance between external costs and benefits of an activity suggests that the actor making the frequency decision has thought reasonably about the impact of the decision on others. As an example, the frequency with which a bus uses the road is likely to balance the probability of an accident – an external cost – with the probability that passengers will enhance the value of stores along the route – an external benefit. When that occurs, the frequency of the bus's trips is not likely to justify judicial intervention. Interestingly, this notion that social benefits and costs of an activity may be equal is related to the corrective justice notion that when risks are reciprocal, liability may depend only on the care exercised. See Fletcher, *Fairness & Utility*, at 543–6 (noting that the risk that the bus imposes on stores along the route is reciprocated by the risk that stores impose on buses; moreover, the bus and the stores are interdependent beneficiaries of each other's success).

that only marginally increase risks to others but express preferences reflecting highly individualistic decisions about the value of time and the ends the actor is trying to achieve.

We have already seen that society tolerates the reasonable risk imposed by a driver subject to an epileptic seizure and therefore does not impose strict liability; this is precisely because we do not want the defendant with a disability to worry about legal liability every time he gets in his car. Instead, we affirm that, except when the driver with epilepsy chooses an unreasonable activity – such as becoming a school bus driver – the frequency with which the epileptic drives is not relevant to the determination of liability. More generally, freedom of movement and freedom of travel suggest that the law ought not generally intervene when individuals decide how frequently to do an activity that can be done with reasonable care.[59] The relevant determination is whether an actor's mode of decision making is one that society would endorse as consistent with the healthy interrelationships that make up a community or that are important for individuals to follow in a social setting. We trust decisions that are embedded in social systems that protect against abuse of the autonomy the law values; we do not want people making claims on the projects and preferences of others that they would not want to be made on them. By this reasoning, many frequency-level decisions are socially benign.[60]

---

[59] The *Restatement (Second) of Torts* recognizes this by providing the following:

> The law attaches utility to general types or classes of acts as appropriate to the advancement of certain interests rather than to the purpose for which a particular act is done, except in the case in which the purpose is of itself such public utility as to justify an otherwise impermissible risk. Thus, the law regards the free use of the highway for travel as of sufficient utility to outweigh the risk of carefully conducted traffic, and does not ordinarily concern itself with the good, bad, or indifferent purpose of a particular journey. It may, however, permit a particular method of travel which is normally not permitted if it is necessary to protect some interest to which the law attaches a preeminent value, as where the legal rate of speed is exceeded in the pursuit of a felon or in conveying a desperately wounded patient to a hospital.

RESTATEMENT (SECOND) OF TORTS §291 cmt. e, American Law Institute (1965). As Stephen Gilles recognized, this "is a ruling on the *merits* rather than a ruling that activity-level claims lie outside the ambit of negligence law." Stephen G. Gilles, *Rule Based Negligence and the Regulation of Activity Levels* 21 J. LEGAL STUD. 319, 340 (1992); see also, *Restatement Second*, § 293 cmt. b (1965) ("A car may be driven at fifteen miles an hour through a city street upon the least important of errands.")

[60] This general point is related to the difficulty of proving that the harm was caused by frequency-level decisions. Professor Gilles has pointed out that even if a plaintiff could convince a court that a railroad had run too many trains, or that the defendant had gone to the grocery store too frequently, the plaintiff would have difficulty showing that the unreasonable activity *caused* the harm. Gilles, *Regulation of Activity Levels*, at 333. He offers this as a reason to adopt strict liability. But the difficulty of proving causation is a reason to have a no-liability regime for those decisions. The causation difficulty reflects the fact that ordinary people do

Accordingly, when an actor decides how frequently to go to the grocery store, social cohesion does not require or expect that decision to be subject to social oversight through tort law (as long as the person drives with due care). We do not expect the actor to weigh the costs and benefits of that trip from a social perspective to determine whether one more trip is reasonable. Instead, we preserve the autonomy of a person to make a private assessment of the costs and benefits of one additional trip because, if courts interposed social oversight on that decision, they would unduly burden the actor's decision making and freedom of motion. This implicit calculus of normative values is reflected in the way people normally think about such choices. When we decide whether to make a trip to the store, we normally think not of the risk of the trip; we normally compare only the time and effort of the trip with the goal of the trip.[61] For this reason, engaging in an activity is rarely an occasion for liability in negligence and we have few instances in which the appropriate frequency level of an activity is zero.[62] Negligence law is replete with instances in which engaging in an activity – even an unlicensed or illegal activity – is not the

---

not make decisions about how often to do something with a view that the decision might "cause" an accident, in the sense of triggering an accident that otherwise would not occur. If you said to the person on the street that their trip to the store caused the harm in an accident because it was an unnecessary trip, they would wonder what concept of causation you were using. The fact that causation would be hard to prove simply demonstrates that when people make decisions about how often to go to the store they are generally unconcerned with safety matters and therefore would not understand that they had caused any harm by the decision if an accident occurs. Causation is a part of individual decision making related to risk only when the decision being made is thought to have an influence on the risk or outcome. People would understand that driving too many miles and becoming tired causes an accident, but not that making an extra trip to the store causes an accident.

[61] As Stephen Gilles has noted,

[the] asymmetry between the courts' willingness to evaluate "high-risk" claims – claims that an actor negligently engaged in an activity that is normally safe but was unsafe on a particular occasion – and their willingness to evaluate "low-utility" claims – challenges to an actor's decisions to engage in an activity on the grounds that, although the activity's utility normally outweighs its costs, on the occasion in question its utility was so low as to require a finding of negligence. Gilles, *Regulation of Activity Levels*, at 321. This is noticing that courts will evaluate risky driving but not the claim that the trip should not have been made. That is because it would unduly impinge on a person's autonomy to inquire into low-utility claims; a finding of unreasonably low utility would disable a person from making these choices. Professor Gilles also noted that increased frequency of activity is often associated with diminishing marginal utility rather than an increase in the risk of the activity. *Id.* at 335. Because of this, if an excess of risk over return might occur in a low-utility activity, the actor is likely to curtail the activity even if the law does not make it the occasion for liability, merely because the return to the activity decreases as frequency increases. That makes the need for legal intervention that much less important.

[62] *Products Liability Restatement* § 2 cmt. E, illus. 5 (1998).

source of liability when harm results.[63] As a general category, frequency-level decisions are not the concern of tort law.[64]

We need not conclude, of course, that frequency-level decisions are never the concern of negligence law. Some environmental risks stem from dumping chemicals too frequently in one location. Driving for too long a time may be unreasonable. A bottle may be reused too frequently. But in instances like these, the information costs of determining whether the frequency decision is unreasonably made are manageable within the negligence regime. We can get the information to understand the frequency "tipping point" beyond which further dumping of chemicals, further driving, or further use of previously used bottles becomes unreasonable.

8.4. LIABILITY FOR RESIDUAL RISK

As we saw in previous chapters, when a court concludes that the defendant's decisions are reasonable, the court is concluding that the defendant could not bring about any different result without imposing unreasonable burdens on society by sacrificing more of her projects and preferences than is warranted for social cohesion. The actor could stop the activity, of course, but doing so would deprive people of the benefits of the activity, which, by the finding of reasonableness, outweigh the expected harm from the activity. Therefore, any convincing theory of strict liability must explain why an actor should be responsible for harms from risks over which the actor has no control – that is, for the residual risk after the actor has made reasonable due care and activity-level decisions. In the realm of abnormally dangerous activities, no convincing theory has been presented.

---

[63] This is true, for example, when the defendant should have been, but was not, licensed to practice an activity and harms someone while engaging in that activity. See, e.g., *Brown v. Shyne*, 151 N.E. 197 (N.Y. 1926) (addressing the liability of an unlicensed chiropractor). Moreover, it is commonly assumed that a kidnapper who gets in an accident while driving carefully after the kidnapping is not responsible for the harm from the accident, even though his activity level should have been zero.

[64] The same general point applies when enterprises make frequency-level decisions. Frequency decisions by enterprises need not be a general concern of the law because market forces generally induce enterprises to make reasonable frequency-level decisions. Why, for example, would an enterprise send out trucks with unreasonable frequency? An enterprise generally has nothing to gain by overusing the transportation infrastructure because using the transportation system costs money and the enterprise will normally want to avoid that cost if the expense yields no offsetting benefit. Moreover, in these special instances in which markets fail, the law can easily identify when an enterprise has a motive to increase the frequency of its activity beyond socially appropriate levels.

There are two barriers to such a theory. The first, practical, barrier, is that we have no way to determine when residual risk is abnormally high and therefore no theory that would keep strict liability from supplanting the negligence regime. The second barrier is normative: A defendant ought not be responsible for residual risks.

8.4.1. *Measuring Residual Risk*

As to the practical barrier, we have no test for identifying the amount of residual risk and no theory as to why large amounts of residual risk ought to be the source of liability while lesser amounts of residual risk ought not.[65] The problem of identifying the level of residual risk is apparent from the negligence standard. The negligence standard revolves around eliminating the unreasonable risk of an activity. The standard is geared toward determining when the defendant should have reduced the risk, but the negligence standard says nothing meaningful about the residual risk that is left over once the unreasonable risk is eliminated (except that the victim should bear it). Indeed, we have no independent concept or test that would help us determine the amount of residual or reasonable risk.

It is sometimes thought that the dangerousness of an activity can be used as a proxy for determining the amount of residual risk, but that is wrong. As is well-known, the negligence standard automatically adjusts as the dangerousness of the activity increases. The more dangerous an activity, the greater the precautions an actor must take and the lower the residual risk. Accordingly, as the dangerousness of the activity increases, the space for strict liability decreases,[66]

---

[65] It is possible to argue that residual risk is related to the technology of precautions: that when an activity is new, the technology of precautions is likely to be underdeveloped, and that we can identify large amounts of residual risk by identifying the underdeveloped nature of the precautions provided by existing technology. Under this view, strict liability would hasten investment in the technology of new precautions and reduce residual risk to acceptable levels. Although this view of residual risk has some coherence, it is not clear by what test we would determine whether the technology of precautions is underdeveloped, for this implies knowledge about what is possible in the future. Moreover, if an actor is not actively investing in the technology of better precautions, or implementing them when they are known, it is likely that the actor would be acting unreasonably. The duty to investigate makes that clear. Finally, the notion that residual risk can be identified by evaluating the technology of precautions implies that strict liability would apply at early stages of new activities but not at later stages, which is not how strict liability is now understood.

[66] See, e.g., *Ergon, Inc. v. Amoco Oil Co.*, 966 F. Supp. 577, 583 (W.D. Tenn. 1977) (finding that the storage of gasoline requires a high degree of care); *Miller v. Civil Constructors, Inc.*, 651 N.E. 2d 239, 245 (Ill. App. Ct. 1995) (finding that the use of firearms requires a high degree of care); *Resteiner v. Sturm Ruger & Co.*, 566 N.W. 2d 53, 55 (Mich. Ct. App. 1997) (addressing a claim that the storage of firearms requires a heightened degree of care).

and this makes it impossible to associate strict liability with dangerousness alone.[67] Conversely, it is sometimes mistakenly believed that a nondangerous activity is likely to have little residual risk,[68] but, as a matter of logic, that is not true. Depending on the type of precautions that are possible, it is conceivable that an activity could have a relatively small risk of harm before reasonable precautions are taken but a high residual risk after reasonable precautions are taken. Think of a water main. There may be few precautions that can help us predict where the water main might break, and most water main breaks might cause relatively little damage. Yet, the damage from some water main breaks could be high, depending on where they occur. Little average danger implies that fewer precautions have to be taken, and that might imply that the residual risk after those precautions are taken is more than trivial. It all depends on the technology of precautions.[69]

In other words, there is no reason to think that the amount of residual risk is related to the danger the activity presents; dangerousness is a poor proxy for determining residual risk. And there is no other known test for determining which activities are associated with high residual risk and which are not.

Even if we had a test to determine the size of residual risk, we have no convincing theory for why *high* residual risk should be shifted from the victim to the injurer while *low* residual risk should not be. Of course, high residual risk is, by definition, more dangerous than low residual risk, but if the law should be troubled by high residual risk, why would the law not also be troubled by low residual risk? No theory addresses this question, for no theory posits

---

[67] See, e.g., *Ind. Inner Harbor Belt Ry. Co. v. Am. Cyanamid Co.*, 916 F. 2d 1174, 1181 (7th Cir. 1990) (refusing to apply strict liability based on the dangerousness of a chemical alone).

[68] The *Restatement Third*, § 20(g), at 287, for example, says that "The absence of a highly significant risk is one of several reasons that courts have been unwilling to impose strict liability for harms caused by leaks or ruptures in water mains: the likelihood of harm-causing incidents is not especially high, and the level of harm when there is such an incident is generally not severe." This seems to equate a low level of average dangerousness with a low level of residual harm after due care is taken.

[69] In other words, when a water main breaks, it could be that the cost of precautions is very high; after all, it is difficult to predict where and why a water main will rupture. That implies that there may be few precautions that can realistically be taken to prevent water main breaks, which indicates that the residual risk would be high. Under the "residual risk" version of strict liability, this would be a good case for strict liability, but strict liability is not generally applied in these cases (apparently because the average danger is not great). See, e.g., *John T. Arnold Assoc. v. City of Wichita*, 615 P.2d 814 (Kan. Ct. App. 1980); *Reter v. Talent Irrigation Dist.*, 482 P.2d 170 (Or. 1971) (applying the same standard to an irrigation ditch). On the other hand, in Chapter Eleven, I show the justification for imposing responsibility on waterworks for water main breaks without resorting to strict liability.

responsibility on the basis of harms alone[70] and thus none posits responsibility on the basis of residual harms.

In this respect, strict liability cannot be justified as an extension of the doctrine of *res ipsa loquitur*. Rather than being complementary concepts, as is sometimes assumed, strict liability and *res ipsa loquitur* occupy separate domains. *Res ipsa loquitur* is relevant where the residual risk is small – that is, where due care eliminates most of the risk. Otherwise, it would be impossible to say that the accident is "of a kind which ordinarily does not occur in the absence of negligence."[71] But strict liability is thought to apply when there is a large residual risk, and that implies that the harm could have occurred even after due care has been taken. So *res ipsa loquitur* applies precisely in those cases in which residual risks are not high, while strict liability applies when residual risks *are* high.

8.4.2. Responsibility for Residual Risk

Even aside from the problem of measuring and evaluating residual risks, strict liability is inconsistent with the requirements of social cohesion because it makes an actor responsible for risks over which the actor has no effective or socially valued control. Once we determine that an actor has made reasonable due care and activity-level decisions, there is no warrant for requiring the actor to further consider the well-being of another because the well-being of another is not subject to the actor's agency.

As we saw earlier, fault-based theories, whether from the corrective justice or economic viewpoint, emphasize that legal and moral responsibility must be centered on the decision making autonomy and agency exercised by the

---

[70] The *Restatement (Second) of Torts* adopted the notion that recovery in private nuisance could be justified if "severe" harm is "greater than the other should be required to bear without compensation." *Restatement Second* § 829A cmt. a (1965) (stating that "[t]he rule stated in this Section applies to conduct that results in a private nuisance, as defined in § 821D"). This appears to be a theory of harms, but, as the *Restatement Third* says, this standard has "not been helpfully clarified by any large number of subsequent judicial opinions." *Restatement Third* § 20(c), at 282. The law could make responsibility depend on the substantiality of the harm that occurs, rather than on the unreasonableness of the harm, but if it did it would have to rework the negligence standard itself. Likewise, it is sometimes assumed that Judge Reid's concurring opinion in *Bolton v. Stone*, [1951] A.C. 850, 864–8 (H.L.) (U.K.), endorses a test that makes responsibility flow for imposing substantial expected harms, without regard to the cost of precautions for avoiding those harms. As explained in the text, however, *Bolton v. Stone* dealt with the substantiality of the harm at that location, and thus implicated only the reasonableness of location decisions.

[71] Dan B. Dobbs, THE LAW OF TORTS 371, West Hornbook Series (2000). This is the traditional restatement formulation from the RESTATEMENT (SECOND) OF TORTS § 328D (1965).

defendant. This focus on decision making as the source of moral and legal responsibility defines both when responsibility should be found and when it should be withheld. Just as there are positive reasons for not imposing liability on a person who has acted reasonably in terms of his quality of care, there are positive reasons for not imposing liability on a person who has made reasonable decisions about the frequency, location, method, or timing of activity. Imposing liability in these circumstances has no positive impact on human behavior; it can only induce people to refuse to undertake activities that benefit society. And it makes a person responsible for conditions over which the person cannot exercise effective moral agency.

Core to this understanding is the notion that imposing liability is unjust if an actor has had no opportunity to make a different decision that would help the victim. From the corrective justice standpoint, imposing liability in this circumstance would deny the agency of the defendant. Here, as we saw in discussing duty and proximate cause, the corrective justice scholars join Oliver Wendell Holmes, who noted that the only possible purpose of introducing this moral element (the actor's choice) is "to make the power of avoiding the evil complained of a condition of liability."[72] Weinrib echoes this in Kantian terms: "The injurer can be liable only for action that flows from the capacity for purposiveness. Such action characterizes the injurer's status as an agent, and differentiates the injurer from an irresponsible force of nature.... An agent, therefore, ought not to be held liable for being active."[73]

A central insight of the economic approach to torts – fully consistent with the corrective justice insight just described – is that it is impossible to force people to make more than reasonable decisions. The law can make people pay for harms, but it cannot, through compensatory damages, make them change the way they exercise their choice in order to be more than reasonable. The rule of strict liability internalizes the cost of harm and imposes a tax on activity, but it does not induce anyone to exercise more care than is reasonable

---

[72] Holmes, THE COMMON LAW at 95.

[73] Weinrib, *Private Law*, at 181–3; see also Alan Brudner, THE UNITY OF THE COMMON LAW 190 (1995); Arthur Ripstein, EQUALITY, RESPONSIBILITY, AND LUCK 50–1, Cambridge University Press (1999). For an argument that human agency supports the imposition of strict liability, see John Gardner, *Obligations and Outcomes in the Law of Torts*, in RELATING TO RESPONSIBILITY 111, 113 (Peter Cane & John Gardner eds., 2001). Ultimately, an appeal to human agency to determine whether strict liability should be preferred to negligence liability begs the question of which aspects of human agency ought to be the source of responsibility. After all, the decision to go for a drive is an act of human agency, as is the decision to drive recklessly, and there is no *a priori* reason to believe that one act of human agency ought to be the source of responsibility and the other not. My proposal – to focus on the aspect of human agency that is unreasonable in order to assign responsibility – honors the concept of human agency, but avoids the question-begging.

in the circumstances. It is always cheaper to pay the judgment rather than to change the reasonable decisions that have been made – because once a reasonable decision is made the expected harm is less than the cost of more precautions. To penalize the reasonable act runs the risk of losing the benefits of action without reducing the costs of the action.[74]

These two schools of thought point in the same direction. It is morally unwise to impose liability when a person has made reasonable choices and impossible practically to induce more than reasonable care by imposing compensatory liability.[75] The object of private law is human behavior, and when we cannot trace harm to human behavior, any imposition of liability would make humans responsible for risk that amounts to forces of nature. While there may be good reasons to relieve the victim of the burdens of harm from such forces, there is no warrant to make another individual responsible for those forces simply because the other set them in motion – unless setting them in motion in and of itself is faulty. Fault as we understand it in the reasonableness standard is the only relevant moral and practical measure of individual and organizational responsibility

8.5. CONCLUSION

Because strict liability offers an appealing normative alternative to negligence liability, theorists have spent a great deal of time discussing the relative merits of the two regimes. But to justify the mixed system of strict and negligence liability that we are thought to have, we also need a theory to explain how the relative merits of each regime relate to the characteristics of various activities and identify those activities to which each regime would apply. We have no such theory, for the only theory that relates responsibility to the dangerousness of an activity is the negligence regime, which automatically adjusts to the danger of the activity. We have no theory or justification that would sustain our present mixed system of responsibility.

---

[74] Oliver Wendell Holmes expressed this thought as well: "[T]he public generally profits by individual activity. As action cannot be avoided, and tends to the public good, there is obviously no policy in throwing the hazard of what is at once desirable and inevitable upon the actor." Holmes, THE COMMON LAW at 95.

[75] In terms that are sometimes used, imposing liability on a person who has made reasonable due care and activity-based decisions is like a tax. See, e.g., Hylton, *Theory & Restatement*, at 1417 (arguing that liability for unreasonable decisions is not a tax, impliedly accepting the notion that liability on any other basis is a tax). The relevance of this is that a liability rule that functions as a redistributive tax would require a different kind of justification than a liability rule that is imposed because of fault.

Fortunately, such a theory is not needed. The negligence regime is both flexible enough in its evidentiary and burden-of-proof requirements and expansive enough in its concept of other-regarding responsibility to impose on activities a full range of reasonable decision making. Under the theory presented here, all of an actor's decisions can be examined under the negligence concept to ensure that they appropriately account for the ways in which risks might ripen into harm, making sure that the actor makes reasonable decisions about due care and about where, when, how, and how often they undertake their activities. This approach to responsibility has two great advantages over the mixed system that we are thought to have. First, it allows courts to look directly at the kinds of decisions people make to determine whether they are reasonable, and therefore invites a more precise examination of the justification for calling a decision unreasonable. As just one example, it will avoid the mistaken belief that decisions about how frequently to drive ought to be a general source of responsibility, even though people normally make such decisions without expecting the risks of more frequent driving to be relevant to their decision. Second, it will avoid holding people responsible for matters over which they have no control, preserving valuable activities that pose no more than reasonable risks and reflecting a concept of responsibility that centers on the human attribute of reasoning toward a just behavioral rule.

The next three chapters elaborate on the nature of fault-based liability as an alternative to so-called strict liability. In the next chapter, I show that because of special circumstances, the *Vincent* case ought to be understood as fault-based liability. In Chapter Ten, I show how product liability law has expanded the burdens of responsibility under the negligence regime to include robust obligations to investigate, design, and warn. And in Chapter Eleven, I show how the fault-based conception of *Vincent* allows us to identify a narrow niche of enterprise liability within the negligence regime.

9   Using Another's Property

A litmus test for any theory of tort law is the *Vincent* case,[1] which I take up now. The central problem is to find a justification for the outcome in *Vincent* that does not either (1) undercut a general theory of tort law by constituting a special exception to a general theory of responsibility or (2) rely on a conclusory, nonspecified assignment of rights. *Vincent* also tests the strict liability concept because *Vincent* is uniformly understood to be about liability without fault. In this chapter, I present and defend a different view of *Vincent*. I claim that justificational analysis allows us to understand *Vincent* in a detailed and precise way that integrates it with the general responsibility of one person for the well-being of another. Under this view, *Vincent* emerges as a case in which the failure to repair the damage *was* faulty even though the conduct that caused the damage was not faulty. Once we understand fault as inappropriate regard for the well-being of others, we can explain why sometimes even reasonable conduct can be faulty.

9.1. THE JUSTIFICATIONAL PROBLEMS OF *VINCENT*

In *Vincent*, the defendant ship owner made the reasonable decision to lash his ship to a dock during a storm, knowingly inflicting harm to the dock in order to avoid the greater harm if the ship had left the dock. Although the choice minimized the social harm from the storm – and was therefore a reasonable decision – the ship owner was required to pay the dock owner for damage to the dock, an apparent instance of liability without fault. Why did the court require the defendant to pay for the use of the plaintiff's property when the defendant acted reasonably? It is conventionally accepted that this is an instance of liability without fault, and therefore an example of some form

[1]   *Vincent v. Lake Erie Transportation Co.*, 109 Minn. 456, (1910).

of strict liability, but the justification for this form of liability without fault is not clear.

The justificational challenges of *Vincent* were laid bare in a penetrating article by Robert Sugarman, who found the then existing *Vincent* scholarship lacking in justificational analysis.[2] The case presents a puzzle. The defendant was privileged to stay at the dock and the defendant's conduct was entirely reasonable.[3] "[T]he character of the storm"[4] was such that it would have been unreasonable to leave the dock or to have permitted the ship to drift away. Moreover, "the record of the case fully sustains the contention of the [defendant] that, in holding the vessel fast to the dock, those in charge of her exercised good judgment and prudent seamanship."[5] It would have been unreasonable to leave the dock, and remaining at the dock was both reasonable and reasonably done. The defendant was in the right location[6] doing the right thing[7] (albeit, given the storm, at an inopportune time). Neither the dock owner nor the ship owner was at fault for causing the damage to the dock. Neither party could have reasonably anticipated the storm and neither party could have taken any action to reasonably reduce the damage that occurred when the storm arose at the same time that the ship was at the dock. The dock owner was not charged with having built a dock that was unreasonably flimsy and the ship owner was not charged with failing to do something that could have minimized damage to the dock or to its ship.

Yet despite the defendant's reasonable conduct and the privilege to stay at the dock, the defendant was liable for the damages its ship inflicted on the dock. Liability was imposed without negligent conduct.

[2]   Stephen D. Sugarman, "The 'Necessity' Defense and the Failure of Tort Theory: The Case Against Strict Liability for Damages Caused While Exercising Self-Help in an Emergency," *Issues in Legal Scholarship*, Vincent v. Lake Erie Transportation Co. *and the Doctrine of Necessity* (2005): Article 1. Available at http://www.bepress.com/ils/iss7/art1 (Sugarman, *Tort Theory Failure*).

[3]   *Ploof v. Putnam*, 71 A. 188 (1908).

[4]   124 N.W. at 223.

[5]   *Id.*

[6]   The reference to the location of the activity reflects the now-accepted notion, discussed in Chapter Eight, that courts should use the strict liability standard when the plaintiff is questioning the location of the defendant's activity rather than the quality of defendant's conduct. See, e.g., Steven Shavell, Foundations of Economic Analysis of Law 193–9 Harvard University Press (2004). In *Vincent* there was nothing unreasonable about the location of defendant's activity – indeed, the unloading was taking place pursuant to contract and therefore (presumptively) at an efficient and reasonable location for that activity. This suggests that a standard justification for applying the strict liability standard would not apply.

[7]   The case does not suggest that the defendant could (or should) have foreseen the approaching storm and taken steps to avoid having to damage either the ship or the dock. It was not negligent for unloading when it did.

Consider the nature of the problem presented by *Vincent*. Though the ship owner made a deliberate choice to allow the harm to the dock,[8] the predicament resulted not from human decision making, but from an act of nature. The case raises the issue of which party – the dock owner or the ship owner – should bear the losses that arise from acts of nature when neither actor contributes in an unreasonable way to those losses. To put the matter another way, the case deals with allocating the losses from the joint bad luck of the dock owner and the ship owner.[9] Either the dock owner or the ship owner must bear the loss, and the allocation of the loss to one party is a benefit (in not having to absorb the loss) of the same amount to the other party. The difference could be shared, of course, but every dollar of loss attributed to one party represents an equal benefit to the other party. Moreover, we want the ship owner to stay at the dock, for that imposes the fewest costs on society. Accordingly, we would not want the court to intervene in any way that would inhibit the ship owner from staying at the dock and minimizing costs.

The *Vincent* problem has not yet been justified under an economic approach to tort law. This is not a case where the obligation to compensate the dock owner is designed to minimize the social costs of the activity (at least not directly), for the ship owner minimized the social cost by acting reasonably and staying at the dock. Nor does focusing on production incentives justify one outcome over another. To be sure, as Landes and Posner argue, if the loss is allowed to fall on the dock owner, there may be less investment in docks.[10] However, as Robert Sugarman has countered, if the loss is shifted to the ship owner, there may be less investment in shipping.[11] There is no a priori incentive basis for believing that a loss of investment incentive in docks is more or less advantageous than a loss of investment incentive in ships, and therefore no way of favoring one outcome over another.[12] The allocation of the loss

---

[8] It is accurate to point out that the ship owner made a choice in the sense of having made a deliberate decision. Glanville Williams, *The Defense of Necessity*, 6 Curr. Legal Prob. 216 (1953). But here the English language defeats us. The ship owner did not choose to put himself in the position where he would have to choose the lesser of two damaging outcomes. What made it necessary to choose, and thereby created the necessity behind the doctrine of necessity, was beyond any possible choice by the ship owner – namely, a powerful and unexpected storm.

[9] The fact that the origin of the harm in this case was bad luck does not eliminate the need for the court to consider whether it should intervene. Nor does it take away the need to understand the justificatory basis for either intervention or nonintervention. To avoid a decision about whether to reallocate the loss is to make a decision that the loss should lie where it falls, which is, of course, an intervention decision.

[10] William M. Landes & Richard A. Posner, The Economic Structure of Tort Law 128, Harvard University Press (1987).

[11] Sugarman, *Tort Theory Failure*, at 29.

[12] Other considerations that are normally associated with efficiency analysis are also inapplicable in *Vincent*. Awarding the rights to avoid the damage to the dock to one party rather

will surely influence the allocation of resources, but the efficient allocation of resources cannot help us determine how to allocate the loss. Rather, we determine what allocation of resources we favor (and therefore which allocation we will call efficient) by determining where the loss *should* fall.[13]

Nonefficiency, distributive methods of allocating losses are also not helpful. The arguments that losses should be allocated to those who can best insure against the risk,[14] or to those who can spread the losses among many customers or shareholders,[15] do not explain the outcome in *Vincent*. The loss distribution rationales might be applied to either the dock owner or the ship owner; there is no a priori distributional reason to prefer ship owners to dock owners as the entity that can redistribute the loss.[16] Under any loss distribution rationale, sometimes the best distributional agent will be the ship owner and at other times the dock owner, depending on the comparative ability of each to pass the costs on.

Finally, as Professor Sugarman argues, we cannot justify a particular loss allocation by appealing to some preexisting right to be free from interference. True, it was the property of the dock owner that was harmed, but the ship had

> than the other will not reduce transaction costs or facilitate bargaining between the parties over the rights. Once the storm came up, bargaining was impossible because decisions had to be made without the possibility of a face-to-face meeting and because the emergency conditions would have skewed the bargaining positions of the parties. Although the parties were in a bargaining relationship when the captain of the ship asked to use the dock space, the dock owner and ship owner had neither the incentive nor the ability to bargain over the risks from a storm. The possibility of a storm was foreseeable, but it is unlikely that the parties had sufficient incentive to address that risk because the nature and effect of the storm was not foreseeable. Remembering that the ship owner had the right to stay at the dock in the event of an emergency, we can approach this case by asking what terms the parties would have bargained for if they had been able to agree on the nature of the risk that they faced. That approach, however, provides a framework for thinking about the problem but does not help us decide what terms the parties would have agreed to. The best we can do is to find a justificatory basis for determining who *should* bear the risk of the storm's damage to the dock and then use that outcome to understand how to define the default term that we think parties would have reached had they reasonably bargained over the risk.

[13] This is not to deny that economic analysis is helpful in understanding the *Vincent* problem. Below I show how the law allocates the loss in order to influence the decisions that the ship's captain must make aligning those decisions with the socially appropriate outcome. This might be thought of as a kind of efficiency function (minimizing social harm given the constraints on conscripting another's labor), but this does not seek to influence the allocation of investment resources to either docks or ships.

[14] Dale Broeder, *Torts and Just Compensation: Some Personal Reflections*, 17 HAST L. J. 217, 231 (1965).

[15] Albert Ehrenzweig, *Negligence Without Fault*, 54 CALIF. L. REV. 1422, 1459 (1996).

[16] Sugarman. *Tort Theory Failure*, at 24–5. Apparently, Broeder recognized the defect in his own theory (*id.* at 25) while Morris had previously disputed the loss spreading argument as applied to *Vincent* (*id.* at 23).

a privilege to be at the dock (in order to avoid the greater harm to the ship), so under emergency conditions does the property belong to the ship or to the dock owner? And property does not exist with predefined content. Its content is defined by analyzing where the burdens and benefits of ownership should fall.[17] Further, it is well enough to believe that justice or fairness require the ship owner to compensate the dock owner, but believing is not understanding.[18] Without an understanding of the concept of fairness or justice that is being invoked, it is impossible to understand the meaning of *Vincent*. Put more broadly, we cannot decide the issue by appealing to some notion of property, fairness, right, wrong, or unjust enrichment without specifying what those terms mean – that is, without identifying the normative content of the notion that we invoke.

9.2. RECENT JUSTIFICATIONAL ANALYSIS

None of the subsequent analysis generated by Sugarman's challenge for greater justification of *Vincent* seems to be adequate.

Professor Keating's justification rests on the fact that the storm threatened disproportionate damage to the ship, and argues that prospective damage can be allocated to the ship owner and the dock owner on the basis of preexisting

---

[17] For a cogent development of this point for students in the context of *Vincent*, see Kenneth Abraham, THE FORMS AND FUNCTIONS OF TORT LAW, 2d ed. 39–41, Foundation Press (2002).

[18] Consider Jules Coleman's explanation: Although the dock owner had a contractual right to cast the ship off, "it would have been wrongful for him to do what he had a right to do.... The fact that it would have been wrong of the dock owner to exclude the ship does not extinguish the right [of the dock owner] or the claims to which the right gives rise. Thus by keeping the ship moored to the dock, the ship's captain infringes the dock owner's right, and commits, in that sense, a wrong." Jules Coleman, RISKS AND WRONGS 372, Cambridge University Press (1992). But what kind of a right is it that cannot be exercised and why does the privilege to stay at the dock not take away the right? In EQUALITY, RESPONSIBILITY AND THE LAW 118, Cambridge University Press (1999). Arthur Ripstein correctly says that the ship owner should not be allowed "to displace risks they face onto others" but does not explain why, instead supporting this proposition with the statement that "people should bear the costs of their choices rather than displacing them to others" (which, of course, is not consistent with the negligence regime, where the costs of an activity *are* displaced to others). He says, also, that in borrowing the property, the ship owner should gain no advantage that he would not have had if he had owned the dock. If he owned the dock, he would have suffered the loss to the dock and he should not be able to gain just because somebody else owned the dock (*id.* at 120). Then, in order to prove that necessity is a basis of liability (a nice way to look at the case), he reasons only by analogy to the common sense notion that people who mistakenly pick up another's similar raincoat or are given the wrong clothes at the cleaner normally rectify the error. He concludes by saying that one should not be able to transfer one's ill fortune or mistake to another. This is an incomplete explanation because, in case of an epileptic seizure, one is allowed to transfer one's ill fortune to another.

notions of property – that is, on the basis of who owned what. He continues: "But it is unfair – or unreasonable – for the ship owners to save its own at
the dock owner's expense. That would mismatch burdens and benefits."[19] This
concept of fairness "boils down to proportionality of burden and benefit, an
idea at least as old as Aristotle."[20]

This appeal to fairness and the proportionality principle is conclusory, not
revelatory. It tells us little about the content of this concept of fairness, except
that proportionality counts. But this tells us little about the proportionality principle, especially about how to identify the burdens and benefits that
matter or how to make sure that the burdens and benefits are proportional.
Keating's later attempt to justify the benefits principle in light of the seemingly
contrary result in the negligence regime (if the defendant acts reasonably, the
defendant gets the benefits and the victim gets the burdens)[21] also lacks justificatory appeal. His argument is that sometimes strict liability applies (in which
case the result is "justified" by the benefits principle) and sometimes the negligence regime applies (in which case the result contradicts, seemingly, the benefits principle). But this does not tell us why the benefits principle sometimes
applies and why it sometimes does not apply, which is to admit that we have
no justificatory understanding of the benefits principle.

None of this, of course, says that Keating is wrong. It says only that his conclusions are not falsifiable because we do not know the basis on which they
are made. They are conclusions without content, and it is the content that
matters for the purpose of analysis. We need not disprove, or disapprove of, the
conclusions to point out that they lack justificatory content.[22] The justificatory

---

[19]   Gregory C. Keating, "Property Rights and Tortious Wrong, in Vincent v. Lake Erie," *Issues
      in Legal Scholarship*, Vincent v. Lake Erie Transportation Co. *and the Doctrine of Necessity*
      (2005) art. 6. Available at http://www.bepress.com/ils/iss7/art6.
[20]   *Id.* at 32. Keating later says: "An ideal of fairness provides the moral basis for this judgment of
      wrongfulness. One aspect of this ideal is captured by the idea of unjust enrichment: Because
      the preexisting baseline of legal entitlement had pinned the lion's share of risk of loss from
      the storm on the ship, it is unjust for the ship to gain by transferring that risk to and impover-
      ishing the dock owner." *Id.* at 53.
[21]   *Id.* at 54–5.
[22]   After articulating his fairness/proportionality approach, Keating immediately interprets it in
      terms of legal doctrine, illustrating another analytical approach that lacks justificatory force.
      Keating shows how the fairness/proportionality approach can be used to understand tradi-
      tional doctrines of unjust enrichment, strict liability (in the form of both *Rylands v. Fletcher*
      and, nuisance doctrine), and the just compensation clause. *Id.* at 32–52. These applications
      appear to bolster the justificatory appeal of his theory. But none of this doctrinal discussion
      explains the content of the fairness/proportionality principle. The discussion simply asserts
      that the results in other cases are consistent with the fairness/proportionality principle, not
      that the content of the fairness/justificatory principle leads to the results in those cases.
      Consistency with the fairness/proportionality principle does not help us understand what the
      principle is or how to apply it.

enterprise demands that we get behind the conclusion to understand the basis on which it is made.

Professor Grodley relies on unjust enrichment to explain *Vincent*,[23] and makes a significant contribution to legal theory by showing how unjust enrichment fits within a scheme that accommodates both tort and contract, going back to the late scholastics.[24] But his analysis assumes the answer to the question he is asking by assuming the plaintiff's exclusive right to the property. Given this assumption, it is unjust that "[r]esources, from which one party had the exclusive right to benefit, had been used to confer on someone else the very benefit to which the first party had the exclusive right."[25] He does not, however, identify the scope of this exclusive right, which is the very issue that the court must decide in *Vincent*. Professor Grodley gets his conclusion only if property rights are thought to be self-defining or self-evident, but the privilege of the ship to stay at the dock indicates otherwise.

Professor Klar adopts the same approach, but he uses the doctrine of trespass rather than unjust enrichment.[26] His justification depends on the following principle: "When defendant directly and deliberately interferes with a plaintiff's right to the security of persons or to the exclusive possession of land or chattels, then the defendant has committed a trespass."[27] Like Professor Grodley's appeal to the exclusive right in property, Professor Klar's appeal to the right to exclusive possession assumes the very issue to be decided, and therefore fails as a justification. He also makes the same argument in terms of personal autonomy,[28] which, from a justificational standpoint, would require a specification of the scope of personal autonomy.

For his part, Professor Geistfeld relies on a theory of responsibility that assigns responsibility to those who make choices that have bad outcomes.[29] The problem with this theory is its use as a justification in the context of *Vincent*. True, the ship owner chose to stay at the dock and the bad outcome (to the dock owner) would not have occurred but for that choice. But this

---

[23] James Grodley, "Damages, Under the Necessity Doctrine," *Issues in Legal Scholarship, Vincent v. Lake Erie Transportation Co. and The Doctrine of Necessity* (2005): art.2. Available at http://www.bepress.com/ils/iss7/art2.

[24] *Id.* at 15.

[25] *Id.* at 22.

[26] Lewis N. Klar, "The Defense of Private Necessity in Canadian Tort Law," *Issues in Legal Scholarship, Vincent v. Lake Erie Transportation Co. and The Doctrine of Necessity* (2005): art.3. Available at http://www.bepress.com/ils/iss7/art3.

[27] *Id.* at 20.

[28] *Id.* at 21.

[29] Mark A. Geistfeld, "Necessity and the Logic of Strict Liability," *Issues in Legal Scholarship, Vincent v. Lake Erie Transportation Co. and the Doctrine of Necessity* (2005): art. 5. Available at http://www.bepress.com/ils/iss7/art5.

was a choice the ship owner was privileged to make, so it is hard to see how that choice can be the source of responsibility. Moreover, it is not clear that the decision can even be considered a "choice" in a sense that is relevant to responsibility. The privilege to stay at the dock reflected that, given the storm and potential damage in the harbor or lake, the ship owner really had no choice, or at least no choice that society would want to endorse. Outcome responsibility in *Vincent* is clearly in the hands of an act of nature – the force that robbed both the dock owner and the ship owner of good choices. Choice has a great deal to do with responsibility (as I acknowledge throughout this book), but it cannot be the choice to stay at the dock that is the source of responsibility to pay for the dock's damage.

If we want to take seriously Professor Sugarman's challenge to explain the outcome in *Vincent*, we must understand *Vincent*'s outcome in terms of a justification that explains how the law allocates unavoidable losses that result from human decision making. I suggest that we view *Vincent* as resting on the fault principle derived from the theory of other-regarding behavior.

9.3. THE OBLIGATION OF THE OTHER-REGARDING ACTOR TO COMPENSATE

My argument that *Vincent* is a fault-based decision is straightforward. To be sure, the defendant's decision to stay at the dock was reasonable, and therefore unobjectionable. The decision correctly minimized the damage from the storm. From a traditional negligence perspective, defendant minimized dead-weight losses to society by choosing the least costly way of preventing harm. For this reason, the defendant ship owner was not negligent in its conduct. But as Robert Keeton and others have emphasized, the privileged decision to stay at the dock was not the only decision the ship owner made.[30] The failure to pay reparations was an independent decision. If the failure to pay reparations was faulty, then the privilege to stay at the dock was, as Keeton surmised, a conditional one, and the breach of that condition by failing to pay reparations would be an independent basis for making the ship owner responsible for the harm. I complete Professor Keeton's theory by specifying what his theory

---

[30] Robert Keeton, *Conditional Fault in the Law of Torts*, 72 HARV. L. REV. 401 (199). Dan B. Dobbs, THE LAW OF TORTS 249, West Hornbook Series (2000); Francis Bohlen, *Incomplete Privileges to Inflict Intentional Invasions of Interests of Property and Personality*, 39 HARV. L. REV. 307 (1926). Conditional fault and incomplete privilege suggest that the privilege to stay at the dock is not complete until the defendant pays for the use of the dock. These notions are descriptively accurate but do not tell us why the privilege is conditional or incomplete. That explanation is given in this chapter.

lacks – a justification for making the reasonable conduct conditioned on pay-ing reparations when in other cases the privilege to impose harm by reason-able conduct is not conditioned on paying reparations.

If we understand other-regarding behavior to be the core element of the fault principle, we can understand why *Vincent* calls the failure to repair the dock faulty behavior. We saw in Chapter Seven, under proximate cause doctrine, that an unreasonable actor will not be responsible for harm if the behavior does not show the actor, in those circumstances, to be inappropri-ately other-regarding. The *Vincent* situation involves the converse proposition. Sometimes, even a reasonably behaving actor is not thinking in an appropriate way about the well-being of the victim if the actor does not compensate the victim. Why would that be?

Normally, of course, if the defendant behaves reasonably, we conclude that because the defendant has thought appropriately about the well-being of the victim the defendant may refuse to repair the victim's harm. If the defen-dant acts reasonably, the victim has no further claim against the defendant for repair and the defendant's reasonable decision justifies the defendant's deci-sion to refuse to repair the damage. But *Vincent* is not the usual negligence case. The decision to inflict harm to the dock was linked in a unique way to the decision to refuse to repair the dock. The damage to the dock was the precaution that a reasonable person would take in order to avoid the greater expected harm from leaving the dock.[31] The burden of preventing the harm from the storm *was* the damage inflicted on the dock, and the damage to the dock was the burden that society wants people to assume in order to be called reasonable. The defendant's decision to refuse to repair was therefore a state-ment that when deciding to stay at the dock the ship owner need not pay for the cost of reasonable precautions.

In other words, *Vincent* inverted the usual situation. In the usual negligence case, an actor is expected to invest *her own* resources (effort, time, or money) in reasonable precautions in order to prevent harm to *others*. In *Vincent* the actor is allowed to impose the cost of reasonable precautions on *another* (by choos-ing to stay at the dock) in order to avoid harm to herself. But this reversal of the usual case, it turns out, does not change how we think about who should bear the cost of precautions. In the standard negligence case, the defendant has a means of preventing expected harm and the negligence concept imposes a duty on the defendant to repair the harm if the defendant did not bear the cost of reasonable precautions. *Vincent* raised the same issue, but with a twist. In *Vincent*, the precaution that would prevent the harm to the ship was to impose

---

[31] One of my students, David Ricco, helped me to crystallize this point.

a cost on the dock owner (at least initially), and the issue is whether that cost (the cost of taking reasonable precautions) should lie where it falls or whether it should be internalized into the activity of shipping. Should the dock owner be required to pay for the cost of reasonable precautions (by absorbing the loss to the dock), or should the cost of reasonable precautions be transferred to the person who is responsible for preventing the harm and who benefits from the reasonable precautions?

In a way, the negligence principle already answers the question: An actor is required to pay for the cost of precautions up to the amount of the expected harm. In the terms used in this book, the projects and preferences of the ship owner should bear the reasonable burdens of preventing harm to the dock owner's projects and preferences. The issue can be put more prosaically: If I borrow my neighbor's garden hose in order to put out a fire at my house, should I not also expect to pay for any damage to the garden hose? The common sense answer seems clear. A reasonable actor borrowing another's property to save his own will, having appropriate regard for the well-being of the other, borrow the property with the implicit expectation of returning it intact. If something happens to the property, the actor will repair it. The refusal to repair shows an inappropriate regard for the other's well-being.

What analysis justifies this intuition?

In *Vincent*, the court wanted to match burdens with benefits in a way that all negligence cases do.[32] In the ordinary negligence case, the law imposes the cost of precautions on the actor who creates or has dominion over the risk because that actor benefits from taking the precautions. The "benefit" is avoiding legal liability for acting unreasonably. Actors can either invest in reasonable care or risk paying damages. Investing in reasonable care benefits the actor by avoiding the greater loss of paying for the harm caused by the activity. Similarly, *Vincent* allocated the cost of precautions to the ship owner because, just as is true in any negligence case, the owner of the ship benefited from the precautions by not having to pay for the harm if the precautions had not been taken. In the normal negligence case, the defendant has a choice between

---

[32] Although theorists have long understood that the ship owner is required to pay the dock owner because the ship owner benefitted from staying at the dock, the theory of other-regarding behavior shows that this understanding is an application of the benefits theory underlying general negligence law. This is the law's embodiment of a concept of fairness – the proportionality of burdens and benefits that is "at least as old as Aristotle." Gregory C. Keating, *Property Right and Tortious Wrong in* Vincent v. Lake Erie 31, Berkeley Electronic Press (Oct. 2005). Available at http://bepress.com/ils/iss7/art6. The law makes the obligation to invest in reasonable precautions a prerequisite for avoiding liability (the fairness of the negligence rule) in order to match the costs and benefits of the chosen activity (the proportionality principle).

paying for the expected harm by repairing the victim's loss or by paying to avoid that loss. In *Vincent*, the defendant had to choose between absorbing the damage to its ship or paying for the precautions necessary to avoid those damages. The benefit theory applicable to negligence cases says that to reap the benefit of avoiding damages, reasonable people should invest in reasonable precautions the cost to the dock, and that is what *Vincent* required.

The benefit theory has an instrumental goal. By requiring the ship owner to pay the cost of precautions, the law matches costs and benefits for an actor so that the actor has before it the information needed to make a socially appropriate decision.[33] In the usual negligence case, the law asks the actor to integrate the expected harm to others into the actor's projects and preferences when making decisions, which ensures that the actor matches benefits and burdens from a social perspective. Matching burdens and benefits is equally important when the actor imposes the costs of precautions on another. *Vincent* internalizes the cost of precautions because the ship owner has superior access to information that is necessary to make a socially useful decision with a minimum of intrusion by the courts; internalizing the cost gives the party with access to the best information the incentive to act on the basis of that information.[34]

If both parties had perfect information, it would not matter who decided whether the ship could stay at the dock. Under *Vincent*, the ship owner is privileged to stay at the dock but pays for damage to the dock, so the ship owner stays at the dock if the expected damage from doing so is less than the expected damage to the ship. Alternatively, the legal system could give the dock owner the right to cast off the ship, provided only that the dock owner would compensate the ship owner if the expected damages to the dock were less than the expected damage to the ship. If the expected damage to the dock was $500 and the expected damage to the ship was $501, the dock owner would not cast off the ship (for it would then have a loss of $1). But it would cast off the ship if the expected loss to the ship were less than $500 (for then it would save money by avoiding damage to the dock). Under either legal regime, if there is perfect information, we can set up the legal system so that either decision maker gets the socially appropriate result and minimizes the sum of the costs to the dock and the ship.

But the dock owner and the ship owner do not have symmetrical access to the information needed to make a decision. Because we are asking the parties

---

[33] George Fletcher may have had a similar rationale in mind when he proposed a corrective justice interpretation of *Vincent* that centered on the dominance of the ship owner over the dock owner, a dominance given by law. George Fletcher, *Corrective Justice for Moderns*, 106 HARV. L. REV. 1658, 1676 (1993).

[34] This line of thought is suggested in Abraham, FORMS AND FUNCTIONS OF TORT LAW at 402.

to make the decision based on predicted losses, we want to put the decision in the hands of the party with the best access to information and the best incentive to interpret the probabilities accurately. The dock owner and the ship owner stand in different positions in this regard.

If the dock owner decided whether to sacrifice the ship or the dock, two types of potential errors could influence the decision. First, because the dock owner lacks shipping experience, the dock owner has a poor basis for predicting the expected loss to the ship in the storm on open waters. Second, for the dock owner, the damage to the dock is immediate and emotional, making it likely that the dock owner would amplify the expected damage to the dock when making the decision between damage to the dock and damage to the ship. Although this error would be corrected by a court if the expected loss to the dock were found to be less than the loss estimated by the dock owner (and if it were less than the expected loss to the ship), such judicial intervention is a waste of resources when the decision can be put in the hands of a decision maker whose decisions are less prone to error. Both the problem of underestimating the potential risk of harm to the ship and the problem of overestimating the potential damage to the dock make the dock owner an unattractive decision maker in this instance.

By contrast, the ship owner has both better access to information and better incentives to act on the information in a socially appropriate way. First, the ship owner has experience with both ships and docks. It has not only sent ships through storms, but it has also considered how to minimize damage that ships impose on docks (because minimizing that cost reduces the cost of using the dock). This puts the ship owner in a better position than the dock owner to predict the expected losses to both the dock and the ship. Although the ship owner can be expected to overestimate the expected damage to the ship (just as the dock owner would overestimate the damage to the dock), for the ship owner, the damage to the dock is immediate and observable (whereas for the dock owner the damage to the ship is in the future and unobservable). Moreover, internalizing the dock damage to the ship owner's decision offsets that bias. The ship owner bears the cost either way and thus is not biased in interpreting the information that it has. Its decisions are therefore more dependable and less subject to reversal or challenge.

In short, the law gives the ship owner the right to decide how to minimize the costs to the ship and to the dock because the ship owner is in a better position than the dock owner to have access to the information that is needed to make a socially appropriate decision.[35] But the law requires the ship owner

---

[35]   The ship owner will not have superior information in every case, of course. We can imagine a case in which the dock owner, but not the ship owner, knows that a dangerous chemical or

to pay for the damage to the dock so that the ship owner has before it both the costs and benefits of its options. This allows private decision making to conform to socially beneficial results with a minimum of intrusion by courts, giving the ship owner's decision important presumptive legitimacy. The cost of evaluating the decision *ex post* is likely to be high, not only consuming judicial resources but also leading the court to make errors. Minimizing those costs by putting the decision in the hands of one who can make the decision with appropriate incentives is a valuable social function of the law.

Consider also the ramifications of a different outcome. *Vincent* reinforces limits on the claims that one actor can make on the project and preferences of another. If the negligence regime allowed an actor who creates a risk or benefits from taking precautions to impose the cost of precautions on others, the actor could make a claim against the projects and preferences of another. An actor who dug a hole in the sidewalk could then look to another to protect people from the risks that the actor's activity engenders, effectively conscripting the resources of another. An actor could dig a hole in the sidewalk and borrow a sawhorse from a neighbor to put over the hole to reduce the risk of someone walking into hole. If this were allowed, it would, in effect, impose a duty on the neighbor to aid the actor in protecting against risks the actor created. This would be a great incursion on the autonomy of the neighbor and on the principle that one person does not have to look out for the well-being of another unless that person is attached to the risk of harm in some significant way.[36]

expensive painting is on the dock, and therefore knows of unexpectedly high risks if the ship stays at the dock. Because the law is looking for a general approach, the best it can do is to assign decision-making authority to the party that in the majority of cases will have superior ability to make a socially appropriate decision. Moreover, tort law can adjust to cases that deviate from the expected norm. Once the decision-making rules are laid out and the decision-making authority is allocated, the parties must adjust to that allocation. In the example given, private information of the dock owner that is relevant to the ship owner's decision would impose a burden – a duty to warn – on the dock owner. The failure to reveal information that the ship owner needed to make a socially appropriate decision would relieve the ship owner of the obligation to pay for the resulting damage. *Palsgraf v. Long Island Ry. Co.* 248 N.Y. 339 (1928).

[36] Of course, *Vincent* is different from the defendant who digs a hole and relies on another person's resources to protect against the risk the hole presents. The ship owner in *Vincent* did not create the risk to his ship and is not connected to that risk in any way, except that the defendant bears the loss if the risk is not reasonably addressed. But the prior discussion of the importance of matching benefits and costs in the person who makes a decision about those benefits and costs shows the way in which *Vincent* is like the general negligence case in an analytically relevant way. Because the ship owner in *Vincent* benefits from the investment in reasonable care and must make the decision about whether to risk staying at the dock or leaving the dock, the ship owner is attached to the risk in a way that is relevant to negligence law. The risk is part of the risk of being a shipper. There is no more warrant in asking the dock

In short, *Vincent* indicates that in making the decision about whether to stay at the dock, a reasonable person would take into account the well-being of the dock owner and would implicitly agree to restore that well-being if the decision adversely affected it. Any other result would allow the decision maker to conscript the resources of the dock owner and thus to ignore the dock owner's well-being. Only by internalizing the costs of the damage to the dock can the law ensure that the decision maker takes into account the well-being of others when deciding whether to stay at the dock. The claim that one can ignore the interests of another is, by itself, unreasonable, for no reasonable person acts with disregard of the well-being of others when undertaking her own projects and preferences. In the normal negligence case, it is unreasonable to ignore the expected harm to another that could have been avoided by reasonable means, for that is tantamount to ignoring the well-being of another. In the *Vincent* case, it is unreasonable to ignore the costs of precautions, for that too would be tantamount to ignoring the well-being of another. Either way, the defendant acts unreasonably when he or she fails to invest in reasonable precautions because that is tantamount to exalting the decision maker's projects and preferences over the projects and preferences of others.[37]

9.4. CONCLUSION

This chapter has presented the argument that sometimes an actor will repair the damage done to another even if the actor has acted reasonably in inflicting the damage. On its face, this conclusion seems inconsistent with the main premise of the reasonable person standard – namely, that an actor need not repair harm to another that is reasonably inflicted. But analysis has shown that the narrow responsibility to repair reasonable decisions when an actor

> owner to contribute to the reduction of that risk than there would be if an actor were to dig a hole in a sidewalk and ask the neighbors to pay to protect against the harms that might occur from that hole.

[37] Although *Vincent* is an important application of the theory of other-regarding behavior, its scope is limited to situations in which an actor uses another's property in order to conserve her own. It is not applicable if an actor chooses to impose harm on one person in order to avoid the greater harm to another person, as where a driver must choose between hitting a boy who darts into the street or swerving and hitting a car coming the other way. If the decision is reasonable under the circumstances, no compensation is required because the actor did the best she could under the circumstances. No self-interest would influence the decision in a way that would require the costs of the decision to be internalized into the actor's decision. Nor is *Vincent* applicable when an actor is forced to shoot in self-defense, although the actor is sacrificing another's well-being to preserve her own. The justification for this result, if there is one, is that others have put the actor in a situation requiring the actor to choose between two social harms and the victim must take that into account when deciding how to approach the actor.

would otherwise impose the burden of precautions on another is subject to the same analytical framework that requires an actor to pay for the burden of protecting another in order to avoid unreasonable decisions. A single principle supports both *Vincent* and the general negligence rule – that an actor should pay for the cost of reasonable precautions that his activity imposes on society. The analysis has therefore integrated *Vincent* into a conception of fault-based liability, where the duty to repair is fully consistent with, and does not undercut, the main premise of the negligence standard.

The underlying problem, it seems, is our belief that the fault concept revolves around acting unreasonably – as in driving too fast – when in fact it revolves around a failure to take into account the well-being of another in an appropriate way. Driving unreasonably fast is one such example, but so too is borrowing another's property to save one's own without agreeing to indemnify the other if the property is damaged. By understanding fault to be the failure to consider appropriately the well-being of others, we have a single standard for evaluating human decision making in interpersonal settings.

10 Product Liability

Social Cohesion and Agency Relationships

The other-regarding behavior of product sellers has been the object of intense scrutiny for over half a century, developing product liability law into a seemingly distinct branch of tort law. Yet the product liability "revolution" has come into focus over the last couple of decades, and it appears now to be different than it initially appeared. When we reexamine developments in product liability law through justificational lenses, we understand them in a new way.

10.1. THE JUSTIFICATIONAL ERRORS

My account of product liability law emphasizes its close relationship to the negligence concept. My account is therefore a major departure from most contemporary stories of product liability. It is generally thought, for example, that "products liability law" is a unique legal regime, self-contained and separated from the negligence regime applicable to other activities. A small industry has grown up advancing this position, producing product liability casebooks, treatises, and restatements, carefully justifying the regime's individual identity and content. Often the regime is thought of as "strict products liability," although I demonstrate below that the term *strict liability* is largely a misnomer when applied to product liability law. Contemporary accounts tell a common story: The rise of the concept of privity to shield manufacturers from responsibility to indirect customers, the erosion of the privity requirement over time and its eventual destruction by Justice Cardozo in the *MacPherson* case,[1] the dissatisfaction with the negligence regime and the inadequacy of the doctrine of *res ipsa loquitur* as a standard for determining a seller's negligence, the penetrating force of Justice Traynor's concurring opinion in *Escola*,[2] where

[1] *MacPherson v. Buick Motor Co.*, 217 N.Y. 382 (N.Y. 1916).
[2] *Escola v. Coca Cola Bottling Co. of Fresno.*, 24 Cal.2d 453 (Cal. 1944) (Traynor, J., concurring).

that patron saint of product liability laid out the justification for switching from the negligence regime to a new strict liability regime, the assault on the citadel of privity by Professor Prosser,[3] the early use of strict liability as the putative basis of responsibility for product sellers in the early California cases,[4] and then (partially) in section 402A of the *Restatement Second*.[5]

But the conventional product liability story seems to be driven by the self-fulfilling belief that the new regime under construction was one of strict or enterprise liability. This belief served to distinguish product liability from activities governed by the negligence regime and also provided a basis for imposing greater responsibility on manufacturers than, say, on doctors. In this chapter, I seek to show that this conventional story lacks justificational focus. It turns on two myths that I challenge here: the myth of strict liability and the myth of a unique field called product liability. In this chapter, I seek to displace those myths by showing that: (1) the regime governing product liability is fully consistent with sound principles of responsibility under the negligence regime and (2) it is therefore not a unique regime that differentiates the responsibility of product sellers from the responsibility of service sellers or other similarly situated actors.

The conventional story is shot through with justificational challenges. Although it is common to refer to the regime governing product manufacturers as one of "strict products liability," that usage appears to be unjustified. Professor Geistfeld, for example, defines "strict products liability" as "A tort that makes a product seller of a defective product liable to a right holder for physical harms proximately caused by the defect, distinguishing it from a rule that would make a product seller absolutely liable for all injuries caused by the product."[6] But the meaning of that definition depends on the requirements for proving a defect. If, as is now broadly (but not uniformly) accepted, proving a defect depends on principles of fault, then we might as well refer to "strict negligence liability" and define "strict services liability" as a tort that makes a service seller liable for the sale of defective services. As long as liability is tied to a defect that must be proven, the word "strict" is surplus; it does no analytical work and cannot signify liability without fault. It might be that those who use the term *strict products liability* have in mind the general expansion of the responsibility of product sellers (which has undoubtedly occurred), but the expansion of responsibility is, as I show below, based on fault principles and

3   William L. Prosser, *The Assault Upon the Citadel*, 69 Yale L.J. 1099 (1960).
4   *Greenman v. Yuba Power Products, Inc.*, 377 P.2d 897 (Cal. 1963); *Vandermark v. Ford Motor Co.*, 391 p.2d 168 (Cal. 1964).
5   *Restatement (Second) of Torts* § 402A (1965).
6   Mark A. Geistfeld, ESSENTIALS OF TORT LAW 406, Wolters Kluwer (2008).

therefore does not implicate no-fault liability. Using the term *strict* to refer to this development does a disservice to our need to understand the justifications for, and limits of, the expanded responsibility.

As one other example of a justificational wrong turn, consider the shadow of privity, which held its force only because of an analytical error. The case of *Winterbottom v. Wright*[7] put the iron jaws of privity around the responsibility of manufacturers, from which it took years to break free. Yet, the limitation on liability in *Winterbottom* was justified on grounds other than privity, for the manufacturer should not have been responsible for the harm that occurred in that case. In *Winterbottom*, the manufacturer had not created the risk,[8] and the case should have been decided on the ground that the manufacturer, even if thinking reasonably about the risk the customers faced, should not have been responsible for the risk. The plaintiff was the driver of a coach that was owned by the Postmaster General and used in transporting mail. The plaintiff was injured when the wheel came off and the coach tipped over. The driver sued the manufacturer of the wheel, but there was no showing that the wheel had been negligently made, or that it contained any defect. The reason the wheel came off was not poor manufacture but poor maintenance.[9] The accident occurred because of normal wear and tear, and the negligence issue in the case was whether the wheel manufacturer or the owner of the coach had negligently failed to inspect the wheel and avoid the harm.

Under normal circumstances, one would expect that the owner of the coach had the duty to reasonably inspect the wheel, and that the manufacturer, having delivered a non-negligent (nondefective) wheel, had relinquished its responsibility for the wheel. Under this reading, the wheel manufacturer would not be responsible and should not have been sued. The plaintiff sued the wheel manufacturer only because the wheel manufacturer had agreed with the Postmaster General to assume responsibility for maintaining the wagon. The plaintiff wanted to take advantage of that contract, presumably because the Postmaster General was protected from suit by sovereign immunity. The finding that the manufacturer owed the plaintiff no duty of maintenance simply reflected the fact that, absent the contract, the manufacturer would have had no duty to maintain the wheel at all. On this reading, the case did not implicate tort law; the only issue was whether the duty that the manufacturer had assumed under the contract with the Postmaster General created a duty

[7] *Winterbottom v. Wright*, 10 M and W 109 (1842).
[8] *Id.* at 110.
[9] *Id.*

to the plaintiff, a simple question of how the manufacturer and the Postmaster General divided the risk of maintenance under contract law.[10]

Although it is not beyond doubt, the court was arguably correct to hold that plaintiff could not take advantage of the contractual duty that the plaintiff had neither bargained for nor contributed to. Plaintiff was claiming the position of a third-party beneficiary of a contract between the manufacturer and the owner of the coach, but it is not clear that their bargain extended to the plaintiff, because it was not clear that the owner's duty extended to the plaintiff. If the Postmaster General really were immune from suit, then the Postmaster General would have paid the manufacturer for this protection simply to restore the value of the coach and not to indemnify its employees who were injured in accidents. The injustice of the case lies in the fact that the law made the Postmaster General immune from suit, not that the manufacturer was relieved of an obligation that tort law should have imposed.[11]

Winterbottom should therefore *not* have been understood as a general limitation on duty to indirect customers under negligence law. It was really the application of the notion, still nascent in the developing negligence law, that an actor has no duty to rescue or aid a potential victim when the actor did not create the risk that subjects the victim to harm (absent a special relationship), coupled with the notion that the contract of service did not create a duty to the plaintiff. Had that aspect of *Winterbottom* been understood, courts and commentators would not have seen the privity doctrine as a general bar in

---

[10] Courts have continually held that when two parties divide the risk that affects a third party, the court will not make the third party a beneficiary of the contract without inquiring into how the parties divided the risk of loss between themselves. *Robins Dry Dock and Repair Co. v. Flint* 275 U.S. 303 (1927).

[11] *Winterbottom* is not an isolated case. Other early cases denying recovery in tort on the ground of privity would also have been correctly decided on the ground that the defendant had not created the risk that led to plaintiff's harm. For example, in *Longmeid v. Holiday*, 6 Exch. 761 (1851), the wife of the purchaser of the lamp was injured when the lamp exploded. She sued the manufacturer of the lamp, and was denied recovery on the ground that she was not in privity with the manufacturer. This was an unnecessarily formalistic holding. The same outcome could have been justified with the simple statement that the manufacturer was not liable because the manufacturer had not breached the standard of care it owed to those who used the lamp. The cause of the explosion was not the fault of the manufacturer, but of a supplier of a faulty part that the manufacture incorporated into its lamp. The parts supplier, not the manufacturer, created the risk. Because there was no evidence that the manufacturer had not reasonably inspected the part or had unreasonably chosen the supplier, plaintiff's case should have been against the part supplier, not the manufacturer. Even if there had been a well-developed duty on the part of the manufacturer to protect consumers, the inability of a reasonable manufacturer to find the defect in the part would have fulfilled its duty to protect the plaintiff. The court used privity to cut off responsibility only because legal analysis was not sophisticated enough to reveal the true nature of the limitation on defendant's responsibility.

negligence cases. Those courts could have (and should have) said that the duty when a manufacturer creates a risk arises from the creation of the risk in the first place, and not from contract.[12]

There is another irony in the conventional story behind the rise and fall of privity. Had the preoccupation with privity not been so great, commentators might have spent more time celebrating Cardozo's other achievement in *MacPherson*. The real significance of *MacPherson* was that the manufacturer had not created the risk; the defect was in the wheel the manufacturer purchased. Yet, Cardozo had no trouble affirming the duty of a manufacturer to inspect (reasonably) the parts that it buys so that the parts, combined in the final product, do not cause harm to others. But this advance in understanding the responsibility of manufacturers to inspect was hidden by the concentration on privity. Product liability law is due for a justificational makeover – a retelling of conventional understanding from a justificational point of view.

10.2. AN OVERVIEW OF THIS CHAPTER

In the view presented here, the product liability revolution turned out to be a revolution in the way we think about the scope of responsibility for product sellers, requiring that product sellers consider more intently and along several dimensions the well-being of those who might be affected by their products and how harm might occur; but it was not a revolution that invoked strict or enterprise liability.[13] Under the negligence regime, product sellers have always been required to be other-regarding. The product liability revolution changed the requirements of other-regarding behavior to reflect a new understanding about the seller–buyer relationship, and a social determination that in an era of specialization social cohesion requires a higher level of other-regarding behavior by sellers. But it was not the application of either strict or enterprise liability; the revolution simply expanded the duty to inspect, warn, and design reasonably given the agency relationships and information asymmetries in product markets.

In retrospect, however, the revolution was not restricted to product sellers. The revolution included a parallel expansion in the scope of other-regarding responsibility in any agency relationship – that is, in any relationship in

---

[12] Indeed, it is worth noting that the erosion of the privity doctrine occurred in cases where the defendant had created the risk – cases that are easily distinguished from those where "privity" was code for saying that the risk belonged to someone other than the defendant.

[13] We must distinguish two meanings of enterprise liability: One is a loss spreading argument and the other is expanding an enterprise's ambit of responsibility to reflect an enterprise's superior access to information and agency obligations. The theory in this book rejects the former but embraces the latter.

which one person relies on another by delegating decision-making authority to the other. The same factors that shape a product seller's obligation to be other-regarding also influence the obligation of service suppliers to be other-regarding, including both sellers of services (landlords, common carriers, and professionals) and nonprofit suppliers of services.[14] When an actor is the agent of another, the agency relationship imposes an obligation to be other-regarding that includes the obligation to take advantage of specialized information on behalf of those who rely on the agent. Accordingly, the separation between product liability law and negligence liability law ought to be extinguished.

This chapter's substantive thesis is straightforward. Under the theory of other-regarding behavior already developed in this book, an actor must reasonably take into account the well-being of others when the actor has either created a risk or chosen an activity that implicates the actor in the risk another faces. Because for-profit and nonprofit suppliers voluntarily enter into relationships that make the well-being of others a part of their activity, and because suppliers have specialized information, they are required to use that information to incorporate the well-being of others into their decisions about the activity. The scope of that requirement flows from the agency relationship between seller and buyer (and between nonprofit supplier and client) and responds to the buyer's justified reliance on the relative superiority of the supplier as an information generator and harm reducer. This puts pressure on the supplier to think more comprehensively and coherently about how the supplier can prevent harms that the users might otherwise encounter from the activity – the obligation to put reasonable effort into inspecting, warning, and redesigning as part of the activity of supplying products or services. And this form of liability has adopted various presumptions and burden-shifting techniques that make it easier to prove that the supplier has not thought sufficiently about how harms from the product or service can be avoided.

But this expansion in the responsibility of a supplier to be other-regarding is fully accounted for by the negligence regime; we need no special regime of strict liability or loss spreading to bring it about.[15] The revolution occurred

---

[14] For-profit enterprises are agents for their customers. Nonprofit enterprises are agents for their stakeholders. For convenience, I will use the term *customers* to refer to both customers of for-profit enterprises and stakeholders of nonprofit enterprises.

[15] We can call the resulting theory one of enterprise liability, but the theory is not built on loss spreading but on the notion that because of the relationship between an enterprise and her customers and the information advantages of the enterprise, an enterprise that is appropriately other-regarding will increase vigilance on behalf of the enterprise's customers. This is a negligence theory that understands the ways in which enterprises must be other-regarding and therefore describes the expanded scope of enterprise responsibility to look out for the well-being of others.

in the precincts of duty and causation *within* the negligence regime. As is shown below, sometimes the revolution modified the requirements for proving causation, shifting the burden of proof to the supplier. In other instances, the revolution reflected the expansive notion that suppliers who do not invest in reasonably preventable harm have caused that harm (even if they are not responsible for the victim being in the position to incur harm). And the revolution expanded the contours of the duty to inspect, warn, and redesign, the key dimensions of protection. Although these changes all increased the responsibility of suppliers, this expansion is based on traditional negligence principles that govern the responsibility of an actor to look out for the well-being of others. And, as I said, it applies to all enterprises – nonprofit suppliers of services and sellers of products and services. Finally, it is not just enterprises that face this expanded duty. The same principles that inform the obligation of enterprise suppliers inform the responsibility of individuals. This is manifest in the negligent entrustment cases, where one person supplies another with a dangerous instrumentality knowing of the risk of doing so.[16] In those cases, too, the actor serves as the agent of the recipient, with the implied obligation to withhold the dangerous instrumentality from the recipient and thereby protect the recipient and others.

10.3. THE DICHOTOMY BETWEEN PRODUCTS AND SERVICES

Although it is common to think of product liability as a regime separate from general negligence liability, the dichotomy rests on an unsustainable distinction between products and services. When referring to for-profit firms, the relevant analytical category is "seller's responsibility." And because the principles governing sellers also govern the responsibility of nonprofit organizations to the people they serve, the responsibility of for-profit sellers (of both products and services) and nonprofit suppliers of services can be understood as part of a coherent system of supplier responsibility.

It is difficult to see any meaningful difference between products and services that would justify separate legal regimes.[17] Services and products share common characteristics that are relevant to determining the scope of an actor's legal responsibility to consider the well-being of others. Both services and products are provided through market mechanisms to consumers. Accordingly, both services and products are subject to the kind of market failures that invite

---

[16]   See, generally, Robert L. Rabin, *Enabling Torts*, 49 DePaul L. Rev. 435 (1999).

[17]   William Powers, Jr., *A Modest Proposal to Abandon Strict Products Liability*, 1991 U. Ill. L. Rev. 639 (1991); Jane Stapleton, *Bugs in Anglo-American Products Liability Law*, 53 S.C. L. Rev. 1225, 1255 (2002).

legal intervention. Providers of services, like providers of products, can cause serious injury if the service is not provided carefully enough; the harm caused by an overturned railroad tank car (when the railroad, a service provider, negligently maintains its track) can be greater than damage when chemicals leak from a poorly made tank car (a product). Moreover, service sellers take the same kinds of precautions to avoid harm as product sellers. Sellers of services and products are both able to investigate, design, and warn in a way that minimizes injuries. An automobile manufacturer, for example, can design the automobile to reasonably protect passengers in a crash; a motel owner can ensure that his guests are reasonably protected from injury by an arsonist or unwanted intruder. Sellers of services and products can both investigate harms that come from what they supply. Both can warn customers when information can prevent injury. In other words, we cannot distinguish between products and services on the basis of the institutional channels through which they are provided, the risks they impose, the amount of damage they inflict, or the nature of the precautions that would avoid harm. Nothing in the normal calculus of risk suggests that we should construct legal regimes for products that are fundamentally different from the legal regime for services.

Services and products are not identical, of course. Services are intangible, products tangible. Services are generally (although not always) delivered directly to consumers; products are often (but not always) provided through intermediaries. Historically, services were generally (but not always) local, while products could generally be shipped efficiently over long distances (and the digital age is fast removing the barrier of distance in the supply of some services). Differences there are, but if these differences were to justify different legal regimes, one would think that the different legal treatment of products and services could be traced to one of these differences, and that when the differences were not present the legal regimes would be the same. Although distinctions are possible, the distinctions should matter only in the application of the obligation to be other-regarding, and only when the distinction relates to the factors that influence the scope of the obligation to be other-regarding.

10.4. HISTORICAL DEVELOPMENT OF THE SCOPE OF OTHER-REGARDING BEHAVIOR OF SUPPLIERS

The distinction between products and services is of historical, not analytical, origin. Service sales were unburdened by the shield of privity; common carriers, innkeepers, and service professionals sold directly to users and worked closely with them. Moreover, *caveat emptor* never infected services as it did products; from early on it was assumed that purchasers of services did not have the information to protect themselves when defects in the services threatened them. And the agency relationship between buyers and suppliers of services – one captured in the common carrier notion – was a relationship that courts could easily understand when dealing with service providers like innkeepers.[18] As a result, from the earliest days of the negligence regime, courts had no problem imposing on service sellers a duty to investigate, warn, and redesign.

However, courts did so *sub rosa*, without openly acknowledging what they were doing. The expansive duties took various forms. One mechanism was to impose on sellers the duty of "utmost care" – a duty that incorporated the duty to investigate, warn, and redesign.[19] In addition, service sellers sometimes became subject to special regimes; for the medical profession, the duty to warn morphed into the duty of informed consent and the duty to investigate got folded into the standards of the profession. In other instances, the duty to reasonably redesign, warn, or inspect got folded into general negligence law. Courts had no trouble determining that, for example, juries could find that landlords should warn tenants that the glass in their shower was not tempered[20] or that a bus company had to be more careful looking for defects in bus seats when doing maintenance and repair work.[21]

By contrast, the law relating to product sellers developed in the shadow of privity. As manufacturers became increasingly separated from their customers, the negligence concept lost sight of the parallels between service seller responsibility and product seller responsibility. Even the removal of privity as a barrier to responsibility in 1916 did not fertilize a more explicit and progressive

[18]   Robert J. Kaczorowski, *The Common Law, Background of Nineteenth Century Tort Law*, 51 OHIO ST. L. REV. 1127 (1990). For example, courts often used analogies to bailment – an explicit agency concept – when discussing common carriers.
[19]   Under the utmost standard of care, a stagecoach company had to warn passengers of the danger of loading the stagecoach onto a ferry so that passengers would have the option of getting out of the stagecoach, *McLean v. Burbank*, 11 Minn. 277 (1966), and to warn a passenger of a group of nearby rowdy soldiers who later injured the passenger, *Flint v. Norwich & N.Y. Transp. Co.*, 9 F. Cas. 277 (1868). And even after a stagecoach driver warned a passenger atop the stagecoach of a low clearance, the company was responsible because the warning was not explicit enough. *Dudley v. Smith*, 170 Eng. Rep. 915 (K.B. 1808). Common carriers were also required to make their products crashworthy – that is, to design them in ways that would reasonably minimize harm in the event of an unavoidable collision. *Railroad Co. v. Pollard*, 89 U.S. 341 (1874) (upholding jury verdict on ground that armrest was not padded well enough). Finally, under the utmost care standard, courts regularly determined whether a common carrier's inspection of its vehicle was reasonable. *Ingalls v. Bills*, 50 Mass. (9 Met.) 1 (1845) (common carrier is responsible for defect in the coach that might have been discovered and remedied under the most careful and thorough examination, but not for hidden and internal defects).
[20]   *Trimarco v. Klein*, 56 N.Y. 2d 98 (1982).
[21]   *Bethel v. New York City Transit Authority*, 92 N.Y. 2d 348 (1998).

negligence regime applied to products. Although, as we have seen, Justice Cardozo in *MacPherson* had no trouble imagining a manufacturer's duty to inspect reasonably the parts that it purchased, negligence law did not overtly explore the concepts of the duty to inspect, warn, and redesign. The lingering spirit of *caveat emptor* – which reflected expectations from an earlier and less specialized era about the responsibility of consumers to investigate products before buying – blocked many explicit attempts to impose higher other-regarding obligations. The notion that product consumers could self-protect – and therefore had a high duty to investigate and address hazards – continued to restrict suits against manufacturers to "hidden dangers" far into the late twentieth century.[22] Because courts did not grasp the agency relationship between manufacturers and users – the analog to the common carrier notion on the service side – courts never adopted the concept of utmost care, which had been so helpful in putting pressure on common carriers to think about the well-being of their customers. As a result, courts never developed the notion that manufacturers must anticipate how they could prevent harm when their product did not cause the accident; as late as the 1950s courts were rejecting manufacturer's responsibility for designing products that would reduce harm from other sources.[23]

But this does not mean that an expanded duty of product sellers to consider the well-being of customers was not developing. Rather than being organized around the concept of utmost care (as on the service side), tort law expanded the scope of product seller responsibility by using *res ipsa loquitur* to allow juries to impose liability on manufacturers who did not reasonably inspect, warn, and redesign their products. This approach, of course, hid, rather than illuminated, the expanded scope of responsibility the law was imposing. This role of *res ipsa loquitur* is poorly understood.

Res ipsa loquitur allows juries to infer negligence from the way the accident happened; its invocation requires the judge to determine, first, the range of probabilities of various circumstances that might have led to the accident

---

[22] *Batts v. Tow-Motor Forklift Co.*, 978 F. 2d 1386, 1392 (5th Cir. 1992) ("there is no strict liability in tort under Mississippi law for a patent – open and obvious – danger"); *J.I. Case Co. v. Sanderfur*, 197 N.E. 2d 519 (Ind. 1964) ("The emphasis is on the duty to avoid hidden defects or concealed dangers."); *First Nat. Bank and Trust Corp. v. American Eurocopter Corp.*, 378 F.3d 682 (7th Cir. 2004) (finding that, under Indiana law, there is no duty to warn of open and obvious dangers); *Campo v. Scofield*, 95 N.E. 2d 802 (N.Y. 1950) (finding a duty and holding a machine manufacturer liable only where a product defect or danger is latent or concealed), overruled by *Micallef v. Miehle Co.*, 39 N.Y. 2d 376 (1976).

[23] *Hentschel v. Baby Bathinette Corp.*, 215 F. 2d. 102 (S.D. N.Y. 1954) (bassinette manufacturer not responsible for using metal alloy that increased the intensity of a fire, because the bassinette and metal alloy did not cause the fire).

and, second, whether the defendant is responsible for those circumstances. For example, as we saw earlier, when a barrel of flour falls out of a second story window of a flour warehouse, the judge must assess the probability of three types of events: that the owner failed to reasonably secure the barrel, that an unexpected tremor shook the barrel lose, and that an intruder snuck into the shop and dislodged the barrel. The shop owner is clearly responsible for the first (high probability) event and clearly not responsible for the second (low probability) event (which the defendant could prove as a defense). As to the third event (the intruder), the defendant's duty to keep intruders out of the warehouse (a duty to inspect) makes it easier to ascribe to the defendant responsibility for that event, and thus easier to invoke *res ipsa loquitur*. The defendant has responsibility both to reasonably secure the barrel and also to reasonably protect against an intruder who might dislodge the barrel, and this (along with the defendant's ability to prove that the harm could not have been reasonably prevented in an earthquake) justifies a jury in holding the defendant responsible for the harm.

Res ipsa loquitur therefore allows a judge to let the jury find that the defendant was unreasonable by finding that the defendant could have done more by way of investigating, warning, and redesigning to look out for the well-being of the victim, even without making the contours of that responsibility explicit. Even before the product liability revolution, then, negligence law imposed a duty to inspect, warn, and redesign the product by invoking *res ipsa loquitur* rather than directly, and the true scope of a seller's obligation to be other-regarding was never understood.

Take the famous *Escola v. Coca Cola Bottling Co.*, a case discussed in Chapter Eight to show that courts understand how to assess alternative methods of delivery.[24] Plaintiff sued when a soda bottle exploded because of a hairline fracture in the reused bottle.[25] At first blush, this looks like a bad case for *res ipsa loquitur*.[26] There was no "commercially practicable" test to eliminate the risk, so the use of used bottles looked to be reasonable. The judge correctly saw, however, that although the hairline fracture in used bottles could not reasonably be identified, the bottler could shift to new bottles with reasonable ease (the cost of shifting to new bottles was less than the harm from undiscoverable hairline fractures in old bottles). By invoking *res ipsa loquitur*, the jury was allowed to determine that a reasonable bottler, knowing of the risk of

[24] 150 P. 2d 436 (Cal. 1944).
[25] *Id.* at 437.
[26] The point is made in Mark Geistfeld, *Strict Product Liability Unbound* in TORTS STORIES 233–4 (Robert L. Rabin & Stephen D. Sugarman, eds.), Foundation Press (2003).

hairline fractures in used bottles and the harm they cause, would have used new bottles (in effect a redesign of its product). The jury, in other words, was permitted to base liability on the failure reasonably to consider a reasonable alternative method of delivering the soda.

Dissatisfaction with the negligence regime for products therefore reflected, in part, the inability of theorists to recognize that the negligence regime was already imposing a duty to inspect, warn, and redesign, and the lingering restrictions placed on the obligation to be other-regarding from the *caveat emptor* notion. Without discounting the desire of some courts and commentators for genuine strict liability (the notion that all harms from use of a product should be incorporated into the cost of the product), the revolution that was started by Judge Traynor[27] in California and Professor Prosser (in his assault on the citadel and the Restatement Second) was really a linguistic one. By making product suppliers responsible for "defects" rather than just for "unreasonable" acts, the courts could explicitly explore a broader range of responsibilities for suppliers. And, as is now widely acknowledged, the exploration led the courts to make explicit the duty of the seller to reasonably inspect, warn, and redesign – enhancing the obligation of the seller to think about the well-being of others in ways that are easily encompassed without the reasonableness concept. But the courts, with rare exceptions[28] (most of which were later reversed), never really got away from the reasonableness standard.

With the benefit of hindsight, we can now articulate a single analytical basis for understanding and evaluating the scope of responsibility of suppliers – one that is applicable to suppliers of services and products and nonprofit suppliers of goods and services. Suppliers are not like the actor who passes the baby on the tracks; suppliers have chosen an activity – providing for the well-being of their customers or clients – that is inherently other-regarding; that choice to be other-regarding gives them the obligation to think about the well-being of others in ways that advance social cohesion. The scope of that obligation – what it means to be other-regarding – is determined by the agency relationship between supplier and customer or client and by the supplier's specialized information. We take up each in turn.

---

[27] *Escola v. Coca Cola Bottling Co. of Fresno*, 150 P. 2d 436, 462 (Cal. 1944) (Traynor, J., concurring).

[28] *Beshada v. Johns Manville Products Corp.*, 447 A. 2d 539 (N.J. 1982), reversed in *Feldman v. Lederle Labs*, 479 A.2d 374 (N.J. 1984); *Hayes v. Ariens Co.*, 462 N.E. 2d 273 (Mass. 1984) reversed *Vasallo v. Baxter Healthcare Corp.* (Mass. 1998); *Green v. Smith & Nephew AHP, Inc.*, 629 N.W. 2d 727 (Wis. 2001).

10.5. TORTS AND AGENCY RELATIONSHIPS

Suppliers are agents for those who purchase or use their product or service. For suppliers, the very act of supplying is the activity of accepting responsibility for the well-being of others. The obligation of suppliers to take into account, in a reasonable way, the well-being of their users is but an application of the theory of duty articulated in Chapter Six. Looking out for the well-being of others is an inherent part of the activity of supplying products and services because the only rationale for the activity is to improve consumer well-being.

Consider the agency implications of organized markets. Perfectly competitive markets form a perfect agency relationship between the buyer (the principal) and the seller (the agent). Because perfect competition assumes perfect information and the frictionless movement of factors of production, the interests of the agent become perfectly aligned with the interests of the principal; the agent (seller) is compensated for her services with a reasonable profit and the customer (the principal) pays no more than is necessary to induce the production of goods or services desired by the customer. Any divergence by the agent from the interests of the principal – any tendency to shirk or be opportunistic – is punished because the buyer can easily detect the disloyalty and find alternative suppliers. Perfect markets therefore result in sellers who are perfectly other-regarding. The buyers choose a level of safety that comports with their projects and preferences (given the cost of safety) and the seller delivers it. If sellers do not deliver it, buyers shift suppliers to those who are more other-regarding. Buyers rely on an implicit social contract of other-regarding behavior; they understand that society has chosen the market system rather than some other social institution of allocation because perfect markets perfectly align the interests of sellers with those of buyers.

Yet we know that markets are not perfect. Market failures – information imperfections, friction in the movement of factors of production, and too few sellers – allow the interests of sellers to diverge from those of buyers. When market failures occur, agency relationships break down and consumers are no longer able to control their agents. When market failures occur, suppliers stop being other-regarding and become self-regarding. As a result, agents earn excess profits or substitute their judgment for those of buyers, their principal. The agency relationship is restored only when society supplements the market mechanism with a different institutional design to align the interest of the agents with the interests of the principals. That is tort law's function. Tort law says to suppliers: Even if the market does not discipline you for diverging from the interests of your principals, you are answerable for their well-being in the same way the market would require were it perfect.

The intellectual concept of perfect markets and market failures are economic analogs to Rawls's veil of ignorance. They ask the supplier to be other-regarding in the following sense: If the supplier did not know whether she was supplier or buyer, but understood the function of supply to be to satisfy the preferences of buyers at least cost, what is the supplier's best conjecture about the mix of safety and low price the fully informed buyer would want? An other-regarding supplier must therefore be able to imagine the level of safety a buyer would want if the buyer were fully informed of the various risks or harm from products and their associated costs. This thought exercise is not foreign to suppliers. They regularly receive, and in the competitive market must seek, information about what makes their product or service attractive to buyers, about buyer use and misuse of the product or service, and about buyer preferences for risk. Once the supplier understands herself as the agent for the buyer and therefore adopts an attitude of other-regardedness, the supplier will sacrifice her own interests that do not also advance the interests of the buyer.

This depiction of markets as agency relationships formalizes our understanding of the relationship between supplier and buyer that has fueled the product liability revolution. In an age of specialization and technological advance, a buyer has neither the time nor the knowledge to inform herself, in any significant way, about the safety-related features the supplier builds into the product or service. As Justice Traynor said: "It is evident that the manufacturer can anticipate some hazards and guard against the recurrence of others, as the public cannot."[29] Nor should consumers have to invest unduly in thinking about how products or services are designed or how injury can be prevented. The agency aspects of the buyer–seller relationship reflect an interdependence on which people ought to be able to rely. Justified reliance on the other-regarding behavior of a supplier – that is, one who has accepted, and is therefore charged with, the responsibility of serving the well-being of another – improves the well-being of both buyer and seller. Social cohesion depends on such justified reliance. As is well known, such justified reliance enhances efficiency by releasing people's energy to work on things that are most important to them; it delegates responsibility to those who can undertake a function most effectively. Even beyond efficiency, however, the dynamics of justified reliance suggest that a common understanding between agent and principal of the nature and scope of the reliance make it fair to impose on the agent the duty to take into account the well-being of the principal that are implicit in the scope of that relationship. The buyer therefore relies on the supplier to make choices that are good from the buyer's standpoint and to

---

[29] *Escola,* 150 P. 2d at 440–1 (Traynor, J., concurring).

keep buyers informed of information that allows buyers to reduce harm. Tort law says that suppliers must be other-regarding in a way that markets would require if markets were perfect.

10.6. TORTS AND INFORMATION

Society relies on markets as institutions of social cohesion because, when functioning without imperfections, markets marshal information that allows society to allocate responsibility for resources (given the existing distribution of wealth). However, markets for information do not always function well, and one goal of law is to overcome the information failures that restrain markets from performing up to their potential. Tort law, in particular, recognizes that within markets information is costly to produce, easy to hoard, and asymmetrically distributed, and that markets may therefore produce too little information or require too high an investment when information has already been produced. Information imperfections are especially prevalent in agency relationships such as those that occur in formal markets. Suppliers may procure information as a part of their work but may have no incentive to either share it or rely on it to improve the well-being of others. Information is costly to use and if suppliers derive no benefits from using information, they will not do so. Information may be misunderstood by consumers who are not used to thinking in probabilistic terms, and who may underestimate the value of the information when they make purchasing decisions. In addition, markets may underinvest in information about risks because, although the social benefit of the information is high, there is no organized institution for ensuring that those who benefit from the information will pay those who incur the costs of the information.

Tort law overcomes these information problems – and thereby improves the social cohesion achieved by markets – by making suppliers into information agents, as well as supplying agents, of their customers. Suppliers generate relevant information in the course of their activities, serving as a central depository of information about customer use and misuse of their product. Suppliers understand the kinds of information that their customers would demand if information markets equated the marginal return on investment in information with the marginal benefit. Suppliers who are under a legal obligation to think about the well-being of their customers have an incentive to share the information they develop with customers. And when information suggests that risk can be avoided by using the information to redesign what is supplied, suppliers can incorporate the information in new designs. Suppliers can therefore improve how markets function – and therefore the social cohesion markets are designed to achieve – by investigating, warning, and redesigning.[30]

The products liability revolution can therefore be traced to the associated revolution in the economics of information, following an intellectual line drawn from the works of Frederick Hayek[31] (who conceived of markets as institutions to generate information) to Joseph Stiglitz[32] and George Akerlof[33] (who helped us formalize our understanding about information failures). The products liability revolution freed courts to focus on the implications of information economics by making suppliers responsible for defects rather than for negligence, but in retrospect this seems to be a focus on defects in the market for information that impaired the supplier's ability to make other-regarding decisions. It never really shifted focus away from the reasonableness of the supplier decision once suppliers were forced to account for the information defects in the markets in which they worked. We can understand the resulting change in the responsibility of suppliers along several dimensions.

The law imposes on suppliers the duty to make products and services crashworthy – that is, to protect buyers in reasonable ways even when the supplier is not responsible for the risk that led to the accident. These cases correspond to cases in the negligence regime in which an actor is not the source of the risk but is in a position to protect the other from the risk and has a duty to do so. Under the crashworthiness doctrine, even when an automobile defect does not cause a crash, the manufacturer, in order to be appropriately other-regarding, must design the automobile to reasonably reduce the harm from a crash. The product supplier is put on the same footing as a service supplier; motels and automobiles must both be designed so that if something goes wrong, even without the fault of the supplier, consumers buy reasonable protection when they buy the product or service. But the requirement of the other-regarding supplier is no more than a reasonableness requirement. The supplier is not

[30] Others have expressed this thought in terms of exerting pressure to reduce costs on the party that is in the best position to avoid the costs. According to Calabresi and Hirschoff:

> [When a] producer is in a position to compare the existing accident costs with the costs of avoiding this type of accident by developing either a new product or a test which would serve to identify [those who are at risk from a product] … the producer is the cheapest cost avoider, the party best suited to make the cost–benefit analysis and to act upon it. Guido Calabresi & John T. Hirschoff, *Toward a Test for Strict Liability in Torts*, 81 YALE L.J. 1055, 1062 (1972).

[31] F.A. Hayek, *The Use of Knowledge in Society*, 35 AMER. ECON. REV. 519 (1945).

[32] Joseph Stiglitz, *Information and Change in the Paradigm of Economics*, 92 AMER. ECON. REV. 460 (2002).

[33] George A. Akerlof, *Behavioral Macroeconomics and Macroeconomic Behavior*, 92 AMER. ECON. REV. 411 (2002).

required to change the nature of the product when doing so would destroy, rather than enhance, the value of the product for fully informed consumers. It is acknowledged that Volkswagens need not be as safe as BMWs, just as it is acknowledged that Red Roof Inns need not be as safe as the Waldorf Astoria.

The duties to investigate, warn, and redesign follow naturally from the obligation to protect consumers even if the supplier did not cause the accident. Because a supplier must be mindful not only of risks that it imposes because of the way it produces its product or service but also of risks from other sources that it can help avoid, the supplier must understand what risks the buyer faces and how they can best be addressed. Hence the duty to investigate, although not explicit in the product liability restatement, is implicit in the duties to warn and design reasonably.[34] In order to be appropriately other-regarding, a supplier must think about how a buyer might be adversely affected by its product or service and whether a warning or redesign best addresses those risks. The level of investment required depends on what the supplier knows about the risks, the supplier's access to information about the risks, and the supplier's claims about the product.[35] A reasonable supplier continually recalibrates the benefits of further investigation as the supplier receives information. Failure to investigate because the supplier feared the information would be unfavorable is itself unreasonable,[36] and the state of the art requirement ensures that suppliers continually investigate technological developments that could reduce product risks.[37]

Information economics has also changed the way that we understand which risks are "open and obvious" (and therefore the responsibility of consumers) and which are not (and therefore are the responsibility of the supplier). When it is more efficient for suppliers to design around the risk than for consumers

---

[34] See, e.g., RESTATEMENT (THIRD) OF TORTS: PRODUCT LIABILITY, American Law Institute (1998) (*Product Liability Restatement*) § 10, Comment C: the duty of reasonable care may "require investigation [and] with regard to…prescription drugs and devices, courts traditionally impose a continuing duty…to test and monitor…," and § 13, Comment C ("when the facts justify investigation and it can be practically accomplished, this section sets up no artificial barrier to recovery").

[35] *Castro v. QVC Network, Inc.*, 139 F. 3d 114 (2d Cir. 1998).

[36] *Richter v. Limex Int'l., Inc.*, 45 F. 3d 1464 (10th Cir. 1995).

[37] *Cover v. Cohen*, 461 N.E. 2d 864, 871 (N.Y. 1984) ("manufacturer or retailer may…incur liability for failing to warn concerning dangers in the use of a product which come to his attention after manufacture or sale, through advancements in the state of the art"); *Moren v. Samuel M. Langston Co.*, 237 N.E. 2d 759, 765 (Ill. App. 1968) (imposing "upon the manufacturer the duty of an expert to keep abreast and informed of the developments in his field, including safety devices and equipment used in his industry with the type of products he manufactures").

to avoid the risk, it makes sense to put the burden of avoiding the harm on the supplier rather than the consumer.[38]

Making suppliers responsible for harms even if the supplier is not responsible for risks that led to the accident also demonstrates an evolving concept of causation; harm that a supplier can reasonably prevent is harm that the supplier caused. But that is not the only way that changes in the application of the negligence regime reflect altered concepts of causation. The "heeding presumption" shifts the burden of proving causation from the buyer to the supplier. By assuming that a victim would have heeded a reasonable warning, courts are shifting to the defendant the burden of proving that even a reasonable warning would not have saved the victim from harm.[39] And a subtle shift in the casual requirement in the *Restatement Third* requires only that a reasonable warning *could* prevent harm, not proof that a reasonable warning *would* prevent harm.[40] This recognizes the difficulty of proving that the defect was necessary to the harm in cases where the manufacturer depends on informed users to avoid the harm.

10.7. MANUFACTURING DEFECTS

Although the responsibility of a supplier to warn, investigate, and redesign is now understood to be grounded on the reasonableness concept, and therefore on the theory of other-regarding behavior, responsibility for manufacturing defects continues to be expressed in terms that seem to embrace strict liability.[41] By explicitly making a manufacturer responsible for deviations from manufacturing standards that cannot be avoided with reasonable care, the test seems explicitly to reject the negligence concept.

But we should put manufacturing defects in context. In many cases, the concept of a manufacturing defect is simply the application of *res ipsa loquitur* to the notion of a defect. If the drive train of an automobile falls out a few

---

[38] Am. L. Prod. Liab. 3d § 28:86 (2008) ("Liability may attach even though the danger was obvious, where an unreasonable danger could have been eliminated without excessive cost or loss of product efficiency."), citing *Thibault v. Sears, Roebuck & Co.*, 395 A. 2d 843, 847 (N.H. 1978).

[39] See, e.g., *Smith v. Rogers Group, Inc.*, 72 S.W. 3d 450, 458 (Ark. 2002); *Tenbarge v. Ames Taping Tool Sys., Inc.*, 190 F. 3d 862, 866 (8th Cir. 1999) (applying Missouri law); Restatement (Second) of Torts § 402A, cmt. j (1965), abrogated by *Product Liability Restatement*, § 2, Reporters' Note, cmt. l (1998).

[40] *Product Liability Restatement*, § 2(b), (c) (1998).

[41] *Product Liability Restatement*, §2(c). Manufacturing defects: 2(c): "when a product departs from its intended design even though all possible care was exercised in the production and marketing of the product."

days after purchase, courts and juries have little trouble concluding that the automobile had a manufacturing defect (unless the manufacturer can show that the defect was introduced by an outsider). The drive train serves the same function as the barrel of flour that falls out of a warehouse window; unless the defendant can explain why the event happened in a way that is not the defendant's responsibility, the way that accident occurred is sufficient proof of the supplier's negligence.

Outside the domain of *res ipsa loquitur*, the justification for treating deviations from the manufacturer's standards as a source of responsibility reflects the theory of compliance error discussed in Chapter Two (Section 2.6). Take the class of cases in which the concept of a manufacturing defect seems to impose liability even if the defect cannot be eliminated with reasonable care, perhaps a case in which the weld used by the manufacturer did not meet the manufacturer's specification and the harm can be traced to that failure. If the weld cannot be made perfect one hundred percent of the time with reasonable investment, why should the manufacturer be responsible for the harm that occurs from those few times when the weld fails to meet the manufacturer's standard?

The defective weld could have come about because there was a better, more reasonable method of making welds, because the reasonable method that was used fails from time to time even though all due care is taken, or because the method chosen was unreasonably executed. The first reason (akin to an unreasonable precaution plan) results in liability because it resulted from an unreasonable decision. The third reason (a compliance error) results in liability because it, too, results from an unreasonable decision. Only the second reason (a reasonable compliance error) lacks a basis for imposing liability in negligence. The question is why a manufacturer should be responsible for a reasonable compliance error.

The number of reasonable compliance errors is probably fairly small. Most manufacturing defects can be, and, I suspect, are eliminated with reasonable care. The technology of assembly and inspection significantly reduces the number of items that come off the assembly line differently than intended. Moreover, the choice that a manufacturer has in selecting a standard for the permissible range of assembly imperfections is itself limited by the obligation to reasonably design the product. If a different design results in fewer assembly errors without otherwise adversely affecting the product, a reasonable manufacturer would choose that design and the law requires it.

As is true for any compliance error, it is impossible to determine whether the error resulted from unreasonable execution of a reasonable precaution plan or whether it resulted from a deviation from the compliance plan that could not have been avoided. Manufacturers, not courts, have the best information about how to assemble their products and what causes reasonable deviations from a reasonable compliance plan. Moreover, the manufacturer can determine whether the compliance error results from circumstances that ought to offer an excuse for the error (perhaps an unanticipated power stoppage). Under these circumstances, establishing a rule of responsibility for compliance errors subject to a defense for unavoidable external circumstances is justified on evidentiary grounds because it avoids cases in which the plaintiff would lose only because the plaintiff could not prove that the compliance error was unreasonable.

In this respect, liability for manufacturing defect is a close analog of liability for doctor's errors. Manufacturers and doctors set their standard of performance and courts generally defer to those standards because they would do more damage if they tried to intervene to review the standards. Manufacturers and doctors both supply highly technical and specialized services; manufacturers do so in assembling goods and doctors do so in providing medical care. In both instances, the supplier chooses the standard of care – the level of protection achieved in delivering medical care or in assembly, and the court adopts that standard as the relevant standard of care. Tort law in effect becomes the enforcer of a standard chosen in the market by suppliers. Compliance errors are owned by the doctor (and the manufacturer) because courts have no ability to evaluate the application of the standards the doctors or manufacturers set and the law therefore holds them strictly responsible for compliance errors (subject to proof that something extraordinary and beyond the defendant's control caused the error).

10.8. CONCLUSION

The development of "product liability law" is important for the way it allows us to understand the other-regarding obligations of those who serve as agents for others. The development has significantly expanded our understanding of the responsibility of one person for the well-being of another. But it is wrong to understand this development as one that is applied only to products, and it is wrong to suggest that the development is one of strict liability. Product liability and service liability ought to be understood as the same phenomenon, one that explores the ways in which an agent must use information advantages on behalf of a principal, even for risks that the agent did not create. Referring to these developments as strict liability misses the justificational analysis that must be done to define the contours of that responsibility.

11   Customer-Centered Enterprise Liability

Thus far, I have claimed that none of the justifications usually given for various manifestations of strict or enterprise liability are superior to the theory of other-regarding behavior as a justification for the level of responsibility courts impose. Another class of cases is sometimes given as an example of strict or enterprise liability that I have not accounted for: cases in which enterprises reasonably impose harms on some customers for the benefit of all customers but courts nonetheless impose a duty to repair the harm (even though the enterprise has acted reasonably). Two cases are representative. In *Lubin v. Iowa City*,[1] the city waterworks consciously decided not to inspect or replace pipes in the ground because the cost of inspection would have been too great. The location of any defect in the pipe was unpredictable, the cost of inspecting the length of the pipe was high, and inspection could not always disclose where repairs were needed. As a result, the waterworks knowingly and reasonably ignored the risk of burst pipes, allowing the costs to fall on the people where the pipes did in fact burst. They were found liable for the harm thus inflicted, even though their inspection policy was reasonable.

Similarly, McDonald's kept the heat of its coffee high, knowing that the high temperature would increase the harm from accidental spills. They did this because they felt that they would lose substantial customer goodwill if they turned down the heat of the coffee. In their view, the high temperature was reasonable because the goodwill it generated in customers outweighed the increased harm from the occasional coffee spill. They, too, were found responsible for the harm from their reasonable practice (after reducing the loss for harm attributable to customer error).

One can see why these cases are understood to be examples of enterprise or strict liability. Each company did the reasonable thing but was still required

[1]   131 N.W. 2d 765 (Iowa 1964).

to repair the harm it caused. In *Lubin*, the company kept the cost of its service low by not investing in expensive and perhaps fruitless investigations, allowing the harm to fall unpredictably and randomly on some customers. In *McDonald's*, the company benefitted its customers by keeping the heat of its coffee high, refusing to reduce customer satisfaction to avoid the harm from an occasional hot coffee spill. If the company did the reasonable thing by not undertaking the inspection or by keeping the temperature of its coffee hot, and yet has to pay, are these not examples of strict liability?

Cases like these are consistent with Gregory Keating's theory of enterprise liability, the general notion that the costs of an activity ought to be spread across the beneficiaries of the activity. But as we saw in Chapter Eight, both judicial decisions and sound theory reject any general theory of enterprise liability. A theory that matches burdens and benefits on distributive grounds is inconsistent with the relational nature of corrective justice because it does not posit a relationship between injurer and victim that needs to be corrected. Moreover, the many cases in which an enterprise acts reasonably and is not responsible for the harm it causes suggest that courts have not embraced the general theory of enterprise liability. Nonetheless, in this chapter, I endorse a narrow and specialized form of enterprise liability that should be understood to be driven by the theory of other-regarding fault developed in this book. I show that cases of this type are driven by the same justification that helped us understand the *Vincent* case in other-regarding terms: When an enterprise benefits its customers by taking reasonable risks, but the cost of those risks falls randomly on some customers, the other-regarding enterprise will compensate those who are hurt. I call this customer-centered liability.

11.1. THE OTHER-REGARDING CUSTOMER

The prior chapter detailed the requirements of the other-regarding supplier – the obligation to investigate, redesign, and warn. We based our understanding of other-regardedness on the agency relationship between the supplier and her customers and the information asymmetries that favor the supplier. But a supplier is often a juridical, not an individual person, and it is helpful to examine more closely the source of the obligation of a juridical person to be other-regarding. Obviously, once an enterprise has the obligation to be other-regarding, those who serve the enterprise have the same obligation, but we can now question more closely why a juridical person has the obligation to be other-regarding.

In the view presented here, the obligation of the supplier to be other-regarding flows from the agency relationship between a supplier and its customers. A supplier exists for the benefit of its customers and is defined by, and confined by, the projects and preferences of its customers. In a perfect market (or, for nonprofit suppliers, through perfect stakeholder satisfaction), customers determine what the supplier does and how the supplier does it; customers therefore determine the kinds of risks that a supplier will impose on society and what steps the supplier will take to address those risks. By their willingness to pay, customers ultimately determine a supplier's investment in other-regarding precautions. If customers do not purchase other-regarding protection against defects when they buy a product or service, the supplier is required to repair the damages that could have been reasonably prevented, and the supplier passes along the costs to its customers. Either way, the supplier's obligation to be other-regarding reflects the obligation of its customers to be other-regarding.

In other words, customers, as principals, control the supplier and this control gives them the same obligation to be other-regarding when they act as consumers that they have when making decisions about other aspects of their behavior. The law obligates suppliers to be other-regarding in order to perfect, and reflect, the obligation of its customers to be other-regarding when market failures or transaction costs prevent the market from bringing that to fruition. Although customers make no decisions about the level of safety the supplier chooses, the customer either pays for the reasonable investment in investigating, redesigning, and warning or the customer sees the damages the supplier pays folded into higher prices.

Once we understand that the supplier's duty to be other-regarding is but a reflection of the customer's obligation to be other-regarding, we can recast and carry forward our understanding of the obligations of a supplier.

First, we can explain why suppliers must take reasonable precautions to protect noncustomers. Information asymmetries are not the only market failure. Customers face ambivalence in their other-regarding role. Individually, customers would like to buy at the lowest possible cost, avoiding investments in other-regarding precautions when the customer's safety is not implicated. Customers might, therefore, be tempted to ignore the well-being of noncustomers. By imposing on suppliers the obligation to be other-regarding toward noncustomers, the law reflects the obligation to be other-regarding that the market would impose on the supplier's customers if the market were fully functioning and without transaction costs – that is, if the customers were fully informed and noncustomers could bargain for reasonable safety without friction. We can see this with a simple analogy. There is no more warrant for a customer to ask a lawnmower manufacturer to omit a reasonable safety feature that protects passers-by (perhaps by keeping the lawnmower from tossing out stones) than there would be for the same person to herself throw stones out of the yard without taking adequate precautions. That is why the other-regarding behavior of a supplier extends to noncustomers, and why the supplier is required to make sure that a customer's use of the product or service does not unreasonably injure noncustomers. Makers of lawnmowers must equip machines with reasonable protective guards and owners of hotels must take reasonable measures to ensure that guests do not injure passers-by on the street by throwing things out the window.

But customers also face ambivalence about the well-being of other customers. As a result, tort law recognizes a narrow kind of enterprise liability. Precautions raise prices or lower quality. If all customers had the same perception about the risk and rewards of the product, they would collectively demand the same price-quality mix. But each customer decides, independently of other customers, what mix of precaution and low price he or she finds to be attractive. Moreover, because the harms from risks of the supplier's decisions are distributed stochastically, every customer makes choices about the risks he is willing to accept without knowing whether he, or other customers, will incur the harm from those risks. This results in a collective action problem. As individuals, customers decide what mix of safety and low price they would like to purchase. They make that choice knowing that if they accept risks in return for low prices or more attractive products, the risks may end up injuring another customer, not themselves. When a customer makes a purchase, the customer approaches the purchase with an expectation about the safety that is built into the purchase, including both the amount of risk any customer takes and also diffuse and impressionistic expectations about the distribution of the risk among the various customers.

Suppliers choose the level of precaution and price they think will be most attractive to customers as a collective, and they adjust that level from time to time as markets reveal more information about customer preferences and technological possibilities. But if customers choose a level of risk that benefits all customers (by virtue of lower prices, greater convenience, or greater customer satisfaction) but disadvantages some (because some are going to be hurt by the product), there may be a mismatch in the socially appropriate distribution of the burdens and benefits of being a customer of that enterprise. The level of risk may be socially appropriate but its distribution may be skewed because it will not reflect the other-regarding obligations of each customer. All customers will benefit from the lower price or higher quality of the product, but some customers will be hurt by the very thing that makes the product attractive to customers in general. We can turn to one of the poster children for tort reform – the McDonald's spilled coffee case – to understand how the theory of other-regarding behavior explains why a supplier is sometimes required to compensate a customer even when the supplier has acted in a socially appropriate way.

11.2. THE MCDONALD'S HOT COFFEE CASE

McDonald's keeps it coffee hot because its customers like it that way; hotter coffee is thought to release flavor from the beans.[2] McDonald's knows that sometimes its customers spill their coffee and get burned, either because the customers behave foolishly or for reasons beyond the customer's control. McDonald's regularly settles claims when customers complain that they have been burned by its coffee. When one customer refused their settlement offer and sued, the judge let the case go to the jury and the jury found McDonald's to be responsible for a portion of the customer's injury (after attributing some of the fault to the customer) and assessed punitive damages. This behavior presents a series of conundrums. How are we to understand that McDonald's regularly settles claims in hot coffee injury cases, the jury's finding of negligence, and the role of punitive damages in cases like this?

We can understand what is at stake in a case like this by asking what burdens ought to count when McDonald's thinks about the well-being of its customers – that is, what impairment of the projects and preferences of McDonald's (and its customers) ought to be within the range of McDonald's contemplation when the supplier considers the well-being of its customers burned by hot coffee. On the one hand, if the relevant burden of preventing the harm is thought to be McDonald's ability to control the temperature of its coffee, then the burden of preventing the harm is relatively small. Lowering the temperature, which reduces the harm, is almost costless, consisting of a corporate decision communicated to the franchisees. If that is the relevant burden, we can easily understand why McDonald's settles the cases, why the judge sent the case to the jury, and why the jury concluded that McDonald's was unreasonable. The communication cost of turning down the temperature of the coffee is clearly less than the harm that would thereby be prevented.

On the other hand, the burden of turning down the coffee's temperature might also include the loss of satisfaction to McDonald's customers from having to buy the cooler (and less flavorful) coffee (at least when they are not

---

[2] Andrea Gerlin, A Matter of Degree: How a Jury Decided That a Coffee Spill Is Worth $2.9 Million, *Wall Street Journal*, Sept. 1, 1994, at A1. The relationship between heat and flavor is discussed in Specifications of the National Coffee Assoc. Available at http://www.ncausa.org/i4a/pages/index.cfm?pageid=71, and SPECIALTY COFFEE ASSOC. OF AMERICA, ROASTING AND CUPPING PROTOCOL (2009) (stating that coffee should be brewed at 200°F and served before cooling to 160°F).

hurt by the hot coffee). If this loss of satisfaction is counted as a burden of protecting against the harm of spilled coffee, the case should not have gone to the jury and McDonald's should not be settling these cases. It would not, under the Hand formula, be unreasonable to keep the coffee hot because the evidence seemed clear that the expected harm from spilled coffee (after adjusting for customer mishandling) is far less than the consumer satisfaction that would be lost if McDonald's turned down the coffee's temperature. By making a credible claim that its customers' welfare would decrease if it lowered the temperature of its coffee, McDonald's made a credible claim that turning down the temperature of its coffee would do more harm than good and was therefore not a reasonable option. So which version of the reasonable supplier should prevail?

Under this model of the *McDonald's* case, the determination of fault seems to turn on the question of what counts as a relevant burden of precaution: the communication burden of directing stores to turn down the temperature or the lost customer goodwill of turning down the temperature. But that creates a dilemma. Under one view of the case, the jury found that the relevant burden is the communication cost of turning down the temperature and therefore imposed liability on McDonald's. Under this view, the jury imposed punitive damages to force McDonald's to turn down the temperature of its coffee (which they would not do if the lost customer goodwill was greater than the amount of compensatory damages they would have to pay). On the other hand, if the burden of precautions is the lost customer goodwill, McDonald's should not have been found to be negligent in the first place and should not have been settling the cases.

Perhaps neither version of the McDonald's story is accurate. If punitive damages were designed to force McDonald's to reduce the temperature of its coffee or increase the effectiveness of its warning, the remedy has been unsuccessful. By all reports, McDonald's has failed to turn down the temperature of its coffee.[3] This could, of course, simply be a failure of the tort system, but I want to offer a different view of the case, one that shows that the dynamic of the *McDonald's* case responds to the theory of other-regarding behavior. As I demonstrated in the analysis of the *Vincent* case in Chapter Nine, sometimes a person may do the socially appropriate thing but still be required to compensate the victim. This allowed us to develop a theory of other-regarding fault that turns not on the defendant's conduct, but on the defendant's failure to undertake the conduct with the expectation of compensating the victims

[3] Mark B. Greenlee, *Kramer v. Java World: Images, Issues, and Idols in the Debate Over Tort Reform*, 26 Cap. U. L. Rev. 701, 721–30 (1997). McDonald's has, however, increased the intensity of its warning, a strategy that puts additional responsibility on the customer.

of the conduct. The fault is not in inflicting the harm but in failing to understand that the way the harm was inflicted requires a reasonable person to agree to compensate the victim for the harm.

We can apply this concept of fault to the McDonald's hot coffee case by asking what regard for the well-being of *other* customers each customer should have. The *McDonald's* case presents a contest between the well-being of two groups of McDonald's customers: the noninjured customers who enjoyed the flavor of McDonald's coffee (or some other attribute of the McDonald's product) and those who were burned by the coffee. To force McDonald's to lower the temperature of the coffee would disfavor those who liked their coffee hot, while to find that McDonald's was not responsible to decrease the temperature of the coffee would disfavor those who got burned by the coffee. If acting reasonably immunizes the defendant from liability, the law must make this choice between the flavor lovers and the victims. But if responsibility is linked to the failure to be other-regarding, then McDonald's can be acting reasonably but still be required to compensate the victims.

Realistically, McDonald's was trying to protect the hot-coffee lovers (by keeping its coffee hot) while settling cases in a way that would protect those who got burned by the coffee (after reducing the award to reflect the customer's own unreasonable behavior). The jury verdict did not upset this scheme. Although the jury award of compensatory damages seems to favor victims over those who like their coffee hot, its award of compensatory damages could not compel McDonald's to turn down the temperature of its coffee. If the aggregate damages from compensating burned customers when the temperature remains high are less than the reduced customer satisfaction from turning down the coffee's temperature (which is what McDonald's claims), McDonald's will not turn down the temperature; it will simply settle the cases when spills occur and build the cost of the settlement into the price of its product. Imposing liability can require that the harm be repaired, but it does not necessarily change a supplier's conduct. McDonald's customers who like the hot coffee but were not hurt would simply pay higher prices to cover the settlement costs for those customers who liked the McDonald's product but *were* hurt.

The justification for that result is that McDonald's derives its obligations to be other-regarding from the obligation of its customers to be other-regarding with respect to each other. All consumers benefit from the omitted precautions in the sense that they are among the class that takes advantage of the consumer satisfaction that is generated by the supplier without the precautions. They are also among the class of people potentially injured by the supplier's omitted precautions. Because the incidence of injury is random (once we have discounted the harm attributable to customer error), each consumer has an other-regarding interest in making sure that the cost of injury is internalized to the supplier. Even if McDonald's did the reasonable thing by not turning down the temperature of the coffee, they are nonetheless required to pay for the damage they impose because, under the negligence rule, those customers who benefit from the omitted precautions ought to be willing to pay those customers who are hurt by the omitted precautions.

The analogy to *Vincent* is clear. *Vincent* was reasonable in staying at the dock, even knowing that it would inflict damage to the dock; McDonald's is reasonable in not lowering the temperature of its coffee, even though it knows that its decision to keep the temperature high inflicts harm on some of its customers. As was true in *Vincent*, the finding of liability does not mean that McDonald's acted unreasonably; the jury could be saying that some reasonable decisions can be made only if the actor simultaneously agrees to compensate those who are injured by the decisions. The decision to keep the coffee hot is conditioned on the enterprise agreeing to compensate those who are injured by the hot coffee. The McDonald's Company and its customers make up an enterprise – a collective of producer and consumer. Within that enterprise, the burdens and benefits of participation are allocated so that there is equality in matching burdens and benefits. Requiring the enterprise to compensate injured customers means that those who benefit from the high temperature without any burden will help compensate those who would otherwise carry the burden of the benefit alone.

If, as I have demonstrated in this book, the essence of the wrong that must be corrected under corrective justice is the failure to think about the well-being of another in an appropriate way, then this form of responsibility is fully consistent with corrective justice. Because a customer influences the choices made by a supplier, and because the customer knows that those choices will affect the well-being of others, the customer has an obligation to take into account the well-being of those who might be adversely affected by the choices the customer makes. Where the customer benefits from the choices the supplier makes but knows that others will be hurt, the customer cannot accept the benefits without agreeing to pay for the burdens. As in *Vincent*, the people who enjoy hot coffee are using the property of those injured by the hot coffee for their benefit. Requiring them to pay for those burdens restores a kind of equality between the parties.

This is also the rule of responsibility that we conjecture would be chosen behind the veil of ignorance. All consumers know that sometimes accidents happen even without the customer's fault. All know that the temperature of the coffee benefits each coffee lover but randomly burdens some. Because no customer knows whether they are in the class of people who will be adversely affected by the high temperature, they are likely to agree to a social contract that authorizes a transfer from those who benefit to those who are hurt.

It is accurate to point out that this form of responsibility looks much like strict liability (subject to a comparative negligence defense). But that illusion stems from the belief that reasonable conduct (here, keeping the temperature on the coffee high to please the customers) cannot be the source of responsibility to others. Once we conceive of the reasonable person as proposed here – that is, as one who has appropriate regard for the well-being of others – we can see cases of this type to be a category of fault cases. It is not misleading to call them instances of strict liability when measured against a conventional fault concept, but we would not want to do that in a way that obfuscates the analysis that determines the source and scope of responsibility.

Assuming this theory has traction, how do we explain the role of punitive damages in a case like this? As already mentioned, one function of punitive damages would be to induce McDonald's to lower the temperature of their coffee. Setting punitive damage high enough would do that. But I suggest a different function for the punitive damages award in a case like this – namely, to induce McDonald's to increase the amount of its settlement offers. McDonald's routinely settles these cases. They make a settlement offer after determining how much of the responsibility for the accident could fairly be attributed to customer error, discounting the harm by the amount they think a jury would attribute to customer error. In the rare case that was tried, McDonald's misunderstood how the jury would perceive customer error; the punitive damages reflected that misperception. By assessing punitive damages (later lowered on appeal), the jury was telling McDonald's that they ought to offer larger settlements, which they would have to do to avoid jury trials. Under this reading, the function of punitive damages is not to punish McDonald's conduct with respect to the temperature of the coffee, but to monitor the decisions they make in the settlement of the cases. This, too, focuses on the nature of McDonald's other-regarding behavior.

11.3. THE GENERAL MODEL

I have described the model of customer-centered enterprise liability in the context of the *McDonald's* hot coffee case. Let me now generalize the attributes of the model and then show the borders that keep the model from overturning the general principle that reasonable conduct is not a source of responsibility to compensate another.

The model of customer-centered enterprise responsibility has the following attributes:

- The supplier imposes risks on its customers in order to benefit customers. In the *McDonald's* case, the benefit was the actual or perceived benefit of better-tasting coffee. In many other cases, however, the supplier takes risks in order to reduce the cost of providing services. A waterworks does not inspect the pipe. To save money, stores keep merchandise on pallets rather than putting them on shelves and the pallets present a risk. In cases like these, the supplier omits a precaution in order to increase customer satisfaction with the supplier's product or service.

- The risk generated by producing this customer benefit is a risk only to customers of the supplier. These are not cases in which the omitted safety feature implicates the well-being of noncustomers, like those where the omitted safety feature allows a lawnmower to kick out pebbles that hurt a passing pedestrian.[4] The circle of those adversely affected by the risk is limited to customers and potential customers. The benefit of not addressing the risk (and thus not building the cost of precaution into the product or service) must be a collective benefit, derived from comparing the adverse effects of higher prices when precautions are taken with the benefits of greater precautions.

- This customer-centered enterprise liability makes sense, however, only when the supplier creates the risk (in the sense discussed in Chapter Seven). It is only in that situation that the decision to impose the risk can be understood to be in the interests of the collective (the enterprise), but not in the interest of the individual. If the risk arises from outside of, and is not controlled by, the supplier, the benefit of not addressing the risk (and thus not building the cost of precautions into the cost base of the supplier) affects the customers collectively and they must be understood to be making a collective decision that binds the individual. For example, if the issue is whether a big box discount store should invest more to protect customers in the store's parking lot, the relevant analytical inquiry is whether the additional costs (in the aggregate) adversely affect customers more than the additional precautions would benefit customers. If the response is that the investment of resources is not

---

4 If the hot coffee burns noncustomers, presumably the victim's recourse, if any, is against the person who bought or was using the coffee. Customers who buy hot coffee must also be other-regarding.

socially justified, then no individual can claim compensation. To give an individual compensation would adversely affect the collective good by raising prices, which is the very thing the law is trying to avoid.

- The expected harm must be less than the burden of reducing the benefits to consumers by changing the supplier's method of doing business. Clearly, if the supplier could reduce the general incidence of harm without sacrificing consumer satisfaction or raising prices, the other-regarding supplier (acting on behalf of its other-regarding customers) would do so.

- Finally, the incidence of harm from the omitted precautions must be essentially random. The law achieves this goal by allowing the jury to determine what portion of the harm is attributable to the inadequate precautions of the customer – the inattention to hot coffee or to the customer's surroundings. Once the jury eliminates the victim's contribution to the harm, then the harm that results is essentially random – a roulette wheel that picks some consumers but not others for the associated harm.

Under this narrow set of circumstances, the customers of a supplier ought to be willing to pay higher prices to allow the supplier to compensate other customers who are hurt by the supplier's risky but satisfaction-producing decisions. Because the customers know that they will be using another person's property to enhance the value of their own property, the obligation to pay reparations flows from the obligation to incorporate the well-being of others into their own well-being when they make decisions.

11.4. CONCLUSION

In this chapter, I have identified a specialized kind of enterprise liability that tort law recognizes, one that is drawn from, and is consistent with, the theory of other-regarding behavior. That liability flows from the responsibility an enterprise has when its decisions benefit all customers but impose randomly distributed costs on individual customers – the responsibility to build into the price of the product the amount necessary to compensate the injured customers for their losses. The justification for this form of customer-centered enterprise liability is that the enterprise represents the decisions of its customers, who themselves have an obligation to be other-regarding toward other customers and the public. In order to be other-regarding, customers who receive the benefits of the enterprise's decisions ought to be willing to compensate those customers who are harmed by the decisions.

This is another example of liability without faulty conduct, but it is not an example of liability without fault. The fault occurs when the enterprise (on behalf of its customers as a collective) makes decisions that knowingly cause harm to some individuals without also agreeing to compensate those individuals. In essence, the enterprise is using the property of the customers who are hurt to benefit customers who are not hurt, and a fair matching of burdens and benefits requires that conferring the benefit be conditioned on also compensating those who would otherwise be burdened. This is an application of the principle of the *Vincent* case discussed in Chapter Nine. Liability in these cases is neither an anomaly nor an example of strict or general enterprise liability. It does, however, represent an important instance in which tort law works out fair terms of interaction between members of a common enterprise by requiring each person to take into account the well-being of other members of the enterprise.

12 Social Cohesion and Knowledge

The Intentional Torts

It is understood that intentional torts chart the boundary between socially acceptable and antisocial behavior – between, for example, offensive and inoffensive contact or between reasonable and unreasonable invasion of another's emotional well-being. The connection with social cohesion is clear. Yet it is also common to think of intentional torts as a different class of torts from those encompassed by the negligence regime. That division is understandable if we consider the paradigmatic case of the person who knowingly and maliciously hits another. The fault in that kind of a case seems to be a far cry from the fault in the case of the person who inadvertently fails to check the blind spot in the mirror when changing lanes.

Yet these two tort regimes are joined together by the theory of other-regarding behavior, for each represents a situation in which one person has failed to appropriately consider the well-being of another. Moreover, the border between negligence torts and intentional torts is far thinner than is normally supposed. For example, the cases discussed in the last chapter are not usually thought of as implicating intentional torts, but they do. In those cases, the defendant knew that harm would occur and that knowledge was one of the reasons they were responsible for reacting reasonably to the harm.

In this chapter, I explore our understanding of the relationship between negligence torts and intentional torts by showing how intentional torts embody the theory of other-regarding behavior developed in this book. I do that to refute the common assumption that intentional torts inhabit a fundamentally different realm of responsibility from negligence torts. I show the analytical and theoretical link between intentional and nonintentional torts and argue that intentional and nonintentional torts embody identical theories of social cohesion, differing in only one respect: Because the actor's state of knowledge is different in intentional torts than in negligence torts, the law changes the burden of proof in intentional torts, requiring the actor to prove that her conduct was reasonable.

12.1. INTRODUCTION

Intentional and nonintentional torts are drawn together if we understand that they both rely on a theory of responsibility that depends on an assessment of how actors make decisions. The theory of other-regarding behavior evaluates the actor's conduct by specifying the information an actor should consider when making decisions that affect another's well-being and how the actor should process that information. Negligence torts focus on the actor's information about risks, while intentional torts focus on the actor's information about the consequences of her actions. In both instances, however, responsibility in tort law focuses on what the actor's conduct tells us about the actor's attitude toward the well-being of others and how an actor would have acted were she appropriately thinking about the well-being of others. As this chapter explains, the two types of tort differ only because the distinction between knowing of risks and knowing of the consequences of one's actions on another justifies the law in asking an actor who knows of the consequences to bear the burden of showing that she acted reasonably.

The intent element of intentional torts focuses on the actor's knowledge that the action she takes will result in the kind of effect that the law seeks to avoid. This can be understood as other-regarding behavior in the following sense. When an actor knows with a substantial degree of certainty that the actor's decision is going to result in specified consequences to another, or acts with the purpose of causing the consequences, the actor is held to have intended those consequences.[1] The actor is then obligated to modify the decision to avoid the consequences or to justify the actor's decision to allow the consequences to occur. The actor's knowledge of the consequences of her action triggers the obligation to be other-regarding; the actor's responsibility is to understand what society means by social harm and under what circumstances the infliction of harm is justified.

At first blush, this formulation looks to be different from the parallel formulation of responsibility in the negligence regime. The negligence inquiry is triggered when an actor knows of a risk for which the actor is responsible

---

[1] As Mark A. Geistfeld has written, "if the actor knows that his or her conduct is substantially certain to produce a consequence, then the choice to engage in the conduct establishes the intent to cause the consequences." Mark A. Geistfeld, ESSENTIALS OF TORT LAW, 115, Wolters Kluwer (2008). The leading case is *Garret v. Dailey*, 279 P. 2d 1091 (Wash. 1951).

but does not know whether the risk will ripen into harm. Then, the negligence standard imposes a duty to act reasonably with respect to the risk, limited only by the victim's reciprocal duty to also act reasonably with respect to the same risk and by circumstances connecting the actor's conduct and harm for which the actor is not responsible. The "excuses" for not doing more for the victim are built into the concept of reasonableness (the limitations on responsibility that, as we have seen, are embedded in the concepts of duty and proximate cause and the victim's own negligence or assumption of the risk). Liability in intentional torts turns on three features that seem to distinguish intentional torts from negligence torts: (1) responsibility flows from the actor's knowledge of the consequences (as opposed to knowledge of the risk); (2) the harm in intentional torts consists of a wider range of antisocial harm; and (3) the concept of justification is available for intentional torts but not negligence torts. It might seem, therefore, and is commonly assumed, that intentional torts must be driven by a different theory of responsibility than the theory that propels negligence torts. However, once we interpret these features in light of the theory of other-regarding behavior, we see that the theory of intentional torts is strikingly similar to negligence theory, separated only by the distinction between knowledge of the consequence and knowledge of the risk.

In this chapter, I maintain that knowledge sufficient to create the requisite intent for intentional torts is the knowledge that would, in a reasonable person, trigger the obligation to take into account the well-being of the victim. That commonality between intentional and negligence torts establishes their shared theory of responsibility. Once the requisite obligation to think about the well-being of another is shown in intentional torts, the actor's responsibility is to either stop the conduct or to justify it by showing that the consequence is lawful (not socially harmful) or not unreasonable (harmful but outweighed by other considerations). Both the concept of social harm and the concept of a reasonable justification for the conduct turn on the reasonableness of one person's consideration of the well-being of another. In the case of battery, for example, once an actor knows with a substantial degree of certainty that forbidden contact will take place, the actor must either prove that the consequence was not "offensive contact" or that the offensive contact was justified. In the case of assault, once the actor knows with a substantial degree of certainty that the conduct will put another in justified fear, the actor must justify the conduct. In both cases, the obligation is to think reasonably about the well-being of the other by continuing the conduct only if it is reasonable to do so – that is, only if the contact is (in the case of battery) not offensive or (in the case of assault) such as would not instill reasonable fear in a victim, or only if the actor inflicts the harm under circumstances that make the conduct reasonable. In other intentional torts, where the justification for the conduct is more ambiguous, the definition of the harm to be avoided generally includes the concept of unreasonable harm, so that the determination of which conduct is reasonable includes determining whether the conduct is justified because of consent, necessity, or self-defense. The protection of both emotional harm and freedom of mobility depend on a finding that the harm was unreasonably imposed. Because the finding of intent is linked to the obligation to take into account the well-being of others, and because appropriate consideration of the well-being of others revolves around the reasonableness concept, intentional torts and negligence torts are tied together by the theory of other-regarding behavior.

The connection to social cohesion is then clear. The goal of social cohesion requires people to channel their behavior into conduct that respects the well-being of others and therefore balances the freedom of expression and movement that advances their own projects and preferences against the security that allows others to advance their projects and preferences. The security that results is reciprocal in the sense that every member of society shares both the burdens and the benefits of that security. Without that security, individuals either reduce investment in their projects and preferences or look for ways of retaliating in order to protect their projects and preferences. Either way, society loses. People either curtail their own contributions to society or invest in unproductive anger and retaliation. The capacity to contribute to society is reduced and the chance of violence is increased.

I amplify these themes in the following three sections, focusing on the relationship between the requirements of social cohesion and the elements of knowledge, the determination of consequences that are antisocial (and therefore harmful), and justifications for inflicting antisocial harm.

12.2. KNOWLEDGE OF CONSEQUENCES AND SOCIAL COHESION

When we ask the jury whether the actor knew that the consequence of her conduct was substantially certain to result, we are asking the jury to determine whether the actor's degree of consciousness about the consequences of her contact was sufficient to trigger the actor's responsibility for the well-being of another. A high degree of certainty about what consequences were about to happen signifies that if the actor did not reverse the decision, the well-being of another would be affected, and this knowledge triggers the requirement that the actor consider the nature of the harm and either reverse or justify the decision. The obligation to consider the well-being of another when the actor has sufficient knowledge of the consequences of her action is the obligation that a reasonable person would take under those circumstances, for the knowledge of the harm from the actor's decision is enough to induce a reasonable actor to think harder about the consequences and their justification. The obligation reflects the same theory of social cohesion and other-regarding behavior that drives the negligence standard.

The standard to determine whether the actor has sufficient knowledge to trigger the obligation to think about the well-being of another is, of course, a subjective standard. The jury is asked to determine what the person knew and what degree of certainty that person actually had about the consequences of her actions. If the actor somehow shows that she did not know that the consequences were substantially certain to result, then the actor has not committed an intentional tort. This seems to separate intentional from negligence torts by relying on a subjective standard for intentional torts and an objective standard for negligence torts. What draws them together is that once a person has the requisite knowledge, if they are to be reasonable (i.e., if they are to make the decision a reasonable person with that knowledge would make), they are required to consider the well-being of the person who would suffer the consequences. The law's reliance on a subjective standard in intentional torts reflects the law's expectation that once people know of the consequences, they know that they have the obligation to govern their conduct by those consequences.[2]

One way to see the relationship between intentional torts and negligence torts is to consider how intentional torts respond to an actor's autonomy and agency in ways that are similar to negligence torts.

Like negligence torts, intentional torts protect the autonomy of the actor. Intentional torts occur only in situations in which the actor is in control of the instrumentality of harm and therefore only where the actor has already taken action that signifies a choice to become enmeshed in another's well-being. It is not an intentional tort for an actor to fail to pick up the baby from the tracks when a train is approaching, even though the actor knows with a substantial degree of certainty that the baby will die if the actor does nothing. Like negligence torts, intentional torts work within a theory of social cohesion that keeps society from imposing obligations on the actor when the actor has not accepted the obligation to think of the well-being of another.

---

[2]   Moreover, of course, the subjective intent – what the actor actually knew – is often proven by what a reasonable person in that situation would have known. This provides a further link between the knowledge requirement of the intentional and the negligence torts.

Like negligence torts, intentional torts also protect the agency of the actor. Contact that comes from spasmodic or involuntary actions cannot form an intentional tort. A minimum requirement of intentional torts is that the actor must have made a decision, and the minimum requirement of a decision is that the actor would have been able to bring about a different result with a different decision. The "but for" concept of causation ensures that if the harm would have occurred even had the actor made a different decision, the actor is not responsible for the harm. And intentional torts embrace a concept akin to proximate cause that absolves the actor from responsibility if the actor is not responsible for taking into account the circumstances that connected his decision to the victim's harm.

Even the definition of what it means to know the consequences of an act with a substantial degree of certainty is congruent with the reasonable person concept. It is accepted that an actor's knowledge that one in a hundred thousand bottles of soda will explode (and that the explosion will risk harm) is not enough knowledge to make the act of selling a bottle of soda an intentional tort. That presents something of a mystery, because the actor with that knowledge literally complies with the requirement that the actor know, with a substantial degree of certainty that forbidden consequences will result. But the mystery is addressed once we understand that if the risk has been reduced by reasonable measures, an other-regarding actor need not consider the possibility that residual risk remains and that it will certainly cause harm. The information relates to a matter that is beyond the actor's agency – something over which the actor has no effective control. It is not information that a reasonable person would take into account when deciding how careful to be, because there is, by hypothesis, no way to reduce the harm except by discontinuing the activity (which, by hypothesis, yields net social benefits). Accordingly, the law does not make the mere knowledge that one in a hundred thousand bottles will explode a basis for imposing responsibility for those consequences (unless the knowledge is enough to invoke the kind of customer-centered enterprise liability discussed in Chapter Eleven).

12.3. UNREASONABLE CONSEQUENCES

The difference between knowledge of risks and knowledge of controllable consequences is this: Sufficient knowledge of the consequences requires the actor either to stop the conduct or to justify the results, which the actor can do by showing either that the conduct is not socially harmful or that the harm to the victim is outweighed by a more important social goal. Once an actor knows that her conduct will result in unjustified (but controllable) consequences, the only way to protect the well-being of the victim is to stop the conduct. Failure to stop the conduct is failure to have appropriate regard for the well-being of the victim. Thus, an actor who knows that bodily contact will occur must be confident that it will not be offensive contact, or that it is justified by the pull of some acknowledged greater good. Under the doctrine of assault, an actor who knows that her conduct will threaten contact with another must be confident that it will not frighten another or that the conduct is justified by some greater good. And a person who knows that her conduct will damage another emotionally must be able to distinguish between emotional harm reasonably inflicted and that unreasonably inflicted.

But the standards for determining whether social harm occurs and the justifications for inflicting harm are, at their foundation, governed by decision-making standards that a reasonable person would use in those circumstances. The standards are ones that promote social cohesion by promoting social interaction that reasonably balances the projects and preferences of different people in a community. Intentional torts are a special case of reasonable other-regarding behavior, applicable when the actor knows that the harm is substantially certain to take place. Intentional torts therefore incorporate the same theory of social cohesion that animates negligence torts.

Take, for example, battery. The restatement formulation – offensive contact – is founded on a reasonableness standard that builds on socially acceptable – and therefore reasonable – contact. In the absence of information to the contrary, an actor is allowed to assume that some forms of contact will be widely understood to be inoffensive under community standards – those forms of contact that signify solidarity or connection. An actor is not responsible for the effects of the contact if that is true, and one who resents such contact must find a way to signal that the contact is offensive. Inoffensive contact is contact that a reasonable person would expect in that situation and that the injurer would endorse if the injurer did not know whether he was the injurer or victim; the reasonableness inquiry is an embedded part of intentional torts. Even when contact is not governed by a specific (and reasonable) social norm, the contact can be analyzed in terms of relative burdens on actor and victim. Where an actor is in a private conference and the door suddenly opens, the contact the actor initiates by shoving the door back on the intruder is not offensive because it is not, under the circumstances, unreasonable. The minimal invasion of the intruder's bodily integrity (the burden on the intruder's projects and preferences) is justified by the actor's interest in not having the private conference burdened by an unjustified (and unexpected) interruption.[3] The actor is entitled to assume that a person desiring to come in will knock first or

---

[3] *Wishnatsky v. Dailey*, 46 Wash. 2d 197 (1955).

otherwise take account of the legitimate privacy preferences of the conferees. Like the reasonable person, the actor who pushes the door into an intruder must take into account the possibility that the intruder will have a thin skull, but the mere fact that the actor closed the door in the intruder's face does not establish an inappropriate regard for the well-being of the intruder.

The concept of offensive contact is also driven by the same attention to information asymmetries as negligence torts. If the actor has specific information about the sensitivities of another, the actor must factor those sensitivities into the actor's decision about what kinds of contact to initiate. Just as one who drives past a truck that is labeled to contain explosives must reasonably take that information into account, an actor must take into account specific information about the proclivities or sensitivities of another.

For intentional torts outside of assault and battery, the definition of what effects are to be avoided revolves more explicitly around the reasonableness standard. When the plaintiff alleges the intentional infliction of emotional harm, the court must compare the plaintiff's harm with the social value of the defendant's conduct, and this is fundamentally a reasonableness determination. The analytical structure that determines whether an actor has thought appropriately about the well-being of others also determines whether an actor is allowed to burden the victim's projects and preferences with emotional harm in order to pursue her own projects and preferences. The comparison reflects the social value of the projects and preferences of the two activities and a social ranking that settles the unavoidable conflict between them. Here, too, the device of the original position allows a court to reason its way to a resolution of the conflict by imagining how an impartial spectator would rank the conflicting claims.

Similarly, an allegation of false imprisonment requires a court to make an analogous determination, this time focused on the victim's freedom of motion and the injurer's goals in restraining another.[4] The social contract determines the extent to which one who is restrained must surrender freedom of movement in order to advance the projects and preferences of the restrainer or, on the other hand, when the restraint surpasses the bounds of socially accepted limitations on physical freedom and commits the restrainer to other means of achieving her projects and preferences.

12.4. REASONABLENESS DEFENSES

Intentional torts are also subject to a reasonableness defense. An actor is privileged to initiate the harmful consequences protected by intentional torts if

[4] *Lopez v. Winchell's Donut House*, 120 Ill. App. 3d 46 (1984).

doing so is justified by, for example, consent, self-defense, necessity, or other privilege. These defenses, too, encompass the concept of social cohesion, for these defenses also require a court to understand the way that social values, interpreted behind a veil of ignorance, would understand the conflicting claims of individual interests. These defenses, too, revolve around the reasonableness concept.

These defenses separate intentional from negligence torts by the fact that the defendant has the burden of establishing the defense. This burden shifting is justified by the fact that both the actor's knowledge of the consequences and the social harm caused by the consequences are socially detrimental enough to require the actor to accept the burden of demonstrating some greater social value. But the divide between intentional and negligence torts in this regard ought not be overemphasized, for the negligence regime also shifts the burden of demonstrating that what appears to be antisocial and unreasonable conduct was in fact serving some larger social purpose or was otherwise beyond the actor's control. As we have seen, burden shifting is an important part of the negligence concept: If a doctor leaves a sponge in a patient, the doctor is allowed to demonstrate some event beyond the doctor's control (like a bomb scare) that justified the conduct. *Res ipsa loquitur* routinely shifts the burden to the defendant to show that the way the accident happened was beyond the defendant's control. And once a victim makes a plausible showing that the defendant omitted an important (and cost-effective) precaution, the court may shift the burden to the defendant to justify its failure to take the precaution.

12.5. CONCLUSION

Rather than being a different species of tort, intentional torts are, under the reading I have given, an application of the obligation to appropriately consider the well-being of another. Intentional torts differ with respect to the nature of the knowledge that triggers the obligation to be other-regarding, for they center on the level of the actor's knowledge of the consequences of her action, but that is the only significant difference between intentional and negligence torts. All other aspects of intentional torts – the determination of whether the conduct was socially harmful and shifting the burden to the defendant to justify the harm – apply reasonableness principles (and principles of other-regarding behavior) that reflect the different nature of the knowledge that triggers the two kinds of tort cases. In this way, negligence and intentional torts can be understood to reflect identical theories of responsibility.

PART IV

SUMMARY AND IMPLICATIONS

In this part, I briefly summarize the implications of the theory developed in this book. I first link the theory developed in the book to a conception of law as a behavioral science and repeat some of the themes and methodologies of the book that flow from this conception. I then present a summary of the analytical framework the book develops to understand and evaluate tort law.

13 The Whole in One

The law's curse is that it sees itself sitting outside the social realm, as if the law were commanding how people ought to act, much like a traffic cop or senior officer. It pretends to reform society from the outside, channeling behavior by creating or recognizing rights and responsibilities from abstract principles or generalized rules that seem to transcend human interaction. In fact, the law operates within the social realm, moving to influence how people *ought* to make decisions by recognizing how people *do* make decisions, endorsing those methods of making decisions that seem to be good for the community and gently inducing people to change those that do not.

Thus, a major theme of this book is a plea to understand private law in a new way – as the institution society has created to work within society by recognizing and endorsing forms of interpersonal decision making that appear to be good for the community and correcting those that do not. This theme suggests that we need a new way of understanding the concept of law – a recognition that private law embodies a methodology of resolving disputes by understanding how people ought to think about their relationships with other members of the community. This, in turn, requires that we understand law as a method of analyzing human decision making and behavior when humans interact, and it implies that the goal of the law is to recognize an assignment of rights and responsibilities that makes each person better off by requiring an actor to sometimes sacrifice the actor's individual interests for the sake of others so that others will sometime sacrifice their interests for the actor. And that means that actors must sometimes make the projects and preferences of others a part of their own projects and preferences.

This book has sought to provide a way of thinking about the obligations recognized and imposed by tort law that responds to this conception of law. If it is successful, it will be because it provides a framework and methodology for understanding the interpersonal, social, and moral dynamics that influence

and shape tort law, allowing people to comprehend the positive and normative aspects of tort law using a new vocabulary and new analytical filters. The
success will not be in adopting the particular applications of the theory that I
have advanced, but in shifting the terms of the debate to recognize, and work
within, the frameworks and methodology portrayed here. These frameworks
will allow us to avoid continuing debate about well-worn questions, like the
relative merits of strict and negligence liability and the differences between
nonfeasance and misfeasance. Instead, it will allow people to focus on a new
set of questions, those laid out later in the chapter, including the following: why we think that people behind a veil of ignorance would choose one
outcome over another, what kinds of personal choices indicate that an actor
has accepted responsibility for the well-being of another, whether the scope of
responsibility for the well-being of others should be extended because of new
principal–agent relationships, and new conceptions of the nature of activities
that allow activities to absorb greater expense without offsetting detriments to
the activities. To me, questions like these are the ones around which analytical debate should revolve.

The responses derived from these lines of questions should allow theorists
to develop a conception of tort law that responds to the three major themes
of the book: the need for greater justificational analysis, the need to integrate
thought across conventional boundaries, and the need to see the law as a
coherent response to the social problems that flow from the fact that people
make decisions that impact others in the community.

The need for justificational analysis reflects the need to explain why the law
reacts as it does when a victim claims that another should repair the injury. If
the law is to operate within, rather than outside, the social system, the law's
justification for its commands must not resort to abstract principles, generalized commands, or legal distinctions that have no social counterpart. Instead,
the law must respond to the question of *why* cases come out one way rather
than another by attaching itself to a conception of how people think about
their behavior and its consequences, both in concrete situations and as a matter of social morality. The law therefore needs to integrate thought across traditional boundaries, for the behavioral issues with which tort law deals are
not within the exclusive realm of any one discipline. If we are to understand
law as a behavioral science (as we surely must under this conception of law),
then we must draw on an appreciation of human behavior that integrates the
behavioral theories of economics, sociology, anthropology, and psychology,
and understand them as a reflection of the moral values developed by a society. Finally, the coherence theme responds to the need to understand law
in the way that people subject to the law understand it: as the application of

socially developed and evolving conceptions of obligation and responsibility that people apply in their daily affairs and that therefore flow from a centralized set of understandings about human behavior. Occam's razor reflects human heuristics and is much needed in the law.

In this chapter, I briefly summarize the distinctive methodologies deployed in this book (Section 13.1) and summarize the framework I offer for analyzing tort cases as we link theory with application (Section 13.2).

13.1. GENERAL METHODOLOGIES

Bottom-Up Approach: As a behavioral science law is understood to be a response to values created in the thousands of interactions between people in a community, as evaluated through a Kantian/Rawlsian approach to social morality. As a result, the building blocks used to construct the legal edifice are social, not legal, and the law is built from the bottom up rather than the top down. We ought not look for a legal principle to apply to a particular situation, we ought instead to look for the maxim that people must be applying when they decide how to behave, and we must construct the law in response to that maxim. We look to precedent, to be sure, but the relevant issue is not the similarity of two situations to each other, but the similarity in the way people make decisions in the two situations (and the law's response to those decisions).

Outputs and Inputs: For this reason, the methodology relied on here does not confuse outputs with inputs. The input into a legal decision is the analysis of human behavior and decision making in a particular situation, and it is that analysis that determines whether an actor has a legal obligation or responsibility. The conclusion we reach in response to the analysis tells us what we need to know about the output – the concept of obligation or responsibility that the law is using – but the concept is the output, not the input. The only way to make the concept that is being deployed into an input is to understand the concept in terms of the content of the analysis that determines how the concept is applied – that is, to understand the concept to tell us what inputs into the analysis are relevant to the justified output.

Evaluating Behavior by Examining the Decision Making That Led to the Behavior: It is conventionally understood that tort law evaluates an actor's conduct to determine whether it was reasonable. Because conduct is the only observable matter from which judgments about the actor's responsibility can be made, this understanding is natural. But when evaluating conduct, we must be asking what decisional methodology led to the conduct and evaluate that methodology. Driving at 80 miles an hour means one thing if the actor is trying to get to the beach in a hurry and a different thing if the actor is taking a heart attack victim to the hospital. What differentiates the two situations is the factors legitimately taken into account by the actor when deciding how fast to go, and that focuses not on the speed the actor chose (the conduct) but the decision-making process the actor used to decide how fast to go. By focusing analysis on the kind of decisional methodology that each of the parties ought to have used, we can link legal analysis with human behavior in a way that productively orients the law toward influencing the attitude with which each individual views her role in the community, and therefore to the Kantian notion that decisions must be made with neutrality and universality in mind. The issue always is: If the defendant had been thinking in the appropriate way about her own interests in light of the interests of others in the community, would the defendant have acted the way she did? The evidentiary focus is on the actor's behavior, but the analytical focus is on the actor's decision-making methodology that led to the conduct. By correcting the way people make decisions – that is, the methodology they use – the law affects behavior in a way that is far more effective than trying to affect behavior in a vacuum.

Generalizability: I conjecture that the theory developed here is a general theory of private law, not limited to tort law, because it influences the causal mechanism that determines behavior, providing the justificational and normative basis for understanding property law, contract law, and unjust enrichment. This conjecture flows from the fact that private law focuses on relationships between people when they face coordination problems. In contract law, the relevant relationship is the one that people develop concerning future opportunities. In property law, it is the relationship that people form over claims to resources. In unjust enrichment, it is the relationship that people form over unearned benefits. Each of these fields can be understood and analyzed by asking in what circumstances social cohesion requires that the decisions of one actor ought to take into account the well-being of another member of the community. Each of these fields requires that in a relationship an actor make decisions taking into account the well-being of other people in the community in a way that the actor would endorse if the actor were behind the veil of ignorance (and therefore possibly in the other's shoes). Once every member of the community makes decisions in that way, the community will be efficient (maximizing the contribution of each member of the community given the need to coordinate activities), fair (because the division of rights and responsibilities is one that would be made behind the veil of ignorance), and stable over time (because the division of rights and responsibilities is widely accepted and can be renegotiated within the community as circumstances and social values change).

The theory developed here is congruent with recognized characteristics of private law. Private law is reactive, created only when people bring disputes to the law. When disputes can be settled without the law, it is because parties in a relationship are either appropriately other-regarding or can negotiate over what appropriate other-regarding behavior is. As preexisting social cohesion increases, the need for law decreases. When the law must intervene, it is because the parties cannot determine whose projects and preferences should be sacrificed so that another's need not be. The intervention is not so much to declare rights and responsibilities based on some abstract preconception of rights and responsibility from outside the social system, but to reason toward rights and responsibilities that would be widely acceptable, even to the person who loses the case, because they appeal to deep-seated values of fairness and efficiency and can be explained and justified. Thus, the function of the law is to consider which adjustment of rights and responsibilities best comports with the values that most people use as they make coordination decisions in the many ways they do every day.

In private law, the dispute provides the justification for the intervention, because the alternative to intervention is to allow the dispute to be settled by some nonjudicial means, which must always be by resort to some form of force or private power. Resort to force or private power to settle disputes or to govern the allocation of rights and responsibilities can never lead to social cohesion, for it can never quell the resentment and anger that it breeds. The goal of the use of judicial power is clear – to resolve the dispute in a way that induces the parties to accept the decision as one they can live with even if they lose the case. And the acceptability of the outcome determines the legitimacy and stability of the force of law on society.

The legitimacy of the law-making through private law dispute resolution is also enhanced by the constraints put on judicial intervention by the limited range of considerations that are relevant to resolving the dispute. The intervention is limited by the relational rights claimed by the parties and by the information base those parties bring to the dispute. The power of the court as decision maker is to adjust the rights as between the parties based on information relating to that kind of relationship. It is distributional only in the sense that it distributes the rights and obligations between the parties and those similarly situated. And because it is based on reasoning behind the veil of ignorance, it does not allow those kinds of decision to be based on such factors as need or private benefit that would be relevant if the issue were one of distributional justice.

Private law is therefore limited to correcting failures to think of the well-being of others by awarding compensation to correct the failure. It is this feature of private law that allowed the efficiency hypothesis to bloom. In the environment of private law, the function of the law is to recognize rights and responsibilities as between the parties, and because that involves minimizing interference between the parties, the result can easily be labeled as efficient. But this does not make efficiency either the goal of private law or the sole determinant of its content. To say that it is efficient to correct imbalances says no more than that corrective justice includes efficiency as one of the determinants of a wrong that must be corrected. The suggestion, now made explicit, is that legal analysis ought to be synthetic rather than antithetic, that we ought to put aside our natural proclivity as lawyers to emphasize differences and divisions, and that if we find differences and divisions to be inexplicable, we search for a new analytical lens through which to understand law. I hope that by identifying the theory of other-regarding behavior as the single guiding star of tort law, I might induce others to search for integrative methodologies and synthetic theories in other private law realms.

13.2. THE ANALYTICS OF TORTS CASES

Justificational analysis suggests that what tort law needs is not more rules, principles, or doctrines, but a framework within which the analyst can integrate ideas from various perspectives about the circumstances, factors, and values that ought to impel a court to decide a case one way rather than another. The law is shaped by the questions it asks, questions that allow us to understand what the law's commands should be. What is important in justificational analysis is not the output of the analysis but the input, and the input must respond to a series of questions rather than a series of rules, principles, or doctrines. The theory developed in this book suggests that tort law can be understood as a response to the following series of questions, moving from the general to the specific.

Distinguishing Intentional Torts from Negligence: To distinguish intentional from negligence torts, the first question is whether the actor has knowledge of the consequences of her decision or simply knowledge of the risks that are legitimately encompassed within the scope of her decisions. If the actor knew of the consequences (or wanted the consequences to occur), we think about the conduct as an intentional tort and ask whether the degree of knowledge of the consequences is enough to require the actor to consider the well-being of those who might be affected by the consequences (which is what the law means when it refers to knowledge that the consequences are substantially certain to result). If the answer to that question is affirmative, the actor is required either to understand correctly that the consequences will not be considered harmful to society (the inoffensive tap on the shoulder) or that the consequences are justified because they are reasonably imposed. If, on the other hand, the knowledge is only about the risks another faces, the actor does not intend any harm simply by intending the risks and the case is a negligence case.

Within Intentional Torts: Once an intentional tort is found, the issue is whether the actor acted reasonably with respect to the knowledge the actor had – namely, whether a reasonable person in that circumstance would have considered the consequence to be socially harmful and whether the consequence was reasonable because it served an important, socially recognized purpose. For intentional torts like the infliction of mental distress, the analysis gets rolled into one question – whether the infliction of emotional distress was reasonable because it served a socially acceptable purpose by socially acceptable means.

Hybrid Cases: Two special instances of substantial certainty bridge the divide between intentional and negligence torts. Sometimes an enterprise knows with a substantial degree of certainty that its decision will result in forbidden harm. If that certainty exists after reasonable care has been taken, the knowledge generally does not result in liability if the social value of the activity outweighs the incidence of harm. In the language of intentional torts, the contact is not offensive. Knowledge that one in a hundred thousand bottles of soda will explode does not lead to liability. In the language of negligence, the harm is not unreasonably imposed. On the other hand, for the reasons given in Chapter Eleven, if the harm is imposed on some customers for the benefit of other customers, the enterprise has an obligation to compensate those harmed. Knowledge of the harm, even when reasonably imposed, is, in the language of intentional torts, offensive unless it is compensated harm.

Within the Category of Negligence Torts: Within the category of negligence torts, the first question is whether the actor has created the risk (i.e., whether, but for the decisions of the actor, the risk would not have arisen) or whether the risk would exist independently of the actor's decisions. If the former, the question of duty-as-obligation has no independent analytical force, for the act of creating the risk also creates the obligation to reasonably address the risk. However, if the actor did not create the risk, the obligation to address the risk arises only if there is a basis for saying that the actor's decisions as to her activities necessarily imply the obligation to reasonably address the risk. This is the "special relationship" between the actor's choice of activities and the risk that creates the obligation to address the risk.

Actors Who Create a Risk: For actors who did create a risk, the responsibility is to reasonably address the risk. This involves questions of breach and proximate cause, for an initial question is whether a reasonable person (thinking appropriately about the well-being of others) would have understood the circumstances that connect the conduct to the harm and have taken them into account when making decisions. If the circumstances are ones that a reasonable person would *not* have accounted for in her decision making, the actor is not unreasonable in failing to take that circumstance into account. This is the case of the speeding trolley on which a tree falls, the attempt to open with a chisel a package (that turned out to contain nitroglycerine), the case of the boy twirling an eight-foot wire near the exposed wires of a trolley, and the case of the passengers who brought the fireworks onto the train platform. If the circumstances are ones that a reasonable person would have addressed, the issue is whether the actor did so. This involves the question of whether a reasonable person in the actor's position, but sitting behind the veil of ignorance and searching for a decision maxim that was neutral and universal, would have done more to protect the plaintiff.

Even if the actor in this class of negligence cases acted unreasonably, there is a narrow class of cases in which an actor who is responsible for the harm should nonetheless not be held liable for the harm. We understand this class of cases by asking whether there are prudential reasons for cutting off liability so that the actor is able to pay other claimants without bankrupting the actor (which would deny full recovery to any plaintiff).

Where the Actor Did Not Create the Risk: Here, there are two issues for the judge. The first is the existence of the obligation to think of the well-being of others, and we get at that issue by asking whether the actor's choice of activities fairly implies that the actor has fairly chosen to accept responsibility for the risk another faces. We ask whether a reasonable person in the actor's position would understand that, given the actor's activity, other people are justifiably relying on the actor to address the risk and whether the harm occurred as a result of that risk. This is now an easy question when the actor is a supplier and the victim a customer, but the obligation extends beyond the supplier–customer relationship. It is settled that the activity of being a landlord implies the obligation to look out for the well-being of tenants and that an auto manufacturer has obligations to those who might be hurt in a crash. Such relationships stem from the principal–agent relationship between victim and actor, allowing the victim to rely on the actor, and the actor's superior access to information, to address the risks reasonably. But such relationships also arise when an actor has undertaken the obligation to another that fairly implicates the well-being of another, even a stranger. The concept of duty is therefore expanded to include school districts that send letters of recommendation to another school district (and unreasonably fail to disclose the extent of the risk) and to psychiatrists who understand from their patients the risks their patients pose to others.

Even in this class of cases, if the actor has an obligation to address the risk reasonably, the judge must consider whether the precautions asserted by the victim are ones that the jury should be allowed to consider when deciding whether the actor breached the duty. The question at this stage is whether the requested precaution would so fundamentally change the activity as to deprive other people of the benefits of the activity in ways that are more socially important than the harm that would be avoided by the precautions. This step is necessary so that juries facing the breach question do not overload the actor's activity with requirements that take away from the actor's central, and socially valuable, activity. This is necessary, for example, so that grade schools and retailers do not have to accept responsibility for every aspect of the well-being of their students or customers.

Merging the Two Kinds of Negligence Cases: Once a court determines in this second kind of negligence case that the actor has a duty and that the precaution claimed by the victim is within the scope of that duty, the two kinds of negligence cases become merged, for the issue that is left is one of the breach of the duty. In the second class of cases, the issue of the circumstances that connect the actor's decision is already likely to have been addressed (for the circumstances are likely to be addressed when the judge considers the scope of the duty), but the jury must still consider whether an actor with the duty to think about the well-being of the victim would have done more by way of precautions than the defendant did.

The Nature of Reasonable Precautions: Under both types of negligence cases, the issue of reasonable precautions implicates both the amount of resources that must be expended to protect the well-being of another and the kind of precautions that are required. The reasonable person pays attention not only to the amount of care, but also to the dimensions of care. We can organize our thinking about precautions around the duty to warn, to investigate, and to redesign. Every case implicates the obligation reasonably to redesign the activity, for precautions often require the actor to redesign the product or service or the way the activity is undertaken. But actors may also have to take precautions in the form of investigating the use and misuse of the activity and how the activity might ripen into harm. This requires the reasonable person to ask whether the additional investment in information production (given its availability and the likely costs and benefits of information) is likely to produce countervailing benefits in terms of reduced harm. And, of course, once the information is gathered, the actor must react reasonably to the information by either warning potential victims or redesigning the activity (depending on the relative costs and benefits of the two options).

In addition, we must ask whether the actor's decisions about where, when, how, and how often to do the activity (the activity-level decisions) have been reasonable. With respect to the frequency of activities (at least), this involves whether a person making the decision in question ought to be taking the frequency of activities into account (for, in many instances, the risk generated by doing the activity more frequently is not an issue that society expects the person to take into account and will therefore not justify legal intervention).

Issues of Evidence and Proof: In all cases, we must determine whether the presumptions that can reasonably be drawn from the way the harm occurred or from the failure to take certain precautions, and the victim's difficulty in getting the evidence relevant to proving negligence or an intentional tort, are sufficient to justify the court in shifting to the defendant the burden of coming forward with the evidence (or the burden of proof). This is not a difficult issue in some negligence cases. Sometimes the negligence can be inferred from the way the accident occurred. Moreover, when an actor makes a deliberate choice, that choice implies that the actor will have evidence about the nature of the deliberations that led to that choice and the actor can be expected to produce that evidence when the plaintiff has raised a plausible implication of negligence.

The Obligation to Compensate for Nonfaulty Conduct: The inquiry into the defendant's reasonableness is often determined by asking whether the defendant's conduct is conduct that a reasonable person would have undertaken if the person were thinking appropriately about the well-being of the victim. In a small class of specialized (and easily identified) cases, however, the relevant issue is not whether the defendant's conduct was faulty but whether the conduct implies the obligation – in order to be appropriately other-regarding – to compensate the victim. To identify this class of cases, we must ask whether the defendant used the victim's resources to save the defendant's resources (the *Vincent* case) or whether the defendant knowingly took risks that benefitted all customers but that hurt a few randomly determined customers (the hot coffee case). In both situations, it is unreasonable to fail to compensate the victim, even though the conduct that led to the harm was not socially destructive.

Cause in Fact: The cause in fact issue is the same for the two types of negligence cases: whether the failure to take reasonable precautions was necessary for the harm to occur or whether the harm would have occurred anyway. However, in the second kind of negligence case, that issue might take a different form and be answered with a different question. Because the harm might have occurred even if the defendant did act reasonably (the mugger might have gotten around even a non-negligent security system in an apartment), courts must resort to determining whether the victim had a chance of avoiding the bad outcome if the defendant had acted reasonably and, if so, what chance of avoiding a bad outcome had been lost. That is the only way of attaching the defendant to harm that necessarily could have been avoided had the defendant acted reasonably.

Harm: I have not dealt with the issue of harm in this book, having assumed throughout that the victim's harm was of the kind that tort law addresses, for the dynamics of the harm included within tort law respond to questions of the scope, not the existence, of responsibility. It is likely, however, that as we think about the two types of negligence cases, we will realize that the infliction of emotional harm is less likely to be absorbed within tort law when the defendant did not create the risk. In that type of negligence case, the person who did create the risk bears the primary responsibility for harm, and therefore would have a wider scope of responsibility in terms of the kind of harm.

Strict Liability: Once the court or analyst has raised and addressed these questions, the court has defined the scope and limitations on the defendant's responsibility. There is, then, no need or warrant for a separate consideration of whether the actor should be responsible without fault.

Index